Bootleggers, Booze, and Busts:
Prohibition in Kern County, 1919-1933

"How Are You Goin' To Wet Your Whistle
(when the whole darn world goes dry)"

…How are you goin' to wet your whistle,
When the whole darn world goes dry?
What are you goin' to do in the morning,
When you need a nip to open up your eye?
Now what of the wedding and the christening,
And the wake when your dear friends die,
Oh, How are you goin' to wet your whistle
When the whole darn world goes dry?

By Francis Byrne, Frank McIntyre
& Percy Wenrich (1919)

Bootleggers, Booze, and Busts: Prohibition in Kern County, 1919-1933

By RICHARD ROUX

GREENHORN MOUNTAIN BOOKS

Published by Greenhorn Mountain Books
Bakersfield, CA
greenhornmountainbooks@gmail.com

ISBN-13: 978-0-6159-4202-5

Notice: A large portion of the research in this book was compiled using public records. It is true and complete to the best of our knowledge.

To Margaret & Eileen

Contents

Contents

List of Photographs, Charts, and Images

A Note to Readers

In 1893, my great grandfather, Octave Augustus Roux, ended up in Bakersfield, California after emigrating from Gap, France. He worked for a short time in a saloon, opened a grocery store, raised a family, and participated in the growing French community. My family's roots, needless to say, run deep and long in Bakersfield. While growing up, family members told stories about early Bakersfield, creating within me an interest in local history, and in particular, how national events affected my hometown. This interest was revitalized while enrolled in a Research Methods class during the Winter 2005 quarter at California State University, Bakersfield. It was during that class that I began to pursue my interest in the topic of Prohibition.

This book is an adaptation of my Master's Thesis completed in June 2013. One of the difficult decisions I had to make when formatting this manuscript for publication as a book was deciding what to do with source citations. As a thesis, sources were cited in footnotes placed at the bottom of the page. This allows for easy access to notes on sources, as well as further explanations. But many readers may find that footnotes clutter the page.

Source citations could have been removed entirely from the book and placed solely in the bibliography, creating an improbable game of hide-and-go-seek for the reader who wants to see and access sources on their own. I have found that many publishers of local history across the nation have chosen to do this, but as a historian, I have several issues with this practice. First, the craft of writing history lies in telling a story that is compelling, as well as a story that can be verified. Second, to assume that the casual reader of history is not interested in sources or will be confused by citations underestimates the reader without giving them the benefit of the doubt. Lastly, citations help maintain academic honesty; writers cannot regurgitate history that they have read as their own work.

As a result, I chose to cite my sources using endnotes organized by chapter and placed at the end of the book. This allows readers to verify sources or get further explanations on what has been written. For readers who find themselves distracted by the numbered endnotes, please bear with my desire to not abandon the process of historical writing. I hope that you will come to see the citations as part of the process that you can choose to access or ignore.

I believe that it is important to note that I write this account of Prohibition in Kern County not as a denunciation of any particular group of people. Dedicated individuals on both sides of the issue maneuvered against each other in the struggle over Prohibition. Violators and those in favor of the repeal of Prohibition believed that the Eighteenth Amendment was fiscally unwise and an attack on liberty. Prohibitionists envisioned a world without alcohol, an item they believed was the root of many social ills. I make no judgment of the parties involved.

There are many individuals who inspired, aided, and urged me on. Dr. Constance Orliski provided the vehicle for what has become a labor of love. Becky Orfila, a fellow student, introduced me to digitized census data, and Ken Hooper saved me endless hours of grief and research time by introducing me to an online newspaper database through the Los Angeles Public Library. Dr. Alicia Rodriquez inspired me with discussions of local history research techniques and shares a peculiar affliction of using large sample sizes, and Dr. Douglas Dodd spent untold amounts of time editing drafts of my thesis in which this book is based on.

The pursuit of photographs to enrich this book has been a sometimes frustrating, long process, but has been successful in many respects. Several individuals I reached out to through online sites provided photographs of family members who were involved in this story. Betty Page Brackenridge, Karen Eliot, Paul and George Giboney, Joey E. Earing, Jr., Georgia Blair, Joe Scott, Marti Sheldon, Marji Turner, Lanie Stussie, Christine Jones Peard, Nancy Fitch, and Charlie Connor graciously allowed me access to personal photographs of individuals and places. Sandra Murch from the West Kern Oil Museum in Taft, California helped find and provide photographs of several places and individuals from the west side of the county. Mrs. Bob Powers, affiliated with the Kern Valley Museum in Kernville, California, allowed me to use a photograph from her husband's collection. And Lori Wear from the Kern County Museum was extremely helpful in tracking down a large number of the photographs that are included in this book. I thank you all.

Lastly, and most importantly, I owe mountains of gratitude to my wife, Margaret, and my daughter, Eileen. Their endless support and understanding has made my research and effort possible. How they put up with me, I will never know.

If you wish to share a family story, photograph, or other document pertaining to Prohibition in Kern County to be included in future editions of this book or other books, please contact me through the following email address:

GreenhornMountainBooks@gmail.com

Introduction

"Prohibition is better than no liquor at all."[1] Perhaps this quote by Will Rogers accurately captures the attitude of many Americans toward prohibition in the United States during the years 1919 to 1933. As one of the last gasps of the Progressive Era, Prohibition laws were a culmination of over one hundred years of effort to promote temperance, abstinence, or the outright ban of alcohol.[2] Prohibition was intended to address absenteeism in the workplace, prevent domestic abuse, institute moral reform, and aid in the assimilation of immigrants.[3] Although passed with good intentions, the Eighteenth Amendment and the National Prohibition Act—Volstead Act—proved to be unpopular and difficult to enforce, largely due to the fact that Americans of all ethnicities and races were accustomed to drinking and the federal government never allocated sufficient resources to enforce Prohibition measures.[4]

Much has been written on Prohibition as a national phenomenon, ranging from studies on gender, economics, public policy, urban-rural conflict, congressional voting patterns, and comparisons to modern drug policy.[5] Many of these publications discuss the role ethnicity played in the reasons for enacting Prohibition and in opposing enforcement of Prohibition laws. In these studies, ethnicity is often discussed in reference to metropolitan areas, especially in the eastern part of the United States.[6] At the very least, attempts to implement and enforce Prohibition are addressed by many historians and commentators of the period in broad strokes as a conflict between the classes or as a middle-class struggle to maintain white, Anglo-Saxon Protestant (WASP) control over the ever-increasing numbers of immigrants who were supposedly changing American culture.[7] That being said, there appears to be a gap in the historiography of Prohibition which needs to be explored. How does a region, such as Kern County, comprised of towns that were neither all metropolitan nor all rural, with a mixed native-born and immigrant population, as well as a mix of religious and political affiliations, fit into existing explanations of resistance to Prohibition? This study of Kern County, with a focus on Bakersfield, contributes to the historiography on Prohibition by testing the relevancy of the major assertions on the role of ethnicity, socio-economic status, and political party affiliation as a cause for opposition to Prohibition. Through an analysis of data, I will prove that, at least in Kern County, ethnicity was a determining factor in the violation of Prohibition, skilled workers or tradesmen were the socioeconomic group who were the most apt to be arrested as violators, and that political party affiliation was not a significant factor in identifying who would or would not be a violator.

Located at the southern end of the San Joaquin Valley of California, Kern County is comprised of over 8000 square miles of desert, mountains, foothills, river and creek bottoms, lakes, marsh, and reclaimed land. During the time period of this study—the 1910s to the early 1930s— the economy of Kern County was largely based on agriculture and the oil industry, drawing a wide variety of people from around the United States and the world to Kern County for economic opportunities. Although this study largely focuses on Prohibition in Bakersfield, other notable towns in Kern County appear in this case study—Delano, Fellows, Maricopa, McFarland, McKittrick, Mojave, Shafter, Taft, Tehachapi, and Wasco.[8] In order to present a detailed and thorough study of the story of Prohibition in Kern County, data and information pertaining to all areas of Kern County will be integrated into this history when possible.

1

Early Prohibition Attempts

The WCTU and the ASL

In the 19th century, the movement to make alcohol illegal in the United States was especially strong in the eastern cities, mid-western states, and many areas of the South. For the most part, the temperance movement was the product of cultural and religious tensions—native-born white Anglo-Saxon Americans versus immigrants; Pietists versus Liturgicals.[1] In essence, promoting temperance was an effort to protect American Protestantism from the growing number of urban immigrant, non-Protestant poor.[2] The Women's Christian Temperance Union (WCTU), the Anti-Saloon League (ASL), and various other civic and religiously oriented organizations led the campaign for temperance and Prohibition nationally and in Kern County.[3]

Founded in Cleveland, Ohio, in 1874, the WCTU aimed to bring about moral reform, advocating social welfare programs and improvements for the underprivileged, in addition to changing American drinking habits.[4] Women across California formed Women's Temperance Alliances, holding daily prayer meetings and circulating petitions for a state local-option referendum.[5] Formed in Sacramento in 1875, the WCTU organized into separate Northern and Southern California branches by 1884, and grew to around 5000 members in the state by 1892.[6] The WCTU attempted to establish itself in Bakersfield in 1891, with Miss Frances Willard (second president of the WCTU) scheduled to speak at an organizational conference.[7] Her appearance, however, was cancelled due to "unavoidable hindrances."[8] Despite this temporary discouragement, women in Bakersfield and the rest of Kern County caught the temperance spirit later in the year when Mrs. Helen Bullock of the National Organization of the WCTU helped form three unions in

1. Arlington Bar in the Arlington Hotel, southeast corner of 19th and Chester. Circa 1890s. Notice the lack of women patrons. *Courtesy of Kern County Museum. Used by permission*

Kern County—Delano, Bakersfield, and Rosedale.[9] Also in 1891, the Southern California WCTU sent Mrs. Mary A. Garbutt to Bakersfield to help women in Kern County further organize.[10] Mrs. Garbutt held meetings all day and every evening for two weeks at the Baptist Church in Bakersfield, and later wrote, "Just to look into the earnest faces of the women was to gain courage for a lifetime, while to the women themselves, this new step of organization was big with promise of work, sacrifice and joy."[11]

Although membership of the National Organization of the WCTU was relatively small (245,299 in 1911 and 344,892 in 1921[12]), the movement was successful in influencing state legislatures, including the California state legislature, to pass laws making it mandatory to study temperance in schools.[13] Mrs. Hunter, the second president of the Kern County WCTU, commented, "Perhaps our most marked effort has been in our public schools. For the first time the question of liquor and temperance was made an issue in the election of a school trustee."[14] Temperance workers in Bakersfield placed books on anti-tobacco, anti-gambling, and temperance in school libraries.[15]

2. In front of the Arlington Hotel, circa 1915. Note the stack of beer barrels. *Courtesy of Kern County Museum. Used by permission*

In 1911, women in California won the right to vote.[16] Women in Kern County actively promoted political, social and moral action through various activities, such as pledge-signing and no-license campaigns, supporting the Prohibition Party and the ASL, and gathering names on petitions—an especially favored method of promoting temperance.[17] The WCTU also promoted a creative measure, the "Home Protection Petition," to make acquiring a liquor license more difficult by mandating that licenses would be issued only if a majority of the voters and women over the age of eighteen approved.[18] Additionally, the WCTU produced a "Petition For War Prohibition" to restrict alcohol during World War I and a "Petition For Constitutional Prohibition" which advocated adding an amendment to the United States Constitution to eliminate alcohol as a national policy.[19] Despite their good intentions, the WCTU's politically weak organization and low membership numbers hampered a united nationwide temperance campaign. Their focus on many aspects of social reform—a "do-everything" policy through departments—drew attention away from the single issue of alcohol temperance, thus, weakening its overall effectiveness in achieving a prohibition amendment without the aid of other organizations.[20] Eventually, a single-issue movement entered the scene to focus prohibition efforts.

The Anti-Saloon League of America (ASL), formed in Washington, D.C. in 1895, used bureaucratic methods to maintain focus on its single emphasis of eradicating the saloon.[21] Unlike the WCTU, where women spearheaded temperance efforts, men served in leadership positions in the ASL.[22] The ASL used professional men as speakers and organizers for alcohol reform in Kern County and the state of California, as well as across the United States. Women continued to be an integral part of the movement itself, although less conspicuously. By the late 1800s and early 1900s, breweries, utilizing technological advances and modern business organization, competed with one another, resulting in a growing number of saloons controlled by breweries for the purpose of expanding revenues.[23] In order to compete with brewery-owned saloons, independent saloons sold beer at reduced prices and offered other

3.   George Helm, a future violator of Prohibition, and Les Dupin inside the Crawford Bar, 1911. *Courtesy of Kern County Museum. Used by permission*

4

services, such as a free lunch (high in salt to stimulate thirst), prostitution, and gambling.[24] Saloons also served as meeting places for labor unions, political machines, and organizational hubs for "wet" forces.[25]

It was the growing political influence of the saloons, the sharp increase in alcohol consumption from the 1870s to the 1910s, and the expanding population of immigrants who accepted drinking as a social custom and the saloon as a tool to maintain cultural and social ties, that motivated members of the ASL to push for local, state, and national legislation to end the influence of saloons. The League's adaptation of a businesslike structure provided for "specialized and departmentalized functions, a central office, and a full-time professional staff in charge of developing strategy, coordinating activities, and fostering organizational growth."[26] Local option elections became the chief vehicle for moving the League's policies forward. These special elections allowed the people in a community to vote on whether they would be "wet" or "dry." As a result of the County Government Act and Municipal Corporation Act, enacted in 1883, city councils in California could pass ordinances regulating the sale of alcohol.[27]

4. Consumption of Beer, Wine, and Distilled Spirits From 1871 to 1915[28]

Year	Distilled Spirits Total Gallons	Wines Total Gallons	Malt Liquors (Beer) Total Gallons	Total Consumption Total Gallons	Per Capita Gallons
1871-80	62,032,085	20,859,695	309,666,658	392,558,432	8.79
1881-90	76,375,208	27,518,873	647,180,365	751,074,446	13.20
1891-95	91,788,636	26,346,208	1,018,007,688	1,136,142,582	16.96
1896-00	82,028,059	26,777,974	1,141,274,857	1,250,080,890	17.01
1901-05	114,161,694	38,954,038	1,425,928,559	1,579,044,291	19.20
1906-10	129,516,812	55,734,669	1,791,093,655	1,976,345,136	21.86
1911	138,585,989	63,859,232	1,966,911,754	2,169,356,975	22.81
1912	139,496,331	56,424,711	1,932,531,184	2,128,452,226	22.05
1913	147,745,628	55,327,461	2,030,347,372	2,233,420,461	22.80
1914	143,447,227	52,418,430	2,056,407,108	2,252,272,765	22.66
1915	127,159,098	32,911,909	1,855,524,284	2,015,595,291	19.99[29]

The Wylie Bill and Local Option

On March 22, 1906, the ASL established a branch in Bakersfield.[30] Twenty people, at the request of G.L. Robertson, met in Judge Mahon's courtroom, electing T.F. Allen chairman and E.R. Long secretary. They created the Kern County Home Protective Association to promote the reduction in the number of saloons (possibly resulting in their eradication) and to shorten their hours of operation, a response to the fact that many of Kern County's saloons remained open twenty-four hours a day.[31] Subsequently, Rev. A.M. Shaw's "Law and Order League" absorbed the Protective Association, although the emphasis on controlling unruly saloons remained.[32] In April 1906, Rev. Shaw articulated the goals of the Law and Order League in a letter to the editor

5. Maier Brewing Co. distribution office exterior with beer wagon. *Courtesy of Kern County Museum. Used by permission*

of the *Bakersfield Californian*, stating that the League is "no fanatical outbreak of religious enthusiasm," and that disreputable establishments, such as dance halls, need to be suppressed because "they corrupt the morals of our people...are a detriment to legitimate business...foster and practice lawlessness."[33]

In 1900, Bakersfield was referred to as a "wide-open" town, a place where a man could easily acquire drink, find a prostitute, and lay a bet in a game of chance.[34] Despite reforms ending gambling around 1902, a large red light district existed and forty saloons operated twenty-four hours a day, seven days a week, for a population of less than five-thousand—approximately one saloon for every one-hundred and twenty residents. As a comparison, the city of San Francisco issued over three-thousand liquor licenses, allowing for one drinking establishment for every ninety-six residents.[35] The vice element present in Bakersfield not only urged some people to call for moral reform, but it also made Bakersfield a special target of criticism by the press in other towns outside of Kern County. An editorial in the *Bakersfield Californian* on March 28,

6. The Del Monte at 1919 Chester Avenue, before 1918. *Courtesy of Kern County Museum. Used by permission*

1906 lamented, "Bakersfield has acquired a reputation for evil throughout the coast, and while conditions here at present are not a whit worse than in many a California community, every agitation for betterment appears to produce the same result—this city is exploited by the press as absolutely the most immoral in the state...."[36] As local ordinances attempted to rein in gambling, dance halls, prostitution, and liquor they served to reinforce the negative image of Bakersfield. On April 1, 1906, the *Los Angeles Times* reported that new Bakersfield ordinances were supposedly in the works to require saloons to close their doors at 10:00 p.m., prohibit back rooms, and banish women from saloons.[37] Despite reporting from Los Angeles—much of which sensationalized problems in Bakersfield—the proposed ordinances were opposed and not enacted. However, the vice element present in the saloons did not escape the attention of the WCTU and the ASL.[38]

Proponents of local option pushed for a law to allow a local option vote every two years, a proposal Chairman of the Board of Supervisors, H.A. Jastro, vowed to oppose as long as he was serving because it would allow agitators to continually raise the liquor issue in the county.[39] Jastro's proclamation that local option was unwise and illegal did not deter organizers. R.H. Young, a field worker for the State Anti-Saloon League of Southern California, held meetings with the local Ministerial Union to organize an anti-saloon campaign pushing for a local option vote.[40] At Young's request, Dr. E.S. Chapman spoke to a gathering of six churches at the Armory Hall and Rev. D.M. Gandier, Assistant Superintendent of the ASL, spoke to temperance workers in surrounding communities.[41]

Initially, temperance workers in Kern County wanted regulation of the saloons, not necessarily their closing. For many proponents of temperance, the problem was not alcohol, but the environment in which it was served; saloons were dens of immorality. The WCTU announced in Bakersfield churches on March 22, 1911, that they were starting a petition campaign to close

7. Henry Jastro. *Courtesy of Kern County Museum. Used by permission*

saloons on Sundays and mandate that saloons be closed during the week from 7:00 p.m. to 6:00 a.m. However, petitioners stated that they would allow saloons to remain open until 10:00 p.m. on Saturdays.[42] Mrs. L.G. Harmon promoted the role women could play in the petition campaign during a meeting of forty WCTU members, including several men,

8. Monte Carlo Saloon on 19th Street, before 1918. *Courtesy of Kern County Museum. Used by permission*

notably Rev. Lloyd C. Smith and Rev. A.L. Paul. Harmon reported that a bill limiting the number of saloons to one per five hundred people in every "wet" city would likely pass in the state legislature, effectively reducing the number of Bakersfield saloons from sixty-four to twenty-five.[43] She also discussed the possibility of the legislature passing the Wylie Bill, allowing towns to hold local option elections to determine the status of alcohol in their individual communities.[44]

Unlike a policy of outright prohibition of alcohol across the United States, local option approaches the issue from the perspective of grassroots democracy. That is, local municipalities and counties know what is best for their communities; local people ruling on a local issue, destroying the evils of drinking by destroying the source—the saloon.[45]

Some contemporaries put much thought into the issue of liquor and saloon reform. Russell Macnaghten, author of a 1909 article in *The North American Review*, writes that true reform is only possible where there is a clear mandate for change. In large towns where there is only a small majority ushering in a dry policy, a large portion of the public would

10

9. Zimmer's Place. East Bakersfield. A.C. Wilber and L.H. Zimmer Proprietors.
    Courtesy of Kern County Museum. Used by permission

undoubtedly turn to illegal sources of alcohol. To avoid this problem, Macnaghten suggests that a two-thirds majority was necessary to approve any "dry" laws. He also believed that if saloons were allowed to exist, they must be limited to one saloon for every one thousand people or even one for every two thousand people, must not be allowed to advertise, should not be allowed to operate in alleys or side streets, and that the bar in the saloon must be banished.[46] Additionally, Macnaghten believed that drinking establishments must have a disinterested management system—profits should be limited to 5 percent and commission should be paid to workers for the sale of food and non-intoxicating beverages.[47]

The eventual passage of the Wylie Bill in California changed the tactics of the WCTU and the ASL in Kern County.[48] Passed by the Assembly 51-21 and the Senate 28-12, the Wylie Bill allowed the local option question on a ballot when 25 percent of the eligible voters in a district submitted a petition to do so. Instead of just limiting the number of saloons allowed in Bakersfield and their hours of operation, the possibility of making the towns in Kern County "dry" enticed many temperance workers to become dedicated prohibitionists. However, their first big challenge was to overcome party loyalty. In the 1890s, both the Republican and Democratic parties were "wet," catering to their urban and immigrant constituencies. Democrats declared they were against regulation; Republicans were against local option and high-license tactics.[49]

Local Option in Kern County

Following enactment of the Wylie Bill, the WCTU, the Bakersfield Ministers' Union, Assemblyman Fred H. Hall of Bakersfield, and the Kern County ASL laid the foundation for local option elections, not just in Bakersfield, but throughout Kern County.[50] T.H. Minor and R.H. Young began to organize Anti-Saloon workers May 18, 1911.[51] After speaking at Bakersfield's largest open-air meeting on temperance at the Pilgrim's Congregational Church in East Bakersfield, Curtis V. Wilbur, a judge in the juvenile court in Los Angeles and a temperance speaker, praised the efforts of reformers in Bakersfield stating, "I will carry back the message to Los Angeles that Bakersfield is evolving from the wild and wooly stage to a place where there is a growing tendency to higher ideals."[52] Seventy-five to one hundred petitions asking for an option election were slated to begin circulation on October 10, 1911.[53] This was an apparent underestimation of the interest in holding a local option election and the time needed to gather the necessary signatures—the required signatures were presented by T.H. Minor to the city clerk on August 23, 1911.[54] ASL workers needed 622 signatures to meet the 25 percent requirement for a local option election to take place. Over 700 signatures were compiled.[55] Despite fears that economic retaliation would be carried out against signers of the petitions due to the *Bakersfield Californian* publishing the list, the ASL assured supporters and opponents

10. Interior of Pasquini and Lencioni Saloon on the first floor of the Bakersfield Hotel, circa 1916. *Courtesy of Kern County Museum. Used by permission*

of local option that petition signers were people participating in democracy who wanted the saloon issue resolved once and for all.[56]

As stated previously, in the fight against the saloon the ASL attempted to work with both Republicans and Democrats in the spirit of Progressive reform. Because Republicans in California tended to be more nativist in orientation and Midwestern in geographic origination, a great deal of the League's efforts was focused on gaining Republican support for local option.[57] And since the League focused on the saloon, not alcohol itself, as the root of evil, local option also attracted supporters from the Democratic party.[58] A sample analysis of names on petitions favoring a local option election in Bakersfield support claims of bipartisan participation.[59] Out of a sample of seventy-two names, political party affiliation was determined for forty individuals.[60] Of the forty, twenty-three (57.5 percent) were registered Republicans, fourteen (35 percent) were registered Democrats, and three (7.5 percent) were registered Socialists.[61] Although the motives for signing the local option petition cannot be determined, it is not improbable that most people who petitioned for the special election genuinely wanted Bakersfield to be a "dry" town. "Wets" may have signed the petition to usher in a vote with the end result of preserving the availability of liquor-selling saloons. A story in the *Bakersfield Californian* on September 2, 1911 states, "Many of those who signed did so because they wish the issue brought to a head and have not expressed themselves one way or another on the election."[62] A desire for a resolution to the saloon question, either way, likely motivated a portion of the petition signers. Another interesting observation of this sample is their occupations. Of the seventy-two people in the sample, the occupations of fifty-five were determined. Professionals made up 23.6 percent (thirteen) of the sample; skilled workers or tradesmen 50.9 percent (twenty-eight); unskilled labor 21.8 percent (twelve); and homemakers 3.6 percent (two). Taken as a whole, professional and skilled workers accounted for 74.5 percent of the sample population; this may be a pronouncement against the saloon and its patrons—that the saloon fostered self-defeatism, poverty, and prevented the lower classes from improving their condition. Regardless, the sample illustrates support for a local option election by members of both

11. Reuben Butterfield, Ed Lechner, Harry Lechner and Elwood Armstrong in the Peerless Saloon, circa 1900. *Courtesy of Kern County Museum. Used by permission*

predominant political parties and people with a variety of occupational backgrounds.

Saloon owners and patrons were concerned enough about regulation and a possible "dry" vote in the early 1900s that they voluntarily attempted to reform the image of saloons. In 1902, the Knights of the Royal Arch, a pro-liquor men's temperance association, was formed in California.[63] Mirroring the fraternal organization of the Masonic Order, the Royal Arch encouraged strict regulation of saloons and elimination of disreputable establishments.[64] A spokesperson for the Royal Arch states, "There is a liquor question in California. It must be faced, and it must be solved. But it is a subject for calm and impassioned discussion by big men with broad, balanced minds. The Knights of the Royal Arch is sincerely and honestly trying to settle the question by elevating the liquor business and encouraging strict regulation."[65] Thomas W. Roulo, commander of

12. Cornerstone dedication for the Woodmen of the World building on the southeast corner of 18th and Eye Streets, circa 1890s. The building would serve as a gathering place for many events throughout the years. *Courtesy of Kern County Museum. Used by permission*

the Royal Arch, urged "morality as [a] means to salvation to the saloon business," and he wanted saloons in Bakersfield to be more respectable and professional in an effort to change the public's perception of the saloon.[66] In response, many saloons attempted to regulate themselves. For example, the Royal Arch in Bakersfield adamantly pledged that all saloons would obey the laws or be subject to punishment, especially laws regulating the minimum drinking age of eighteen.[67] In addition, all Bakersfield saloons except for one agreed to close their doors by 1:00 a.m., not reopen until 6:00 a.m., not allow card games for money, and to remove or cover up nude art.[68] This voluntary regulation was codified in early October 1911.[69] Despite efforts to reform, the local option vote was scheduled for October 31, 1911—Bakersfield's residents seemed more inclined toward regulation, not prohibition.[70]

13. Harriet F. Buss, 7/23/1942, served as the Kern County president of the WCTU several times. *Courtesy of Kern County Museum. Used by permission*

While proponents of a local option election found gathering signatures quite easy, supporters of prohibition diligently solicited votes favoring their position. For instance, on September 11, 1911, T.H. Minor and R.H. Young of the Anti-Saloon League held a meeting at the Woodmen of the World (W.O.W) Hall[71] advising women that through "collective work" they could play an important role in the fight against the saloon.[72] Three days later, on September 14, thirty-five women gathered at the offices of the ASL to form the Women's Civic League of Bakersfield. Pledging to clean up the city, aid the temperance fight, and improve the city with parks and boulevards, the group sought to enlist at least 500 women in their organization.[73] An especially favored

14. Attorney Alfred Siemon spoke out against saloons. *Courtesy of Kern County Museum. Used by permission*

tactic of "dry" forces was to hold meetings at the W.O.W. Hall or in church facilities, usually with guest speakers providing inspirational words to rally the troops. At one meeting for the ASL on September 18, Ms. Harriet Buss gave her speech, "The Campaign and the Young People," and Attorney Alfred Siemon spoke on "The Beleaguered City."[74] Then, at the W.O.W Hall on October 9, Dr. F.W. Mitchell presented a physician's point of view why saloons should be defeated, citing medical problems associated with the consumption of alcohol.[75] In an attempt to bring as much leverage to the "dry" cause in Bakersfield as the League could, G.W. Wylie, author of the Local Option Bill, was scheduled to speak to crowds at the W.O.W. Hall and the Methodist Church in East Bakersfield on October 15, and McFarland and Delano on October 17.[76]

Women, perhaps motivated by "dry" political agitation, not only collectively participated in gathering signatures on petitions, organizing meetings, and promoting the cause of prohibition, but they also registered to vote in the local option. One hundred women registered on October 16 and three hundred by October 18.[77] Optimistically, in preparation for a rally featuring Dr. E.S. Chapman of the ASL, flyers circulated urging supporters to "Come and help drive nails in the saloon coffin."[78] The League even took to street meetings to maximize the number of people they could mobilize for a "dry" vote.[79]

"Dry" proponents also utilized newspaper advertisements to generate possible votes in the local option election. An advertisement in

17

the *Bakersfield Morning Echo* on October 22, 1911, attributed the majority of crimes committed in Bakersfield and the state of California to alcohol. Moreover, E.M. Dearborn, Justice of the Peace in Kern County, reported that of the seventy-one males arrested and imprisoned in the Kern County jail between January and October 1911, nine out of every ten prisoners was under the influence of alcohol at the time of their alleged crime. Additionally, the advertisement reported that experts in varying sociological fields agreed that alcohol contributed to a large portion of the expenses associated with social problems—70 percent for the insane; 84 percent for crime; 85 percent for paupers; 70 percent for the feeble minded; and 60 percent for orphans. The sum total of expenses caused by or related to alcohol in the state of California was $3,254,281.51. Such statistics and financial considerations could potentially go a long way to sway undecided voters.[80]

After reading the "dry" argument in the advertisement, some voters may have supported the anti-saloon cause because it made economic sense. Perhaps even more people were shamed into support. A person reading, "Be fair an[d] square with yourself and with your town and country. Vote dry. The saloons have got to go eventually, anyhow. Let them go now. Vote dry. Booze joints promote crime, insanity, accidents and property loss. Get rid of them. VOTE DRY," might feel guilty if they did not vote "dry."[81]

"I Am Still Strong For The Boy," is another advertisement that ran in the *Bakersfield Morning Echo* on October 29, 1911.[82] It argued against the saloon on the grounds that it was detrimental for children and business. The advertisement also suggested that children, both boys and girls, are robbed of a father because of the saloon's influence. "It is all the same whether booze gets the best of *your* son or *your* son-in-law, *you*, as a grandfather, will be trotting a drunk's kids on your knee anyhow. Either way, you are in bad. Think it over and Vote Bakersfield Dry." Such arguments could be compelling and persuasive in an atmosphere of moral reform. Responding to counter claims that the end of the saloon would hurt businesses, "dry" forces responded that the death of saloons in other parts of the United States has not hurt business. Furthermore, it was best "to place the boy before business!! And let it go at that," arguing that protecting youth was more important than making money born of immorality.

The "dry" forces were better at organizing and holding public gatherings, but anti-prohibitionists held their share of rallies, too.[83] On October 21, 1911, Senator A.S. Ruth of Olympia, WA. spoke on behalf of pro-liquor forces, urging regulation of saloons, not their banning.[84] To counter religious claims used by "drys" to promote prohibition, Rev. E.A. Wasson, pastor of St. Stephen's Episcopal Church in Newark, NJ, spoke at Hill's Theater arguing, "Prohibition is Not Christian Doctrine."[85] "Wets" even attempted to bring Clarence Darrow up from Los Angeles to speak against prohibition, although it is unclear if he ever made an appearance.[86] A few days before the scheduled election, a meeting of more than sixty African Americans at Winter's Hall, declaring to be for regulation, not prohibition.[87]

"Wets" also used advertisements to garner votes for saving the saloon. Advertisements, such as one on October 21 in the *Bakersfield Californian*, called for residents to hear A.S. Ruth speak on 'The Folly Of Prohibition.'[88] The *Bakersfield Morning Echo* ran a simple advertisement instructing voters how to vote "wet."[89] It was as simple as marking "yes" in favor of licensing alcoholic liquors in Bakersfield, effectively shown by an illustrated hand and an "x" marked in the proper box.

Perhaps the most interesting advertisement dealing with the local option election was one run in the *Bakersfield Californian* on October 28 by Redlick's Mercantile.[90] The owner of Redlick's, Joseph Redlick, signed the petition for merchants against the local option election, but his business savvy saw a way to use the election to generate business.[91] Regardless of who wins, "wets" or "drys" the advertisement promised, "We will return the money for any purchases made Monday and Tuesday to the shopper who guesses the nearest majority on either side…Shoppers may make as many guesses as they make purchases." Redlick's opposition to the eradication of the saloon did not stand in the way of increasing sales.

Other businessmen joined with Joseph Redlick in signing a petition against the local option and a "dry" Bakersfield.[92] An analysis of names on this petition reveals bipartisan opposition. Of the 101 names listed on the petition, voter registration information was found for 57 individuals.[93] Nineteen of the petition signers were registered Democrats, thirty-seven were registered Republicans, and one was a registered Progressive. Further examination of the occupations of these petition signers reveal that 24 of the 111 signers of the petition had an interest in the saloon or the alcohol industry: six produced or sold cigars; nine had retail stores or promoted retail establishments; three supplied towels or ice to businesses; and thirteen used alcohol in one form or another in their business. Contrary to what might be expected, only 14 of the 111 petition signers were born in other countries, although 23 of the remaining 97 had at least 1 parent born outside the United States. Ethnicity may have influenced some of these businessmen to oppose local option, but the bottom line, however, was that businesses supported free-market principles of supply and demand; restriction of one type of business could lead to the restriction of others.

15. Redlick's Department Store, circa 1920. *Courtesy of Kern County Museum. Used by permission*

20

Prohibitionists and local option proponents across the nation charged that ethnic immigrants, especially Germans, Irish and Italians, used the saloon to perpetrate immoral acts and challenge the cultural values of white Anglo-Saxon Protestants. This claim, however, is questionable when applied to Bakersfield and Kern County. In 1910, Bakersfield had a total population of 12,727—10,150 were native-born white; 262 were black; 1,734 were foreign-born white; and 2,224 were native-born whites with at least one parent who was foreign-born.[94] To broaden this snapshot, Kern County had a population of 37,715—22,233 were native-born white; 369 were black; 7,219 were foreign-born white; and 3,689 were native whites with at least one parent who was foreign-born.[95] It does not seem likely that 13.6 percent of the population of Bakersfield (4.55 percent for Kern County), or even 35.5 percent—foreign-born plus native-born with foreign-born parents of the population—(14.33 percent for Kern County) were the sole group fueling the saloon industry as proprietors and patrons. Of course, these numbers do not take into account the number of children present in the ethnic population, nor does it segregate the number of women present in the adult population. The impact of ethnic voters on the results of the local option election held October 31, 1911 is also unclear.

16. Foreign-Born Whites and Native-Born Whites With Foreign Parentage in Bakersfield, 1910.

Foreign-Born White: *Born In:*		Native White: *Both Parents Born In:*	
Australia	12	Austria	21
Austria	47	Canada	81
Canada	165	Denmark	12
Denmark	27	England	72
England	182	France	126
Finland	25	Germany	232
France	170	Ireland	175
Germany	211	Italy	61
Greece	10	Norway	9
Holland	4	Russia	18
Ireland	103	Scotland	29
Italy	155	Sweden	24
Mexico	352	Switzerland	9
Norway	10	All Others	363
Portugal	24		
Russia	31		
Scotland	35		
Spain	31		
Sweden	55		
Switzerland	39		
Turkey	10		
Other	36		

17. Foreign-Born Whites and Native-Born Whites with Foreign Parentage in Kern County, 1910.

Foreign-Born White: *Born In:*		Native White: *Both Parents Born In:*	
Australia	30	Austria	49
Austria	367	Canada	160
Canada	536	Denmark	38
Denmark	118	England	235
England	598	France	303
Finland	46	Germany	688
France	539	Ireland	615
Germany	737	Italy	192
Greece	335	Norway	20
Holland	NA	Russia	165
Ireland	540	Scotland	109
Italy	572	Sweden	76
Mexico	1492	Switzerland	45
Norway	60	All Others	994
Portugal	122		
Russia	250		
Scotland	154		
Spain	180		
Sweden	174		
Switzerland	155		
Turkey	19		
Others	152		

Whatever their views or motives, voters responded to the local option election with intense interest. Election Day saw more people casting votes than ever before in the history of Bakersfield and its outlying areas.[96] 6348 people registered to vote and automobiles shuttling "wet" and "dry" voters to the polls were busy all day.[97] In the election frenzy, an automobile driven by election workers carrying voters to Courthouse Square struck and seriously injured Mrs. Emma Rinehart. Amazingly, election workers continued on to their destination and did not stop their vehicle to assist her. More than likely they never realized that they hit Rinehart in the first place.[98] Both sides remained confident and claimed victory in this hard-fought battle.[99] Despite their best efforts, however, "dry" forces lost the election and the measure was defeated. In Bakersfield, "wets" prevailed by a majority of 1158 votes—a 2 to 1 margin.[100] Twelve Bakersfield Precincts voted "wet" and one "dry," with the overwhelming support for licensing saloons catching both sides by surprise.[101] Results from other areas of Kern County were similar to Bakersfield. The town of Tehachapi, and County Supervisorial District One, District Two, and District Four voted majority "wet." Supervisorial District Three and Five were majority "dry."[102] Altogether, the ASL and their allies were disappointed.[103]

Important conclusions can be drawn from an examination of the early attempts to combat saloons and promote temperance and prohibition. Despite strong support for "dry" towns in some corners of Kern County, most residents preferred the strict approach of licensing and regulating saloons rather than eliminating them altogether. Women were instrumental in supporting the activities of temperance organizations, such as the WCTU. But it was the focused agitation of the male-led ASL that made local option elections possible in Kern County. Based on the sample, the majority of those supporting local option elections were Republicans, although large numbers of Democrats also supported these elections, and the majority of the supporters, at least in Bakersfield, were professionals or skilled workers. Both "dry" and "wet" forces utilized rallies and advertisements to mobilize voters and both sides were confident in victory. In the end, prohibition was not embraced by the residents of Bakersfield, Tehachapi, and a majority of the Supervisorial Districts in Kern County, but temperance advocacy continued. These preliminary findings are aligned with historian Gilman Marsten Ostrander's assertion that support for prohibition in California can be geographically divided at the Tehachapi Mountains: Northern California was anti-prohibition, Southern California for prohibition. Bakersfield and Kern County lie north of the dividing line and the majority of residents opposed prohibition, consistent with Ostrander's characterization of Northern California communities.

2

The Passage of National Prohibition

Rationing and a Wartime Measure

Despite the disappointments of the 1911 local option election and other efforts to regulate saloons in Bakersfield and other areas of Kern County, many prohibitionists did not give up hope that the battle against the saloon, and ultimately, against alcohol, could be won. These sentiments echoed those of temperance reformers across the United States throughout the 1910s.

At times, prohibition forces pushed through federal legislation to regulate the alcohol industry. In 1913, the Webb-Kenyon Act was passed, making it illegal for liquor dealers to transport alcohol across state lines into "dry" states.[1] The Hobson Resolution, proposed in 1914, called for a prohibition amendment to the Constitution, and prompted one of the first debates over the merits of national prohibition. Those in favor of the amendment argued that it was necessary to preserve liberty; the liberty of the mind and body from alcohol, not the liberty of citizens to do whatever they wanted.[2] Floyd W. Tomkins, writing in 1923, argued that personal liberty must be restrained by law or there is no liberty at all; for the greater good, as well as the good of the individual, liberty must be restrained.[3] Harry Warner, a contemporary, stated that Prohibition was 'the liberation of the individual from the illusion of freedom that is conveyed by alcohol' and that the desires of the individual must be balanced against those of the family and society.[4] Prohibition was as much to save the individual from the corrupting force of alcohol, as it was to promote the greater efficiency of the nation as a whole.

As with any public policy, there was opposition to the Hobson Resolution. Representative Julius Kahn, from San Francisco, California, argued against the amendment (as well as against Progressivism it seems), stating, "We are trying to regulate all human conduct by laws, laws, laws. Efforts of that character are as old as the world. And they have invariably resulted in failure."[5] President Wilson believed that "government is merely an attempt to express the average conscience of everybody," but if

18. Rep. Julius Kahn argued against a prohibition amendment. *Library of Congress*

government moved faster than public opinion, then legislators needed to stop their actions or reassess the speed of implementation.[6] Many opponents of a national prohibition amendment believed that the issue should be resolved on a state-by-state basis, an affirmation of the grassroots advocacy of local option. Ultimately, a narrow majority of the House (197 to 190) voted for the Hobson Resolution, but it failed to win the two-thirds majority needed to amend the Constitution.[7]

Not to be detered, promoters of prohibition continued to push until national prohibition became a reality in 1920. A combination of continued Progressive agitation and the United States' involvement in the Great War (World War I) made possible the enactment of prohibition as national law. Efforts to conserve food for the war effort provided the vehicle for an amendment to the Constitution prohibiting alcohol.

With the beginning of World War I, prohibitionists recognized the opportunity that mobilization and patriotism presented for their cause. As soon as the United States declared war on the Central Powers, efforts began to organize the nation for war. Influenced by the

Progressive impulse for efficiency and bureaucracy, President Wilson's administration created new agencies, such as the Food Administration, Fuel Administration, Railroad Administration, and the War Industries Board to manage the war at home.[8]

Led by Herbert Hoover and promising that "food will win the war," the Food Administration encouraged farmers to increase production through a combination of patriotic exhortation and the government's guaranteed crop purchases at high prices.[9] The Kern County Farm Bureau, like Farm Bureaus across the United States, worked with the government to boost agricultural production.[10]

Hoover's Food Administration also hoped to make more food resources available for the war by promoting a food conservation program, a program many in Kern County vigorously supported. Bakersfield City Clerk Frank E. Smith led the county's efforts to conserve meat, wheat, and sugar by urging households to sign a food conservation pledge. By November 3, 1917, 5300 had joined the effort.[11] Nationwide, the program reduced the amount of foodstuffs consumed by American households, but mobilization required more.

Despite the patriotic spirit that accompanied America's entry into the war, some residents of Kern County, as well as the United States, begrudgingly conserved food, complained about it, or outright refused to participate. Several editorials appeared in the *Bakersfield Californian* attempting to convince the public of the virtues of food conservation. One editorial appearing on January 7, 1918, reminded audiences that German propagandists used every tool and issue available to them to create division within the United States in order to undermine the war effort. In addition, the editorialist advised all patriotic men and women to be aware that most of the political opponents of the Food Administration were also opposed to the war in the first place. Opponents were characterized as unpatriotic and pro-German.[12] Another editorial from January 26, 1918, admonished that participating was "A Patriotic Duty" and that support for the Food Administration was the right thing to do.[13] Most Americans dutifully adhered to conservation efforts. Those who did not were eyed with suspicion.

The national food conservation campaign opened the door to restricting alcohol through the prohibition clause attached to the Lever Food and Fuel Control Act of 1917. With this act, the President could restrict the use of foodstuffs in the manufacture of fermented liquors and confiscate distilled spirits held in warehouses. In addition, the use of foodstuffs in the manufacture of distilled spirits, as well as their importation, was not allowed.[14] Food Administration officials claimed that eleven million loaves of bread a day could be produced by completely withholding foodstuffs from liquor manufacturers.[15] Wilson, in an effort to allocate food resources for the war, reduced the amount of alcohol allowed in beer to 3 percent, decreasing the amount of grain used for brewing purposes by an estimated 30 percent. Brewing beer was not banned outright, however, due to the Food Administration's fear that American citizens would drink whiskey, considered morally inferior, of which there was a two to three year supply.[16] It was stated that "The social question involved…must be given equal consideration with that of food conservation."

The United States government not only reduced the amount of foodstuffs used to produce alcohol, they also continued to tap into the liquor industry for tax revenue. Between 1870 and 1915 the federal Liquor Tax constituted between one-half and two-thirds of the whole internal revenue of the United States.[17] More than $200 million—71 percent of all internal revenue—was collected from taxes on alcohol.[18] The burden of paying for the Great War mandated a concentrated effort to collect taxes, including those on liquor. The *Bakersfield Californian* reported that Bakersfield businesses selling liquor and cigars had to comply with the taxes on their products. Distilled beverages were taxed $2.10 a gallon and beer $1.50 per barrel. There was also a proposed tax on wine, but the amount was undetermined at the time.[19] Even though it was in their best interest and their patriotic duty to pay their taxes, some in the liquor industry attempted to evade taxation. Internal Revenue officers discovered that approximately 5000 liquor dealers across the country did not comply with orders to report their liquor stocks in compliance with the War Revenue Taxes. These liquor dealers were assessed a 200 percent fine, totaling about $2 million.[20]

Faced with the daunting task of fighting the nation's first war on European soil, there was a genuine fear that alcohol could hinder soldiers' training and combat effectiveness. In the early months of the war, soldiers were not allowed to have liquor in their homes, but the rule was eased (with some restrictions) after February 1918. With the changes implemented by the War Department, only family members could serve soldiers; non-related hosts could only serve soldiers if they were "bona fide" guests.[21] The Kern County Board of Supervisors and the Kern County Council of Defense did their part to aid soldiers in their sobriety by instructing Bakersfield City Clerk Smith that it would aid the War Department if "…all saloons in the town or cities bordering the railroad be closed during the passage of troop trains."[22] This, however, did not prevent all saloon owners from plying their wares to soldiers. The Kern County Board of Supervisors and the Kern County Board of Defense heard charges against Theodore Kelm, a Mojave saloonkeeper, accused of selling liquor to soldiers on December 23, 1917.[23] Kelm's liquor license was revoked as a result of his actions.[24] After hearing complaints that Martin Olson's saloon in East Bakersfield sold liquor to soldiers passing through town, Superior Court Judge Milton T. Farmer called for a grand jury investigation into all saloons in Bakersfield and threatened to close them all. In addition to Olson's saloon, the saloon of S. Scapena and Dibini was investigated for selling liquor to soldiers as they stopped in town in route to training camps. Upon hearing that Olson did not know the group of about one hundred men were soldiers (they were not wearing uniforms nor ribbons identifying them as such) and that the police did not notify him soldiers were in town (even Police Chief Munsey was unaware of the troop train in town), the city council dismissed the charges against all three men and allowed them to keep their liquor licenses.[25]

The Bakersfield City Council, in support of the war effort, promoted food conservation and periodically considered the possibility of further restricting saloons. In early January 1918, the council proposed rejecting applications for liquor licenses for 1918, not because the Kern County Defense Council requested this action, but because the council believed this action would reduce the consumption of alcohol, and thus, the use of foodstuffs.[26] The council eventually decided to issue new liquor licenses, but with a clause maintaining the council's right to revoke the license at any time, for any reason, without benefit of a hearing.[27] In February 1918, the Kern County Grand Jury proposed to the Bakersfield City Council that all saloons within the city should be closed by July 1, 1918. The council voted five to two to decline the proposition.[28] Still, the Grand Jury, with the backing of the Kern County Council of Defense, pursued the issue of closing saloons in Bakersfield and Kern County until the conclusion of the war for the sake of promoting efficiency—efficiency

19. In order to support the war effort, saloons such as The Hermitage Bar (circa 1910), located between 18th and 19th Streets, were required to close their doors when soldiers came through town. *Courtesy of Kern County Museum. Used by permission*

in mobilization, conserving foodstuffs, and labor.[29] Before the Grand Jury adjourned in April 1918, they issued an indictment of the liquor industry, printed in the *Bakersfield Californian*, stating:

> A careful survey of labor and moral conditions in Kern County shows that most of all vice and crime and labor trouble is traceable to the sale of intoxicating liquors; shows that the sale of intoxicating liquors is the only business that does not conserve anything, and that it is the only business that is absolutely wasteful to our resources and manpower in these war times; that it is the only business insisting on special privilege to the extent of disloyal violation of war department rules by selling liquor to soldiers, thereby bringing national disgrace upon, and bringing into question the loyalty of our community.[30]

Their efforts, though, were for naught. Likewise, additional efforts to curb saloons during World War I, such as high license fees, were voted down by the Bakersfield City Council, albeit by a narrow margin. At the end of February 1918, City Manager Benson proposed to the council that the liquor license for wholesale houses be raised from $600 a year to $1200, licenses for retail houses be raised from $900 a year to $1200, and licenses for cafes be increased from $300 a year to $900.[31] Three of the council members voted against the measure, three for it, and one was absent.[32] Even though appeals to control saloons during the Great War failed to produce meaningful restrictions, the sense of wartime urgency and the usefulness of the crisis pushed prohibitionists to pursue their goals through additional methods.

Prohibitionists not only used wartime necessity to enact temporary prohibition measures, they also used wartime propaganda and patriotism to promote permanent prohibition measures to secure the United States from the influence of the Central Powers, especially Germany. Temperance was identified with "Americanism," and by default the liquor interests were labeled as treasonous; brewers and the saloons were hailed as collaborators with the Kaiser.[33] During the 1918 campaign in California for a "Bone-Dry" proposition, a law to enact complete prohibition of liquor, radical prohibitionists claimed that the:

> Foreigner, alien to the principles of Americanism, sets a trap for the boy and girl and cultivates the appetite that is later exploited by the owner of the brewery stock in Germany who uses his tainted wealth to buy poison gas or liquid fire to torture the troops of the Allies.[34]

The proposition lost by only 30,845 votes, a narrow loss that demonstrated the effectiveness of tying alcohol to the enemy in earning votes.[35]

Numerous stories in the *Bakersfield Californian* illustrate the genuine distrust and animosity Americans, and in particular, people in Bakersfield and Kern County, had for the enemy. After making pro-German statements, an un-named man working in a garage owned by Dr. Fox was forced to kiss the American flag and was then fired.[36] A.J. Jacobsen, owner of Pioneer Dye Works, was arrested for violating the Espionage Act by attempting to interfere with the draft.[37] The Kern County Board of Supervisors voted unanimously to ban the teaching of the German language in both public and private schools in order to "combat the Kaiser's unseen forces."[38] German agents were suspected of hanging posters in local communities urging oilfield workers to assert their rights by going on strike.[39] West of Bakersfield, 50 tons of alfalfa and barley hay and 250 tons of hay were burned within a week of each other.[40] German agents or sympathizers were suspected in both. An intricate spy system was uncovered to promote agitation amongst workers across the United States.[41] A woman was arrested as a German spy in Hanford, and an Industrial Workers of the World (I.W.W.) agitator was arrested and held in Visalia as an agent of Germany.[42] Even an ex-resident of Bakersfield, Charles F. Petersdorf, was arrested in Tucson, Arizona, as a German spy.[43] Many worried that enemy agents had infiltrated California,

20. Unreinforced and dilapidated, the remains of the Bakersfield Brewery were demolished in November and December 2013. *Courtesy of Charlie Connor*

surrounding communities, and even Bakersfield. In an attempt to keep tabs on potential agents, the United States government ordered that all German enemy aliens in the United States register, the task of registration in Bakersfield falling into the hands of Chief of Police Munsey.[44]

Oddly enough, people in Bakersfield seemingly focused less on the supposed connection between alcohol and nationality than on the threat war dissenters and enemy aliens posed to the war effort. A search of the *Bakersfield Californian* reveals that not one story in the *Bakersfield Californian* between 1917 and 1918 claimed enemy agents were using saloons to promote war dissention or to harbor enemy agents.[45] Even with the arrest of John Baumgartner, Jr., president of the Bakersfield Brewing Company, for violating the Wartime Prohibition Law by selling six barrels and six-dozen bottles of beer containing more than one-half of one percent alcohol, the papers did not focus on his German heritage.[46] Prohibitionists promoted an end to alcohol because it aided the enemy, but this propaganda appears to be less of a concern at the local level in Kern County.

Clinging to the Old

Still, liquor dealers in Bakersfield presented themselves in a positive, patriotic light whenever there was an opportunity to do so. For example, the Bakersfield liquor industry saw a public relations opportunity when the Children's Shelter Fund attempted to raise money for children in war-torn Belgium. The Bakersfield Bartender's Union "generously" donated $10 to the Fund, bringing the total to $1,256.54.[47] Bakersfield Lodge No. 9 of the California Wet Association gave $100 to the Shelter Fund and guaranteed to pledge an equal amount every year, presumably as needed.[48] Bartenders also tried to improve their image in the community by sponsoring dances. The Bartenders' Local No. 378 held an informal dance and meal at the Labor Temple Hall. They also planned to hold a big ball in April.[49] Instead of being perceived as a corrupting force, the liquor industry hoped to be viewed as loyal Americans willing to sacrifice and contribute to the war effort, both monetarily and by providing entertainment and support.

But then again, anti-liquor forces also appeared as a positive and patriotic force. The California Congress of Mothers and Parent-Teacher Associations selected Bakersfield as the site for their eighteenth convention and pledged their

21. Bartender's Local Logo, 5/8/1941. *Courtesy of Kern County Museum. Used by permission*

support of the government in the war, food conservation, and wartime prohibition.[50] The WCTU raised money for War Relief, sought to raise money to purchase a "Trench Kitchen" and ship it to the war front in France to serve American soldiers hot meals, and hoped to raise $2000 for a War Activity Fund.[51] Bakersfield was also chosen as the location for the state WCTU convention held in May 1918, bringing out of town money to the local economy.[52] In a competition for publicity and public image, both sides did what they deemed necessary to garner support and acceptance.

22. Labor Temple at 2121 Eye Street, 10/25/1941. *Courtesy of Kern County Museum. Used by permission*

Wartime necessity mandated food conservation, however many producers and consumers of alcohol believed restrictions on producing alcohol could be the beginning of a campaign for national prohibition. This was especially true for the wine and grape industry. The California Grape Growers Association and the California Grape Protective Association attempted to oppose restrictions and prohibition efforts by appealing to pride in California's history. They claimed that California was the only state capable of producing premium European-style wine grapes (360,000 acres of grapes with a total investment of $150,000,000), had no alternative uses for grapes produced for wine, and that wine was a morally superior beverage and was actually a temperance drink.[53] The wine industry united with other "wets" to defeat the two prohibition amendments on the California state ballot in 1916, but eventually broke with the saloon interests out of self-preservation.[54] With the support of the wine industry and the collection of at least 74,000 signatures, the

Rominger Bill was placed on the November 1917 ballot. This bill proposed to close saloons, but allow the continued production, sale, and consumption of beer and wine below 10 percent alcohol in content.[55] What many of the Grape Association seemingly failed to account for with their Rominger proposal, according to an editorial in the *Bakersfield Californian*, was how staunchly prohibitionists adhered to their principles—acceptance of the Rominger Bill, even if the (ASL) supported it, was contrary to the goals of radical prohibitionists who wanted nothing short of complete prohibition.[56] The California Grape Protective Association, united loosely with brewers, attempted to preserve their respective industries by sacrificing the saloon and whiskey. However, brewers were not shy in voicing their desire to modify the Rominger Bill to better suit their needs.

At a conference of the California State Brewers' Association in San Francisco, brewers pledged to support the closing of saloons but allow the sale of light wine and beer in eating establishments without having to purchase meals. Agreement with the grape industry on supporting the Rominger Bill with amendments did not entail satisfaction with the events at hand. The Brewers' Association, representing over 90 percent of California's brewers, wrote that the sponsors of the measure hoped to accomplish partial prohibition by:

> methods entailing unnecessary and unjust hardships on capital legitimately invested in the grape, wine, beer, barley, rice and other allied industries by methods which will work an enormous and uncalled for displacement of labor in these industries and will throw out of employment many thousands of men...[and that] The Rominger measure discriminates unjustly among the laboring man in favor of the man of means in the matter of obtaining beers and wines, whose consumption the act permits. It requires the laboring man to buy a meal in order to get a glass of beer or wine.[57]

The California Wet Federation, promoting the interests of hard liquor, met March 7 in San Francisco to discuss tactics to oppose the Rominger Bill and suggest an amendment to the California state constitution to protect their trade. The Federation-supported amendment would abolish the saloon, allow the sale and consumption of liquor containing more than 21 percent alcohol as long as it was securely packaged and not consumed where purchased, and allow the sale and consumption of beverages with less than 21 percent alcohol at tables in eating establishments with or without being served a meal. In addition to

23. Fred and Laura Gunther. Fred served as a trustee with the California Wet Federation.
Courtesy of Christine Jones Peard

discussion of the proposed amendment, the convention elected officers for the Federation. Fred Gunther of Bakersfield was elected trustee for the coming year.[58]

Despite the efforts of the wine and beer coalition, the Rominger Bill was defeated, but so was the Bone Dry proposition proposed by the Bone Dry Federation of California. Efforts to avoid both state and national prohibition were successful to that point, but the "wets" could see that the struggle was far from over. One problem the liquor interests had was unity. It was not until the 1910s that the "wets" joined together, as seen with the Rominger Bill, but it was at the cost of one portion of the faction—producers of wine and beer turned on distillers to preserve their own individual industries. They also had to combat the plethora of literature produced by the ASL. Between 1909 and 1923, the League produced over 100,000,000 pamphlets and leaflets attacking the saloon.[59]

The "wets" managed a printing campaign of their own. By 1915, "wets" printed more than 450,000,000 pieces of literature in defense of saloons.[60] Unfortunately for the "wets," food conservation measures during World War I proved to be their undoing.

Unrelenting "Drys"

In California, prohibitionists continued their quest for a "dry" state. The California Dry Federation held a convention in Fresno in February 1918 to determine whether to support a prohibition amendment to the state constitution or focus on electing representatives willing to sign a national prohibition amendment if the occasion should arise. The Federation also considered the Rominger Bill proposed by the California Grape Protective Association. D.M. Gandier, the legislative agent and field representative of the ASL, presented the majority faction opinion of the convention that like-minded politicians were necessary to enact prohibition statutes. By a vote of 355 to 170, the convention decided to focus on the election of sympathetic politicians, a representation of the spilt between the official Prohibition Party and the ASL.[61] In addition, the convention chose not to comment on the Rominger Bill, more than likely perceiving any compromise with the liquor industry as contrary to the cause.[62] An editorial in the *Bakersfield Californian* pondered the importance of the 1918 election. With 100 members to elect in the state—80 assemblymen and 20 senators—and 20 senators not up for re-election, the future of California's acceptance of a national prohibition amendment was in question.[63] The specter of a national prohibition amendment, however, appeared to be not *if* it would happen, but *when* it would happen.

In December 1917 both houses of the United States Congress approved a "dry" measure that included beer and light wines in its scope—the House by a vote of 282 to 128 and the Senate 17 to 8.[64] Typical of the Congressional opposition to the measure was, again, Representative Julius Kahn of California. Commenting on the measure, Kahn states, "You cannot curb intemperance by law," and that with passage of the measure, "You make sneaks, liars and hypocrites of men when you attempt to put in force laws of this kind."[65] When it was passed,

President Wilson had the authority to limit or prohibit the use of foodstuffs in the production of alcohol on a broader level. Whether President Wilson would invoke it, however, was not definite, and Congressional action on a national prohibition amendment was yet to be determined.

Delegates meeting in Chicago for the Thirteenth National Convention of the Prohibition Party proclaimed that wartime prohibition was the goal for now, but national prohibition added to the Constitution was their ultimate goal.[66] This goal, however, could only be accomplished by taking small steps. Prohibitionists, under the pretext of maximizing resources for the war, attached a rider to the Food Production Bill. Even though an armistice had been signed, President Wilson signed this bill, approved by the Senate on September 6 and by the House with a vote of 171 to 34, on November 21, 1918.[67] The bill sought to increase agricultural production and related food products, as well as their distribution. However, with the addition of the rider, any use of grains or food products in the production of beer, wine or other intoxicating liquors for beverage purposes was prohibited after May 1, 1919 until the end of mobilization. The sale of liquor after June 30, 1919 was also prohibited.[68]

Bainbridge Colby of the United States Shipping Board, Food Administrator Herbert Hoover, and Postmaster-General Burleson were all against the Food Production Bill with the added prohibition rider.[69] Hoover believed that the restrictions on wine making would not aid food conservation during the war.[70] Even President Wilson, the same day he signed the Food Production Bill, recommended that it be repealed in regards to light wine and beer. Of course, the issue of wartime prohibition would be moot once demobilization was complete. The threat of war passed with the signing of the Armistice on November 11, 1918, but Wilson could not declare mobilization to be over. Moreover, Attorney General Thomas Watt Gregory advised Wilson that he had no authority to remove restrictions on alcohol until mobilization was clearly over.[71] Wilson was also hesitant to press the issue, choosing to leave it to

Congress, because he did not want Democrats to be branded as "wets" in the upcoming 1920 election.[72]

A Constitutional Amendment

Added to the confusing issue of wartime prohibition and demobilization was the enactment of the Eighteenth Amendment to the Constitution. Influenced by prohibitionists and Progressives alike, Congress introduced a joint resolution in August 1917 for a constitutional amendment enabling national prohibition. The resolution was reintroduced during the regular session and adopted on December 28, 1917, passing in the House (282 to 128) and Senate (65 to 20).[73] Of the politicians casting a vote, 140 Democrats and 138 Republicans were in favor of the Amendment, 64 Democrats and 62 Republicans were against it.[74] The relatively even spilt of Republicans and Democrats favoring the Amendment is demonstrative of the influence the ASL, Progressives, and prohibitionists had on politicians at that time. Elected with their support, representatives supported the Amendment proposed by those who helped elect them into office. The ASL Yearbook tracked voting patterns between 1913 and 1919.[75] During the tracked time period, over 67 percent of Congressmen from anti-prohibition districts and 40 percent from other districts abstained from voting instead of being recorded by the ASL as opposing prohibition measures.[76] It is also interesting to note that 66 percent of freshmen Congressmen moved to support Prohibition and 53 percent of incumbent Congressmen changed their voting patterns toward Prohibition, leading to passage of the Eighteenth Amendment.[77] Thus, with the approval of Prohibition, the Amendment was passed on to the states for ratification.[78]

This is an illustration of punctuation politics—long periods of a stable government policy coupled with negative public feedback, increased attention to the issue and desire for policy change, a change in policy, and then stability in the situation with the return of negative public feedback. Before World War One, a stable alcohol policy, generally supported by the public, based on taxation and state-by-state regulations reigned in the United States. Twelve states left the liquor question to their

41

counties, four states had prohibition through state law, and thirty states addressed the "wet" or "dry" issue through statewide referenda, resulting in fifty-two referenda between 1900 and 1919.[79] However, desire for wartime efficiency and mobilization increased agitation for changes in alcohol policy and anticipation that changes would succeed. Between 1915 and 1919 there was five times as much coverage of prohibition issues in the press, the majority of which was positive coverage arguing for prohibition.[80] Prohibition was posed as a response to a national emergency and the expediency at which the Eighteenth Amendment was formulated—it was debated for six hours in the House of Representatives—caught many people by surprise, as did the fact that the Amendment was ratified within a matter of months, not the three to four years as was expected.[81]

Ratification of the Eighteenth Amendment was the major issue concerning the California legislature in 1919. With a Senate vote of twenty-four to fifteen and an Assembly vote of forty-eight to twenty-eight, California was the twenty-fourth state to ratify the Eighteenth Amendment on January 13, 1919.[82] On January 16, 1919, three-fourths of the states (thirty-six) ratified the Amendment, allowing it to become effective in one year on January 16, 1920. In all, every state except Connecticut and Rhode Island ratified the Eighteenth Amendment, ushering in national Prohibition.[83]

Opponents of the Eighteenth Amendment argued against ratification for obvious reasons. Both Theodore Roosevelt and William Howard Taft opposed Prohibition on the basis that it trampled on a citizen's liberty of choice.[84] Will Rogers humorously quipped that, "Prohibitionists are the originators of Camouflage, They made drinking look worse than it is," and "If you saw a man drunk in the old days it was a sign of no will power, but if you see one drunk now it's a sure sign of wealth."[85] Various groups and organizations rallied unsuccessfully against the Amendment—the Association Against the Prohibition Amendment; National Wholesale Liquor Dealers' Association; National Resale Liquor Dealers' Association; National Association of Wine and Spirit Representatives; and the United States Manufactures' and Merchants'

Association.[86] Samuel Gompers, leader of the American Federation of Labor (AFL), wrote to newspapers in 1917 that national prohibition would displace approximately two million workers and would be, in effect, class legislation.[87] The wealthy would still acquire their alcohol, but the workingman, dependent on the saloon for their beer, would be discriminated against.

Ironically, patriotic support for Prohibition was already on the decline, but the nation was locked into the policy because it was difficult to

24. Minnesota Rep. Andrew H. Volstead, sponsor of the Prohibition Enforcement bill (Volstead Act). *Library of Congress*

change.[88] By the time the Amendment was ratified, Wilson repealed wartime prohibitions on the manufacture and sale of beer and wine. In response, Congress passed the Prohibition Enforcement Bill (H.R. 6810), also known as the Volstead Act. The Eighteenth Amendment outlawed the manufacture, distribution, and sale of "intoxicating" beverages. However, the term "intoxicating" was not clearly defined. The Volstead Act stipulated that any beverage over one-half of 1 percent alcohol was considered "intoxicating." Wilson vetoed the bill on the grounds that the Eighteenth Amendment and wartime enforcement should not be included on the same measure. In short, Wilson believed the bill to be unconstitutional.[89] Wilson's veto was overridden in both the House and Senate, making the Volstead Act the document of enforcement for the Eighteenth Amendment.

The beginning of 1920 witnessed a flurry of activity preparing the United States for the beginning of Prohibition. Wholesale and retail liquor dealers were ordered to report the amount of liquor in their stocks to their district collector of the Internal Revenue Service (IRS) by January 27. Businesses not returning their notification form would have their names and addresses turned over to the Prohibition commissioner in Washington, D. C. for further action. Notification did not, however, apply to individuals holding private stocks of alcohol—all bonded alcohol purchased and possessed before the implementation of Prohibition was perfectly legal. In addition, after January 17 transporters of alcohol for non-beverage purposes were required to have a permit.[90] The federal government hoped to have all the necessary mechanisms for the administration and enforcement of Prohibition by the time it began. William A. Kelly, supervising Prohibition officer for California, Oregon, Washington, Nevada and Arizona, began to organize agents to enforce Prohibition in early January 1920, placing Frank M. Silva as the agent in charge of northern California, a region including Kern County.[91]

Individual states also passed enforcement legislation, "Baby Volstead" Acts, to prepare for Prohibition. In 1919, California passed the Harris Prohibition Enforcement Law, effective in January 1920 if approved by voters in a referendum.[92] The Enforcement Bill, proposed by Assemblyman T.M. Wright, created a special fund to pay for administrative costs of Prohibition enforcement by levying a $5 fee for licenses issued to druggists and other individuals to sell liquor for non-beverage purposes.[93] However, the Harris Bill was defeated in a public referendum 465,537 to 400,475 and a state enforcement law was not enacted until 1922 with the Wright Act.[94]

Last Gasps of Legal Opposition

Some people argued that the passage of Prohibition would result in the death of those attempting to drink their fill before it was illegal to do so. Surely, many people consumed too much alcohol while grieving for their impending loss, and it is possible some drinkers died from alcohol poisoning. But most deaths from consuming alcohol were related to the type of alcohol consumed, not the quantity. Philip Winser criticized the *Bakersfield Californian* for insinuating that the ratification of the Eighteenth Amendment resulted in increased deaths due to overconsumption. The true culprit for these deaths was the consumption of wood alcohol. If anything, Winser optimistically argued, the law will do its best to prevent deaths by eliminating the production and sale of liquor.[95] An exclusive interview with Surgeon General Rupert Blue of the United States Health Service by the *Bakersfield Californian* echoed Winser's sentiments. The Surgeon General warned that consuming bootleg liquor carried a very real danger of blindness and death, and advised, "Don't take any chances. Better be safe than sorry, blind or worse."[96]

Even with the passage of the Eighteenth Amendment and the Volstead Act, the liquor interests continued to fight for their survival. Jacob Ruppert of New York brought a suit all the way to the Supreme Court over the constitutionality of the Volstead Act.[97] Ruppert claimed the Volstead Act interfered with the regulations of the Lever Food Control Act, which allowed beer with 2.75 percent alcohol. The Supreme Court agreed that 2.75 beer had been legal, but only until the Volstead Act was enacted. They upheld the Volstead Act and Prohibition in one swoop, although the vote was five to four.[98] This did not fully discourage "wet" forces. Levy Mayer, counsel for some in the liquor industry, indicated that the "wets" had only began to fight, and the state of Rhode Island filed two suits against the Eighteenth Amendment.[99] In one of those cases, Rhode Island filed a suit on behalf of the James Hanley Brewing Company, claiming that the Eighteenth Amendment and the

Volstead Act were both null and void, named United States District Attorney Harvey A. Baker and the collector of the IRS, George F. O'Shaunessy, as defendants, and asked for an injunction to stop Prohibition enforcement.[100] Representatives of the California wine industry hoped to provide aid to Rhode Island's challenge to Prohibition, declaring Rhode Island's "null and void assertion" to be correct because liquor holdings were confiscated without financial compensation and in violation of rights guaranteed by state and national constitutions.[101] Counsel for the ASL, Wayne B. Wheeler, claimed that once legislatures ratified the Eighteenth Amendment, which they did, it could not be repealed. As a basis for his position, Wheeler cited Chief Justice John Marshall's claim that, "The principle is asserted that one legislature is competent enough to repeal an act which a former legislature was competent to pass…if an act be done under a law, a succeeding legislature cannot undo it."[102] Although this position was put to the test in 1933 both sides of the argument continued to promote their respective stances throughout the period of national Prohibition.

In addition to questions over the constitutionality of Prohibition, others warned of the social ramifications enforcing Prohibition would have on the United States. Reverend Dr. C. Campbell Morgan, pastor of Westminster Chapel in

25. Wayne Bidwell Wheeler, General Counsel for the ASL and author of the Volstead Act. *Library of Congress*

London, believed that Prohibition will be good for the United States, but it would take time for society to adjust. Until then, he states, "Whenever a great country banishes strong drink it must prepare for a revolution. When a man stops drinking he begins to think." Morgan used Russia's banning of vodka as a prime, and relevant, example of social angst and revolution.[103] Perhaps Morgan's assessment of American societal response to Prohibition was a bit extreme. However, it is important to keep in mind that there are many types of action that may be labeled a "revolution" or rebellion. It is also interesting to note that prohibition legislation was enacted in ten countries, but by 1932 all of those countries, except the United States, repealed their prohibition laws.[104]

26. Attorney Theodore A. Bell tried to broker a deal for the liquor interests at the beginning of Prohibition. *Library of Congress*

Some individuals challenged the impending change to liquor laws by liberating government-bonded alcohol from guarded warehouses and by illegally producing their own liquor at home, a precursor to the rampant bootlegging found throughout the United States after the enactment of Prohibition. In San Francisco, $10,000 worth of whiskey—ten barrels—was stolen.[105] Thefts became so problematic that the federal government planned to use 2500 guards to watch over 69 million gallons of liquor held in government-bonded warehouses.[106] Before the official beginning of Prohibition, under the authority of the Wartime Prohibition Act, officers from the IRS and the Bakersfield Police Department found a brandy still, two tubs of grape mash, three barrels of moonshine, twenty gallons of brandy and all the equipment needed to run the operation in East Bakersfield.[107] In addition to the discovery, four Italians and one Finn were arrested.[108] M. Plantier, a French national living in Bakersfield, was charged in Federal Court for violating the Wartime Prohibition Act. Plantier pled guilty for possessing 150 gallons of grape juice, but claimed that it fermented without his knowledge. Despite this creative excuse, Plantier was fined $150.[109]

The IRS attempted to ease some of the burden on the liquor industry. An Option Plan created by Theodore A. Bell, attorney for various liquor interests, allowed wine purchased by an individual, not a third party, before Wartime Prohibition to be sold.[110] Many in the liquor industry tried to secure profits and eliminate their stocks by selling millions of dollars' worth of their products to foreign markets in Mexico, South America, and Europe.[111]

Despite verbal arguments, court injunctions, legal challenges and disapproval from many segments of the population, Prohibition was now the status quo. On the eve of Prohibition an article appeared deep within the pages of the *Bakersfield Californian*. The writer assessed the coming impact of Prohibition on Bakersfield, stating,

> The Zero hour is approaching. Tomorrow midnight the land of the Red, White and Blue (the wets are very blue) will be as dry as a Shredded Wheat Biscuit. Judgment Day is at hand for spirituous liquors in the United States— including Bakersfield.

> John Barleycorn, Esq., accused of misdemeanors and felonies on every count conceivable to the mind of a prohibitionist, stands convicted of each and every one by Congress and the United States Supreme court, and is condemned to die at midnight, January 16. Today he sits in the death cell, not, however, with head bowed and haggard countenance, but with a brave smile on his lips. He hums gaily to himself, "Eat, drink and be merry, *for* tomorrow I die."[112]

Perhaps that smile on John Barleycorn's lips was the realization of how difficult enforcement of Prohibition would be. From 1920 to 1933, Americans did "Eat, drink and be merry," but Mr. Barleycorn's demise was only a statutory inconvenience for millions of Americans. Where there was a will to drink, there was a way to acquire a variety of libations. National Prohibition may have been the legal mandate, but old habits die-hard.

3

Enforcement of National Prohibition

A Slow Start—Kern County on the Sidelines

With the enactment of Prohibition on January 16, 1920, Kern County, along with the rest of the nation, was officially "dry" on paper.[1] The old social institutions—saloons—no longer legally served their traditional wares. In fact, saloons became a thing of the past. For example, Bakersfield listed thirty-four saloons in the city directory in 1919. No saloons were listed in the 1920 directory. However, fifteen of the previous thirty-four saloons and two additional businesses opened their doors as soft drink parlors, providing patrons with non-alcoholic beverages while providing a familiar social atmosphere.[2] Saloons, however, were not the only institutions affected. Cafes, restaurants, and other businesses serving intoxicating beverages had to change their offerings. The only brewery in town in 1920, the Bakersfield Brewery, attempted to survive by producing beer with less than one-half of 1 percent alcohol—"near beer"—but closed their doors by 1926.[3]

27. Bakersfield Saloons, 1919.[4]

Name Of Saloon	Location	Status in 1920 / 1921
Gildo Agnetti	1813 K St.	Closed --- Farmer
American Bar	1931 L St.	Closed / Soft Drink Parlor
The B. B. Bar	1240 19th St.	Soft Drink Parlor / Closed
H.E. Baker	1819 Chester	Closed --- Mechanic
Clemente Borsi	2021 L St.	Soft Drink Parlor / Soft Drink Parlor
H.E. Brammel	1300 19th St.	Closed
Dante Da Costello	1314 19th St.	Soft Drink Parlor / Closed
Davini & Cocco	1930 L St.	Closed
H.T. Dillon	1927 Chester	Soft Drink Parlor / Soft Drink Parlor
Jas Dusserre	723 Humboldt	Closed
Alonzo Giboney	1438 19th St.	Closed
Gray & Haight	1919 K St.	Soft Drink Parlor / Closed
Marius Grimaud	705 Humboldt	Soft Drink Parlor / Furnished Rooms
G.W. Helm	1823 Chester	Soft Drink Parlor / Billiards
The Hermitage	1809 Chester	Soft Drink Parlor / Soft Drink Parlor
J.P. Johnson	705 Sumner	Leader Cigar Store
C.C. Karnes	1812 Chester	California Garage
Kosel & Co.	1102 19th St.	Hotel Kosel
Martinez & Grimaud	1207 19th St.	Soft Drink Parlor / Closed
Mecca Bar	709 Sumner	Soft Drink Parlor / Closed
Miller & Hink	1919 Chester	Closed
Giuseppe Moretti	1217 19th St.	Soft Drink Parlor / Soft Drink Parlor
Occidental Hotel Bar	1201 19th St.	Soft Drink Parlor / Soft Drink Parlor

Name Of Saloon	Location	Status in 1920 / 1921
Pasquini & Co.	1131 19th St.	Closed
Pasquini & Lencioni	1200 19th St.	Closed / Pasquini & Melone Cigars
Jean Philipp	711 Humboldt	Universal Hotel
Price & Carey	1308 19th St.	Soft Drink Parlor / Closed
H.J. Sollers	1330 19th St.	Sollers Motor Company
J.L. Swett	1434 19th St.	Soft Drink Parlor / Soft Drink Parlor
Tibbet & Daniel	1309 19th St.	Closed
The Turf	1401 19th St.	Turf Rooms
Weichelt & Burger	1400 19th St.	Closed
A.E. Wilson	809 Baker	Soft Drink Parlor / Closed
L.H. Zimmer	800 Baker	Closed

28. Alonzo Giboney and his wife. Giboney's bar closed with Prohibition. He was arrested in 1921 for violation Prohibition laws. *Courtesy of Paul and George Giboney*

For nearly five months, all was quiet in Kern County. Either law enforcement officials were unprepared or unwilling to enforce Prohibition or residents were careful in their activities. The people of Kern County remained spectators to the unfolding drama and dilemma of enforcement throughout the United States as reported in the *Bakersfield Californian*. Readers followed reports of raids and violent confrontations between Prohibition agents and bootleggers in Michigan, Wisconsin, New York, Oregon and other locations during the early months of Prohibition and throughout the era.[5]

Readers also followed the legal challenges posed by several states. Governor Edwards of New York vehemently opposed Prohibition on the grounds that it violated personal liberty and states' rights.[6] Rhode Island argued against

29. Jean Philipp, owner of the National Hotel. Philipp's hotel bar was raided in 1920 and he was arrested. *Courtesy of Marti Hardwick Sheldon*

Prohibition along the same lines. Their presentation to the Supreme Court called for the Court to keep Congress and Amendments to the Constitution "within the scope and jurisdiction of federal authority" and to "maintain that line of division between federal and state powers."[7] Distillers in Kentucky filed a brief against Prohibition, legislators in New York attempted to legalize beer containing 2.75 percent alcohol, and an attempted amendment to the Colorado state constitution called for the legalization of beer containing up to 4 percent alcohol and wine with up to 10 percent alcohol.[8]

The *Bakersfield Californian* reported on the economic impact Prohibition might have on the economy, especially the California grape industry.[9] There was a genuine threat that wine grape growers were destined to lose not only their economic investment in vineyards, but also their livelihood. Justice A. Wardell, U.S. Collector of Internal Revenue, proposed a plan to guarantee compensation to vineyard owners based on pre-Prohibition values and for states to purchase vineyard land for

30. Cartoon, "The Great American Home," *Bakersfield Californian*, February 16, 1921, 4.

colleges to conduct agricultural research and experiments.[10] The California Grape Protective Association diverted energy from fighting against Prohibition to finding new markets for wine grapes and raisins.[11] Grape growers in Kingsburg, California toyed with the possibility of making syrup from wine grapes.[12] Ultimately, the grape industry had little to fear. As more Eastern states became "dry," the value of grapes from California increased.

The lighter side of Prohibition also entertained readers of the *Bakersfield Californian*. Residents read reviews of Prohibition-themed theatrical productions running in Bakersfield and amusing stories concerning Prohibition. Playing at the *Bakersfield Theater* was the production "Wet and Dry," a comedy lampooning Prohibition.[13] "The Bootlegger," also playing at the *Bakersfield Theater*, received negative reviews for its lack of action and humor.[14] One story posited the question: "Can Horse Drink Champagne Under New Amendment?"[15] Apparently, a wealthy show-horse owner allowed her horse to drink a gallon of champagne before each show so it would have more pep in its step. The Collector of Revenue for Southern California advised that it was permitted as long as the horse signed an affidavit that the alcohol was for medicinal purposes. Ultimately, the horse competed in the show without its customary drink beforehand. Another story revealed the willingness of Prohibition officials to limit First Amendment rights in the quest to enforce Prohibition. According to officials, *Drinks As They Are Mixed*, written by an ex-bartender from San Francisco, could not be published, even for export.[16] "The Great American Home," printed in the *Bakersfield Californian*, poked fun at a relative's "wet" tendencies when the man turned down a baby bottle, stating "Uncle Charlie, that's the first time I've seen you refuse a drink!"

Enforcement Arrives

News of Prohibition and its impact routinely made front-page appearances in the *Bakersfield Californian*, but the imprint of enforcement was slow to make an appearance in Kern County. The first thrust of enforcement occurred when three Prohibition agents arrived in town with

31. Police Chief Charles H. Stone, 1919-1923. *Courtesy of the Bakersfield Police Department*

search warrants to search soft drink establishments—former saloons—for liquor.[17] Their efforts produced no contraband, and the proprietors of the businesses searched were cooperative with agents, a response to Prohibition agents that was short lived. This raid was the beginning of many to come over the next thirteen years. Bakersfield City Ordinance No. 42 allowed law enforcement officials to enter and search soft drink parlors without a search warrant, a condition all proprietors of these establishments agreed to as a condition of their

permit for operation.[18] Eventually, the Bakersfield Police Department, led by Chief Charles H. Stone, found the first violator of Prohibition in Bakersfield.[19] Joe Espitallier, owner and operator of the Hotel Des Alpes in East Bakersfield, was arrested on May 3, 1920, for possessing wine, brandy, whisky, and French currant juice for sale.[20] Espitallier—arrested three times in two years, twice in 1920 and once in 1921—became the first of many arrested under a tier of laws enforced by national and local law enforcement officers. Federal, state, county, and

32. Agent Maurice Tice was active in enforcing Prohibition in Kern County. Photo taken April 1928. *Courtesy of Kern County Museum. Used by permission*

33. Agents Maurice Tice and Sid Shannon destroying illegal booze taken during a raid. *Courtesy of the Bakersfield Police Department*

municipal laws were enacted to enforce the Eighteenth Amendment and support the Volstead Act.

Many of the 1727 individuals arrested in Kern County for violating the Volstead Act were arrested by special agents (such as Agents Maurice Tice, Sid Shannon and Thomas Nicely) assigned to federal Prohibition enforcement squads or referred to federal authorities by local law enforcement officials, and then tried in the federal court system, usually in Fresno, California.

In California, the Wright Act—a "Baby" Volstead act—passed in 1922 as a referendum in with 445,076 votes in favor and 411,133 against.[21] This Act called for the Eighteenth Amendment and the Volstead Act to be adopted into the California State Constitution, any changes to national enforcement laws would be reflected immediately in California, and the burden of prosecution shifted from the federal courts to local police courts.[22] The Wright Act set California's commitment to enforce Prohibition until its repeal in 1932, impacting county and municipal definitions of what was considered illegal and how it would be prosecuted.[23]

Before the Wright Act was passed, many municipalities and counties, including Bakersfield and Kern County, passed ordinances to aid law enforcement agencies and add funds to city and county coffers through fines. By September 1920, the ten arrests in Bakersfield were numerous enough that Chief Stone requested a new city ordinance to aid in Prohibition enforcement.[24] The Bakersfield City Council responded by passing Ordinance No. 64. Virtually identical to the Volstead Act, it transferred jurisdiction of violators within the Bakersfield city limits from the federal courts to the police courts.[25] Municipal authorities were initially allocated $1000 for enforcement, with 25 percent of each fine—a minimum of a $250 fine for first time offenders—going back into the enforcement program.[26] Not to be left out of an opportunity to pad the Kern County general fund, a county Prohibition enforcement ordinance, nearly identical to the city ordinance, was created and enforced by the Kern County Sheriff's Department.[27] Later, Bakersfield Ordinance No. 165 and 168 were passed to enforce Prohibition. Ordinance No. 165, adopted April 30, 1923, made it illegal to manufacture or possess for sale intoxicating beverages, with intoxicating defined as anything over one-third of 1 percent alcohol; Ordinance No. 168 allowed for the confiscation and auction of vehicles used to transport alcohol.[28] Of the stories in the *Bakersfield Californian* that reported the fine paid by an offender, $317,127 was collected in Kern County between 1920 and 1933; an amount that would be greatly inflated if all of the fines paid had been reported in the newspaper.[29]

The Difficulties of Enforcement

With the mechanisms in place to enforce Prohibition, federal, state and local law enforcement agencies set out to stem the tide of violations, a task that proved to be easier said than done. It was estimated in 1920 that national enforcement efforts annually would amount to $98,000,000.[30] However, federal money allocated to enforcement was never enough and fell far short of the 1920 projection.[31] In 1923 $6,750,000 was spent on enforcement and $8,500,000 was spent in 1924 to hire about 1500 investigators and agents. These men were attempting to capture smugglers by patrolling 18,700 miles of coastline and borders. They attempted to enforce Prohibition for a population of about

105,000,000 people living within 3,000,000 miles of total area for the United States. According to these statistics, each agent was responsible for 12 miles of border and/or coastline, 2000 square miles of interior, and 70,000 people.[32] Statistically, the chance complete prohibition of liquor in the United States would succeed was improbable given the lack of funding and agents, as well as the geographic enormity of the United States. Additionally, Prohibition was destined to fail unless the majority of people believed in the cause and respected the law.

Perhaps no state had a more difficult time enforcing Prohibition than California. With a 1920 population of 3,426,861 and a total of 158,297 square miles, California presented a special sort of frustration for law enforcement officials.[33] California's vast deserts, mountains, farmlands, and metropolitan and rural areas were ideal for producers of illicit booze, the porous border between California and Mexico was a corridor for smugglers, and California's 1200 miles of coastline presented innumerable opportunities for liquor to be brought in from ocean vessels.[34] Add to these the fact that there were at most thirty-six federal agents assigned to California, ten of which were assigned to clerical and office work.[35] Statistically speaking, each agent in California was responsible for approximately 4397 square miles and 95,190 people. The vast area of California made Prohibition enforcement difficult and frustrating, and the fact that there were many ways to circumvent enforcement added to the feeling that this was a losing proposition.

In 1926, Joseph K. Willing analyzed the profession of bootlegging, noting that there were essentially six groups in this specialized profession—the smuggler; the redistiller; the doctor and druggist; the brewer of strong beer; home brewers and sellers of accessories; and the maker of ciders and wine in the home. Smugglers viewed themselves as beneficial to society. They sneaked illegal, but legitimate, good quality liquor into the United States, providing the eventual customer with whiskey that was 45 to 60 percent ethyl alcohol by volume, aged three to four years. It was not the potentially poisonous liquor produced by the redistiller who extracted the denaturant (nicotine, methyline blue, isopropyl, quinine, brucine, or diethyphthalate) through

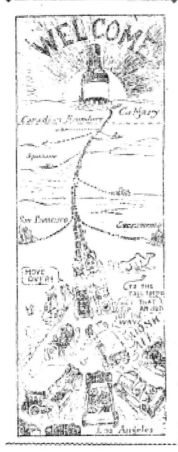

34. "New 'Rum Route' Is One Long Lane That Has No Turning; Is Much Patronized Highway," *Bakersfield Californian*, March 13, 1920, 9.

the distillation process. Denatured alcohol was much cheaper per gallon at .50 to .90 cents compared to grain alcohol at $4.18 with the government tax. Redistillers cooked the denatured alcohol, added caramel or prune juice to give it color, and then flavored it with charred wood or fusel oil to give it an authentic taste, producing a concoction that is up to 97 percent alcohol by volume. Doctors and pharmacists often acted as bootleggers in their own way. A doctor was allowed to withdraw six quarts of whiskey and five gallons of alcohol per year for laboratory purposes. They were also given 100 blank prescription forms for alcohol for a 90 day period, each prescription good for up to 1 pint of whiskey or 1 quart of wine to any single patient every 10 days. Prescriptions were filled with authorized druggists who usually sold high quality liquor. Brewers were allowed to produce beer that was less than one-half of 1 percent alcohol, but it was not illegal for beer to contain higher amounts of alcohol during the manufacturing process. It was not unheard of for some of that high powered beer to disappear from the brewery. Many stores provided the materials necessary for home production of alcohol, and many patrons set about to produce their own liquor. Lastly, as long as individuals kept to themselves and did not produce cider or fruit juice that fermented—and would not be sold—then

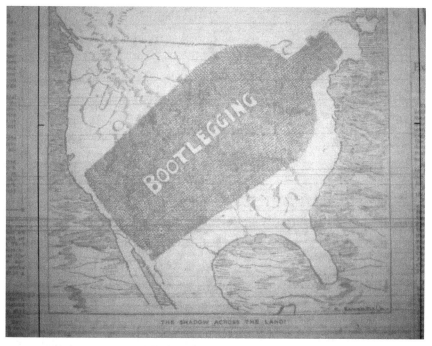

35. "The Shadow Across the Land," *Bakersfield Californian*, April 6, 1921, 9.

authorities had no cause to pay a visit.[36] These six types of bootleggers appeared throughout Kern County between 1920 and 1933, providing evidence of resistance to Prohibition enforcement.

Enforcement of Prohibition was not made easier by the availability of legal alcohol across the United States border in Canada and Mexico. Many "thirsty" Americans made regular trips to Canada and Mexico to drink their fill and attempt to smuggle alcohol back into the country. The pilgrimage to acquire alcohol from Los Angeles, through Spokane, Washington, and on to Calgary, Alberta, Canada, was notable enough to be covered in a story with an accompanying map by the *Bakersfield Californian*. Americans in Mexican border towns such as Mexicali, Nogales, Juarez, and Tijuana, as well as in the Mexican state of Baja California, spent an estimated $1,000,000,000 on liquor.[37] A man and woman were arrested south of Bakersfield as part of a smuggling ring that supplied San Francisco with drugs and liquor from Mexico.[38]

Smuggling alcohol into the United States made enforcement difficult, but it paled in comparison to the difficulty agents had with bootlegging. Booze was readily available for anybody willing to put a little bit of effort into producing or buying it. The constant flow of illegal booze made enforcement difficult and respect for the law laughable. With a relatively small amount of fruit or grain, sugar, yeast, and patience inexpensive alcohol such as "raisin jack," "bathtub gin," or "apple jack" could be produced. Those with the technical knowledge of distillation could turn out "white mule," "moonshine," or the many other names given to homemade grain alcohol in a short amount of time.[39] At least sixty-eight large stills—liquor manufacturing plants—capable of producing large amounts of alcohol were periodically discovered within or near Bakersfield and around Kern County as recorded in the *Bakersfield Californian*. For example, agents discovered five 50 gallon stills concealed in caves on a farm seven miles south of Bakersfield. Smokestacks arising out of a hog pen revealed the location of the operation.[40] On a different occasion, a 1000-gallon vat and 75 gallon still was discovered beneath a

36. Equipment seized in a Kern County raid, June 20, 1922. *Courtesy of the Bakersfield Police Department*

haystack and chicken coop on a ranch east of Bakersfield.[41] In 1932, a liquor manufacturing plant that produced approximately 100,000 gallons of whiskey in two months was discovered on a farm.[42] More often than not, though, dry agents discovered small stills within the city of Bakersfield and the surrounding farmlands capable of producing ten to fifty gallons of liquor in each run.[43]

In 1927, the Jones Act was passed by the United States Congress, making it a felony to own a device capable of distilling liquor and punishable with a prison sentence of one to five years.[44] John W. Harrelson was the first person arrested in Kern County for violating the Jones Act. Represented by Attorney J.K. Lilly, Harrelson plead guilty in Superior Court and asked the court for probation, stating he was just trying to support a wife and seven children. Judge R.B. Lambert granted him probation, an action that greatly upset the WCTU.[45] Unfortunately for Harrelson, he was arrested again after selling liquor to operatives five times. Judge Lambert sentenced Harrelson to one to five years in San Quentin and a fine of $1000.[46] Authorities in Kern County also attempted to reduce home production of liquor by punishing merchants who sold materials to construct stills and breweries. Joseph Fanucchi, Alesandro

Melone, and Albert Pacini were arrested in 1933 for owning stores that bought and sold components that could be used to make a still. Placed on trial by federal authorities for conspiracy to violate the Volstead Act, all three were acquitted.[47]

37. Judge Robert Lambert, 1937-1939. *Courtesy of Kern County Museum. Used by permission*

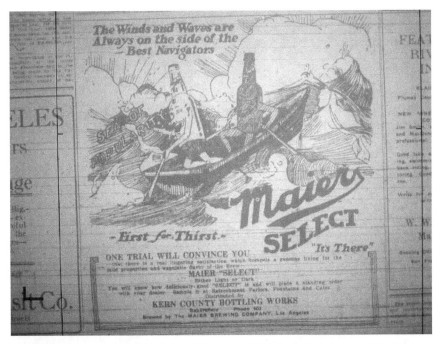

38. Advertisement for Maier Select "Near-Beer." *Bakersfield Californian,* May 21, 1921, 5

The Volstead Act allowed for the production of "near-beer" and "non-alcoholic" beverages. Many breweries across the United States, including the Bakersfield Brewery, attempted to remain in business by producing soft drinks and beer containing less than one-half of 1 percent alcohol. There was a market for "near-beer," with advertisements appearing in magazines and newspapers. By 1925, almost one-billion gallons of near-beer were produced by such companies as Anheuser-Busch.[48] However, some of the "near-beer" produced was nearer to actual beer than allowed by law. Occasionally, real beer was diverted from production lines before it was reduced to "near-beer."[49] The Refreshments Committee for the 91st Division reunion in Bakersfield scheduled for September 24 and 25, 1921, decided not to serve near-beer out of fear that real beer may be substituted, and thus, bring legal problems and bad publicity to the organization.[50] In a statement to the Senate Finance Committee concerning the impact of home-brewed beverages and cereal-based soft drinks, John F. Welch claimed that juice

39. Businesses, such as the Star Soda Works at 406 Grove Street (circa 1912), tried to provide a non-alcoholic alternative to consumers. *Courtesy of Kern County Museum. Used by permission*

sales were hurt by the production of near-beer and cereal based soft drinks.[51] Welch's company apparently had not found a niche in the current market.

Home brewed beer was easy to make and abundant as well. Many recipes for beer implied how it could be brewed full-strength—over one-half of 1 percent—by including warnings that the liquor needed to be diluted to avoid being illegal. One

40. Utica Brew beer label. Notice the alcohol content. *Owned by the author*

particular set of raids in Bakersfield on September 4, 1928, netted 3650 bottles of beer.[52] Raids in July of 1931 resulted in the discovery of 1200 bottles of beer, 157 gallons of whiskey, and fifteen gallons of gin.[53] The brewing of beer in the home was recognized as a big enough problem to warrant the sale of hops and malt illegal to all except confectioners and bakers.[54]

Even easier to make than beer was wine. Despite initial fears that the grape industry would suffer with Prohibition, grape growers continued to prosper with the sale of grapes to individuals for the manufacture of "non-intoxicating" juice for personal use and to bootleggers to produce wine. Wine grapes, commanding $10 per ton before Prohibition, were sold for $40 a ton in March of 1920.[55] By May of 1920, offers of $55 to $60 per ton were made.[56] Farmers rushed to plant more acreage in wine grapes in April of 1921 because of their profitability.[57] 250,000 tons of wine grapes were bought in the summer and fall of 1921 at record prices—for as much as $284 a ton—causing a shortage of grapes.[58] An editorial in the *Bakersfield Californian* concludes that the only logical explanation why raisin grapes ranged in price from $20 to $60 a ton was because they were used to violate Prohibition laws.[59] Between 1920 and 1926, grape shipments—wine, table, and raisin

---

Add to 2½ gallons boiling water 3 ounces loose Hops. Let boil 20 minutes, add 2½ pounds of **Ernst Special Malt Syrup**, 2 lbs. sugar. Stir well so sugar will not go to bottom and burn. Let boil 10 minutes. Total boiling 30 minutes. Strain liquid into crock through piece of muslin and add one package of Clarifying Powder and 2½ gallons cold water. When lukewarm add 1½ cakes of fresh Fleischmann's yeast, dissolved in a cup of liquid, and stir. Set in even temperature.

Cover crock with cloth and let ferment 4 to 6 days. Skim every 24 hours. Filter and bottle. Keep bottles in a dark cool place for 2 weeks.

TOO MUCH FOAM IS CAUSED BY BOTTLING BEFORE IT IS THROUGH FERMENTING
Do Not Have This in Sun's Rays at Any Time.

Be sure your yeast is fresh and that it is not added when liquid is too warm.

REQUIREMENTS of LAW—Such Beverages must not contain more than ½ of 1 per cent. which requires reducing 7 times with water.

---

41. Recipe for home-brewed beer. Notice the legal formality warning home-brewers to mind the alcohol content of their product. *Courtesy of Ken Hooper*

grapes—increased 125 percent.[60] As evidenced by the large amount of wine grapes sold and wine confiscated during raids, the legal and illegal production of wine was a substantial problem for enforcement agents. A raid of Mike Ansolebhere's ranch eight miles northwest of Bakersfield revealed 2000 gallons of aging wine and four tons of fermenting grapes hidden in caves on his property.[61] Raids on French and Italian homes and businesses in Kern County invariably turned up various quantities of wine. Prosperity for grape producers continued until success crippled the grape industry in 1927 due to overproduction.[62] The grape industry had no qualms with Prohibition when the price per ton of grapes was high. With depressed prices beginning in 1927 grape producers renewed their call for the repeal or modification of the Volstead Act.[63]

Several loopholes in the Volstead Act also made enforcement

difficult. As stated earlier, a patient could secure a prescription for medicinal alcohol from their physician. The prescription could then be filled at a pharmacy or other designated place of business licensed to dispense medicinal liquor.[64] United States Attorney General A. Mitchell Palmer determined that certified

42. United States Attorney General A. Mitchell Palmer. *Library of Congress*

distilleries could continue to produce alcohol for non-beverage purposes, i.e. medicinal purposes, and that physicians were allowed to write a prescription for individual patients every ten days. The limitation, however, was left to the 'good faith' of the physician.[65] As with any practice lacking strict oversight, there was potential for abuse of the prescription system. In 1928 alone, physicians in the United States earned $40 million prescribing medicinal liquor.[66] Not only could physicians falsify prescriptions, but druggists could also take advantage of their authority to fill prescriptions. Between 1920 and 1933 there were eleven arrests of pharmacists or workers in pharmacies in Kern County—one in Bakersfield, four in Fellows, five in Taft, and one in Wasco. Five of the

43. Blank prescription for medicinal alcohol (front). *Owned by the author*

individuals were arrested for violating the Volstead Act, five for violating the county liquor ordinance, and one for violating the Bakersfield liquor ordinance. Two individuals, Sam Munger and John Van De Luyster, were acquitted in jury trials.

Section 29 of the Volstead Act allowed for families to make "non-intoxicating" fruit juices and cider for use in the home.[67] The vague terminology used in Section 29—"non-intoxicating"—allowed for somewhat liberal interpretations of the alcoholic content allowed in home-made beverages. Families were allowed to produce up to 200 gallons of wine or cider—non-intoxicating, of course—per year for personal consumption. The Collector of Internal Revenue in San Francisco had to be notified of a family's intentions and the amount to be produced.[68] It is easy to infer that not all the wine produced by individuals was reported and not all of it was produced for individual use in the home.

Fresno-based Fruit Industries, Inc., eased the production of non-intoxicating fruit juices in the home with an original product called "Vine-Glo" in 1920.[69] Available in one quart, one gallon, and five gallon containers, consumers could produce a refreshing drink reminiscent of wine for about 2.5 cents a glass that was assured by the manager, Donald D. Conn, not to ferment.[70] Not surprisingly, Vine-Glo concentrate could produce a beverage with a relatively high, and illegal, alcohol content of approximately 12 percent in sixty days.[71] Eventually, the company hired

Mabel Walker Willebrandt, former Assistant Attorney General in charge of Prohibition, as counsel. Under her direction, Fruit Industries, Inc., stopped home-delivery of Vine-Glo, made the product available only from stores

44. Once a defender of Prohibition, former Assistant Attorney General Mabel Walker Willebrandt went to work for Fruit Industries, Inc. *Library of Congress*

and claimed the company was not responsible for what consumers did with their product.[72] Due to threats from the Justice Department, Vine-Glo was removed from the market in 1931.[73]

Not only did agents have to deal with smuggling, bootlegging, home-brew and near beer, but they also had to determine if liquor possessed by potential offenders was pre-Prohibition stock. Personal stocks of alcohol possessed by individuals before Prohibition were legal as long as it was not sold and as long as it was consumed by the owner.[74] Personal stocks across the United States provided legal comfort, but it did not guarantee that private stocks were safe from "liberation." Between 1920 and the beginning of 1922 several homes in Bakersfield were burglarized and legal stocks of liquor taken. One gentleman had a gallon of wine and five pairs of pants stolen.[75] Joseph Vivian, later arrested for violating city liquor laws, had 140 bottles of old wine and 5 quarts of whiskey stolen from his home—a modest supply to tide a person over during Prohibition.[76] Homer Johnstone was so irate over the theft of liquor and a pistol from his home that he sought federal aid in the arrest of the burglars for illegally transporting alcohol.[77] Whether or not he was successful in attaining federal aid was not reported in the *Bakersfield Californian*. The theft of legal alcohol held by individuals could be personally insulting and perhaps soul wrenching, especially since the prospect of recovering the lost property was slim.

Even government officials and law enforcement officers were not immune to the problem of theft. In the early days of Prohibition, the United States government had to provide storage for bonded liquor— liquor produced legally by distillers for various uses and officially licensed by the government. Republican Senator Warren of Wyoming requested that the government establish warehouses to store bonded liquor on the request of distillers or through seizure by the government.[78] The *Bakersfield Californian* frequently ran stories of bonded liquor stolen from guarded government warehouses.[79] A whopping 50,550,498 gallons of bonded whiskey was stored in government warehouses in 1920. By 1933, the end of Prohibition, only 18,442,955 gallons of government-bonded whiskey remained in warehouses.[80] Surely, 41,000,000 gallons of whiskey was not stolen, much of it was allocated for legitimate uses. However, it was not uncommon for stock to disappear. The theft of bonded liquor was not isolated to government warehouses. Between Caliente and Tehachapi, a Santa Fe Railroad car carrying sixty cases of pre-Prohibition bonded whiskey from San Francisco to Tijuana was disconnected. 720 quart bottles with a retail value of approximately $15,000 disappeared along with a boxcar without being noticed. Residents of the mountain communities of Caliente and Tehachapi expressed "unease" about having stolen liquor in their midst.[81] The unease may have been genuine fear of a criminal gang operating in their community. It may have also been because of the knowledge that Prohibition agents would diligently search for the missing cargo and inadvertently discover unassociated bootlegging operations.

Another problem that interfered with the success of Prohibition had to do with corrupt law enforcement officers in Kern County, as well as in other communities around the United States, who had their hand in bootlegging. The Prohibition Bureau was run on the spoils system for eight years, requiring no specific training for agents until 1927.[82] In that time 17,972 people were appointed to the service, of which 11,982 quit or were let go without prejudice and 1604 were dismissed for bribery, theft,

69

or other criminal acts.[83] Deputy United States Marshall Sid Shannon, instrumental in many Kern County raids, was arrested in Venice, California, for participating in a conspiracy by federal agents to protect prominent politicians from being arrested under Prohibition laws.[84] Bakersfield Traffic Officers F.M. Matthieson and R.M. Beagle were arrested as part of a liquor smuggling ring.[85] Police corruption did nothing to aid in the crackdown on violators. Where there was potential profit to be made, many a person's personal convictions or professional responsibilities were easily compromised. However, the majority of law enforcement officers in Kern County honestly attempted to uphold the liquor laws. One, William Washington "Bud" Wiles, gave the ultimate sacrifice, becoming the only Prohibition officer killed in Kern County. While raiding a cabin near Woody, Louis Lowe shot and killed Wiles. Tried on charges of First Degree Murder, Lowe claimed self-defense and a jury eventually convicted him of manslaughter with a sentence of ten years in Folsom Prison.[86]

45. Early photograph of Louis Lowe, convicted of manslaughter for killing Special D.A. Investigator William Wiles. *Courtesy of anonymous donor*

Probably the biggest factor in the difficulty—even impossibility—of enforcing Prohibition was the lack of public support for the crusade. Federal Prohibition Commissioner John F. Kramer recognized that sentiment was against Prohibition and that it was unsuccessful at the time due to bootlegging, lack of cooperation by the states, and the abundance of licensed dispensers of medicinal alcohol. Assessing the current situation Kramer stated, "You can't turn the current of history overnight."[87] Even Benjamin Owen, National Boy Scout Executive, observed that Prohibition was not a success and was doomed to fail because "Prohibitionists took a big factor out of American life without providing a substitute."[88] This assessment from the leader of one of the most patriotic organizations in the United States only one month into Prohibition was somewhat prophetic or at least realistic. Reality, however, was not always the case for ardent supporters of Prohibition. John Exnicios, appointed United States Prohibition Agent in charge of the Pacific coast states, optimistically planned to take a hand-picked group of agents to 'Sweep California dry from one end to the other inside of a month' and then move on to Oregon, Washington, and Nevada to systematically make them bone-dry.[89] A large portion of the people in California and the rest of the United States, however, did not share his enthusiasm and idealism. Their opposition to Prohibition was expressed time and again through their words and actions.

46. John F. Kramer, first National Prohibition Commissioner. *Library of Congress*

Some expressed the belief that Prohibition was an irrational reaction to the negative impact alcohol had on some people by asserting that it makes as much sense as outlawing the production, sale, and use of small, concealable firearms.[90] Others sought a modification to the Eighteenth Amendment to allow light wines and beer. Delegates in the Maryland Democratic Convention voted to send representatives to the Democratic National Convention with a petition to allow the production and sale of wine, cider, and beer in its original package for home consumption.[91] Arguments in the California State Senate raged over Senator Crowley's proposal of a joint resolution to ask Congress to amend the Volstead Act to allow wine and beer.[92] The California State Assembly passed the Badaracco Resolution 43 to 34, calling for wine and beer to be legalized.[93] The Sanity League of America, incorporated under the laws of California and headquartered in Los Angeles, opened a Bakersfield office at the Tegeler Hotel. Interviewed by the *Bakersfield Californian*, the Sanity League issued a statement claiming, "We are not trying to repeal the Volstead Act, but merely hope to secure an amendment legalizing beer and light wines as beverages in permitting their sale, which was a decision handed down by the Supreme Court." In other words, the Supreme Court ruled that the Volstead Act could be legally amended at any time,

47. Tegeler Hotel at 19th and H Streets, circa 1920s.
Courtesy of Kern County Museum. Used by permission

and the League wanted to pursue that avenue for change. Hoping to appeal to wider audiences, the Sanity League was against whiskey, saloons, and blue laws.[94] A Republican from Michigan, Representative Brennan, sought to legalize beer and wine and add a .04 cent tax to help raise money for the soldier's bonus.[95] The Volstead Act was not modified, but proponents of wine and beer called for compromise throughout the reign of Prohibition.

Many of those arrested for violating liquor laws asked for jury trials, often finding sympathetic juries and judges. A deluge of cases across the United States clogged the court system, so much that United States District Attorneys and local prosecutors and judges pushed for plea bargains, short jail terms, or low fines for a plea of "guilty."[96] After 1922, the number of people convicted of violating prohibition averaged 35,000 a year.[97] Over 5000 cases awaited trial in San Francisco alone with 50 new cases added a day in 1924.[98] As reported in the *Bakersfield Californian*, there were eighty-five instances where suspected Prohibition violators requested a trial by jury.[99] Twenty-four trials resulted in guilty verdicts, eight resulted in hung juries, thirty-one resulted in acquittals, and the results of twenty-four went unreported.[100] So many jury trials were requested and resulted in acquittal or hung juries in 1920 and 1921 that the Bakersfield police court informed the public that no more trials would be held in the police courts and all future cases would be turned over to the Federal courts in the future.[101] The simple fact was many of the peers serving on juries were hostile to Prohibition and impacted courts had to cut deals with violators to keep the docket manageable.

Some violators, instead of taking their chances with a jury, challenged the constitutionality of Prohibition laws. S.C. Crookshank was arrested around December 12, 1920 for violating Bakersfield's municipal Prohibition ordinance.[102] Instead of pleading guilty and paying a $250 fine, Crookshank received a writ of habeas corpus by U.S. District Judge Benjamin F. Bledsoe in Los Angeles to challenge Bakersfield's Municipal Ordinance No. 64 on the grounds that it was unconstitutional.[103] The case itself was closely watched by officials from other cities in California, as well as by other states. A successful challenge by Crookshank's legal team

could void local Prohibition laws around the country. The City of Los Angeles recognized the importance of this test case and pledged aid to Bakersfield City Attorney Wesley Grijalva.[104] Grijalva filed to have the case remanded back to Bakersfield, claiming that the Federal Court had no jurisdiction in the case.[105] Eventually, Federal charges against Crookshank were dropped and he was put on trial in Bakersfield, an end result that would have saved time and money had Crookshank taken the plea deal in the first place.[106]

48. Bakersfield City Attorney Wesley Grijalva. *Courtesy of the Grijalva Family Archive*

Still, a multitude of others in Bakersfield and around the United States showed their disdain for Prohibition simply by disobeying the law. Untold numbers were arrested for drunkenness or for possessing contraband liquor across the nation. But the creativity and determination of some violators in Kern County is remarkable—and humorous— enough to note. Charles Yowell, arrested and fined $250 for violating Bakersfield's liquor ordinance, operated a still in his home. His operation was discovered when city workers encountered a large amount of corn mash clogging the sewer in his neighborhood.[107] Disposing of evidence, an apparently large amount, down the drain probably seemed like a good idea at the time. When Aliprando Bandetini was arrested in a sting in McKittrick, $52,000 in cash and checks was found stuffed in his pockets—potential evidence illustrating how lucrative the bootlegging trade could be. His $700 fine for transportation of liquor was easily

49. The Hunter Cash Market, owned by J.B. Estribou, is seen three buildings to the left of the First Bank of Kern (the corner building). *Courtesy of Kern County Museum. Used by permission*

paid.[108] Two unwise prisoners in the Highway Commission Folsom Prison Work Camp, Mark Carey and Frank Hooper, were arrested on a Kern Canyon road project for making liquor with potato peels and sugar in a guarded camp.[109] So blatant—or mischievous—was Edmund C. Rose of Taft, arrested in 1928, that his profession was listed as a "bootlegger" in the 1930 census.[110]

A few violators, such as Paul Burubeltz and Henry Kaman tried to elude law enforcement officers via their mobility.[111] That is, instead of selling liquor from a stationary business, they became what the law called "walking bars." With liquor concealed on their body, often straight grain alcohol diluted with water, "walking bars" plied their wares while walking the streets and cruising soft drink establishments. This was not necessarily a bad ploy to make money, but all it took was to offer the wrong individual alcohol or to act suspicious around law enforcement officials, let alone draw the ire of an honest businessman or businesswoman who did not want the negative attention in their establishment.

And many sought to avoid detection by hiding their booze in unusual places. Two Italian men attempted to hide forty-five gallons of moonshine and wine in a radish patch behind a grocery store.[112] Some

50. Mrs. and Mr. Egidio Pasquini, Mrs. and Mr. Dante Pasquini, and Mrs. and Mr. Sam Ghilarducci at a family bon voyage party, 3/16/1949. Egidio was arrested for violating Prohibition four times (1927, 1928, 1929, 1932) and Dante was arrested twice (1921 and 1927). *Courtesy of Kern County Museum. Used by permission*

buried their liquor in yards and garages while others stashed it underneath floorboards.[113] A bartender at the Kosel Bar used flexible tubing and a siphon system to deliver liquor from a secreted location.[114] Three men were arrested in an East Bakersfield soft drink parlor for possession of liquor—hidden in a baby carriage.[115] J.B. Estribou, owner of a meat market at 807 Baker St., found himself a target of law enforcement officials on two different occasions. His business was first raided in June 1921. Officials found a large quantity of moonshine and a hole in the wall between his market and a soft drink establishment, a convenient and sneaky way of supplying liquor to a business already scrutinized by the law.[116] Seven months later, Estribou's luck ran out again. This time Bakersfield police officers found alcohol cached throughout his business—behind quarters of meat, underneath steaks, and in pickle barrels.[117]

J.B. Estribou, however, should not feel unlucky; he joined a growing club of men arrested more than once for violating prohibition laws. Between June 1921 and January 1922, six months, Vernon M. Buskard, owner of the American Bar, was arrested four times and faced four Federal Prohibition

51. Amerigo Ripoli, pictured in his later years, was arrested for violating Prohibition three times (1922, 1929, and 1931). *Courtesy Joey E. Earing, Jr.*

charges.[118] A bartender at the Universal Bar, Andre Escallier, was arrested three times in a month.[119] James Hamilton, bartender at the Mecca Bar, was arrested three times in two months and then a fourth time four months later.[120] Not to be outdone, Albert Martin, proprietor of the National Bar soft drink stand, and Fred Harvey were arrested seven times between 1921 and 1931. All told, between 1919 and 1933, 2111 arrests of individuals were made in Kern County for violating Prohibition laws —1726 arrested at

52. Raefello Parenti was arrested for violating Prohibition three times (1921, 1921, and 1930). *Courtesy Joe Scott*

least once; 248 arrested twice; 89 three times; 30 four times; 11 five times; 5 six times; and 2 seven times.

Sadly enough, some drinkers pursued dangerous, and even deadly, avenues to become intoxicated. Some people were desperate enough for alcohol that they bought "Canned Heat," a flammable jelly-like substance packed in canisters and used to heat food, squeezed the liquid out of the jelly, and then drank it. Called the "Doan Special" after Officer Doan who first discovered it being used

53. One of the oldest Prohibition violators (age 75 at first arrest), Frank Soto was arrested four times (1923, 1924, 1926, 1928). *Courtesy of Georgia Blair*

this way, drinkers of the liquid became extremely intoxicated.[121] Four individuals, although not arrested for violating Prohibition, were discovered in a canal trying to cool their insides and quench their thirst from the burning sensation the "Doan Special" left them with. Perhaps more deadly was the consumption of wood or industrial alcohol. More than one hundred people died in the United States from drinking whiskey made with wood alcohol.[122] Others died from drinking straight wood alcohol. James Carroll and four friends bought some wood alcohol to enjoy on the banks of the Kern River beyond the recreation park. Carroll died from the poison. The surviving partygoers claimed that wood alcohol was cheaper than real booze and gave more of a kick. For James Carroll, wood alcohol was more costly than he anticipated.[123] At least five people died in Kern County between 1920 and 1933 from poison liquor and Canned Heat.

An assessment of attempts to enforce Prohibition leads to the conclusion that it was a war of attrition. Law enforcement officials attempted to enforce the laws—some were more enthusiastic than others—and a large portion of the public was willing to break the law. Franklin P. Adams published a poem in the New York *World* that summed up the opinion of many across the United States:

> Prohibition is an awful flop.
> We like it.
> It can't stop what it's meant to stop.
> We like it.
> It's left a trail of graft and slime,
> It don't prohibit worth a dime,
> It's filled our land with vice and crime,
> Nevertheless, we're for it.[124]

As long as enforcement efforts were underfunded and the public was not coerced to obey the law or seek other alternatives, Prohibition was a losing endeavor. As the years ticked off from 1920 to 1933, a growing public tide moved to revise or even repeal the Eighteenth Amendment. It was only a matter of time before the United States government reversed their position on Prohibition, but nobody knew it would take thirteen years.

4

A Profile of Resistance: The Average Violator

Research Methodology

It is pertinent to note that this chapter focuses on developing a profile of Prohibition violators in Kern County. To do this required a massive amount of research. Arrest records for the Bakersfield Police Department and the Kern County Sheriff's Department, as well as the court system, are either non-existent or unavailable at this time. This presents a particularly difficult research problem. The only way to identify violators is to glean information from the pages of newspapers. As a result, I either searched through the *Bakersfield Californian* on microfilm at the Beale Branch of the Kern County Library or the digitized archive of the *Bakersfield Californian* available through the online database of the Los Angeles Public Library. Additionally, some violator documentation was accessed in the *Los Angeles Times* and Bakersfield *Morning Echo*. In all, approximately 60,000 pages were browsed to identify violators. That in itself warrants a caution on the data collected—only those listed in newspapers are included in this study. It is plausible that many violators were not reported in the newspapers. That fact opens the door for a more extensive study on this topic when future documentation is discovered. Identified violators are then processed, on average, three different ways through the Ancestry.com database to identify census and political party affiliation data, but, that too presents other limitations. Not all individuals show up in census data or individuals cannot be definitively identified. In many cases, individual names were cross-referenced with data about their arrest to identify individuals on the database. Individuals were also cross-referenced with other sources—*Lest We Forget: the French in Kern County*; *Basques to Bakersfield*; and *Italians in Kern County*—to positively identify violators whose data was less than complete.[1] Throughout the analysis of violator data I will identify the limitations, assumptions and suppositions I have made in creating a profile of violators in Kern County.

Location, Race, and Age

One way in which a profile of the average violator in Kern County can be created is through an analysis of where violators were arrested. Between 1919 and 1933, 2111 arrests were made of 1726 individuals. During the research process, the location of arrest for 203 people was not identified. Within the city limits of Bakersfield, 864 violators were arrested, with the remaining 1044 arrested throughout the county. Many towns, besides Bakersfield, are represented in the documentation of arrests. Seven people were arrested in Arvin, ten in Buttonwillow, thirty-one in Delano, eighteen in Fellows, seven in Isabella, thirty-six in Maricopa, six in McFarland, sixty-seven in McKittrick, twenty-four in Mojave, fourteen in Randsburg, twenty-one in Tehachapi, and twenty-five in Wasco. Taft alone had 192 arrests. 586 other arrests were scattered throughout the rural areas of Kern County such as the Greenhorn, Tehachapi, and Temblor mountain ranges, the foothills of the Sierra Nevada, the Mojave Desert region, areas along the Kern River and Poso Creek, along the Ridge Route to Los Angeles, in the oil districts, and farmland areas across the

54. Don Hanning (front-left) was said to be the best producer of moonshine in the Kern River Valley. He was only arrested and fined one time (1930). *Courtesy of Bob Powers.*

county. To take this analysis further, the specific location of arrest can be analyzed. Newspaper stories indicate that 340 arrests were made at the person's home and 160 arrests occurred on ranch or farmland. Businesses accounted for 385 arrests, including 117 at soft drink parlors and 11 at pharmacies.

Another aspect of creating a profile of violators in Kern County is an examination of race. Statistical data on race is available for 707 individuals.[2] The overwhelming number of violators identified in Kern County were white—648 people (91.65 percent). No other group comes close—black Americans numbered 33 (4.66 percent); Mexicans 16 (2.26 percent); Chinese 5 (.70 percent); Japanese 4 (.56 percent); and Native Americans 1 (.14 percent). As a comparison of population statistics for Kern County as a whole, in 1920, whites composed 97.05 percent of the population, Native Americans, Chinese, Japanese, and all other races were 2.03 percent, and black Americans were .90 percent.[3] In some areas of the

55. Roadhouses, such as the Buckhorn Club off of the Bakersfield-Taft Highway, often operated as old-time saloons during Prohibition. *Courtesy of the West Kern Oil Museum*

United States, namely the South, black Americans were accused of being a barrier to Prohibition enforcement. Jeannie M. Whayne conducted a study of Prohibition and race, class and family in two small towns in Arkansas. She found that it was not black Americans in particular, but gender and class that presented the biggest obstacle to Prohibition enforcement. Single males—black and white—from the lower class were the main source of Prohibition violations.[4] Whayne's study and this study are hardly comparable in nature—black Americans in Kern County made up a smaller portion of the total population of residents between 1920 and 1930 than did black Americans in Arkansas. In 1920, 499 black Americans lived in Kern County (38,763 in California) and 2142 as of 1930 (81,048 in California). The population of black Americans in Arkansas was 272,220 in 1920 and 472,220 in 1930. But Whayne's findings are still relevant as a comparison of geographic differences between Prohibition violators in the South and in Kern County. This is especially true when the comparison moves from race to age, gender, and socioeconomic status.

The average Kern County violator was middle-aged. However, it is a category that begins to complicate the analysis of Prohibition violators

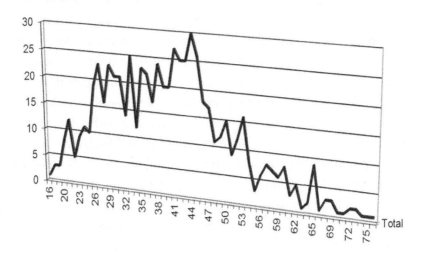

56. Horizontal axis indicates age at first arrest; vertical axis tallies the number of violators in each age category

in Kern County. Identifying the age of an individual at the time of their first arrest either depends on that information being noted in newspaper accounts of the arrest or through census data. With census data, age at the time of first arrest is figured by comparing the age at the time of the census and the year in which the individual was arrested. Of course, analysis is only possible if individuals are found in census data and if the census data indicates their true age, in a legible manner, at the time the census was taken. With that being said, the ages of violators at the time of their first arrest were found for 687 individuals. Ages range from 16 to 87 (the median age is 46), with the average age of a violator in Kern County being 39.97 years old at the time of their first arrest.

Gender, Marital Status, and Education

An examination of gender reveals that of the 1726 violators in Kern County, 1535 were males (89 percent) and 191 were females (11 percent).[5] The general perception, reinforced by a lack of research in historiography and popular culture, is that violating Prohibition was a male event and that female violators were involved in some aspect of the vice industry.[6] Tanya Marie Sanchez's study on female bootlegging in New Orleans paints a picture of female violators that somewhat counters traditional perspectives. Sanchez found that female violators in New Orleans—violating Prohibition to earn extra income or because it was seen as a cultural imperative—were typically of immigrant stock (Italian, Irish, Jewish, Spanish), ranged in age from sixteen to eighty-three, tended to be widowed, divorced or separated, and were usually mothers.[7] Some women in Sanchez's study claimed that they were either forced by their husbands to bootleg or to take the blame for their husband.[8] A study by Mary Murphy further explores the issue of women as bootleggers by claiming that Prohibition created new economic opportunities.[9]

Both studies offer a comparison to violators in Kern County. Age and census data were found for 68 of the 191 females arrested in Kern County. Violators ranged from eighteen to sixty-seven, the average age being thirty-seven. As with black males, black females were specifically identified by race in the newspaper. Women not identified as black are

84

assumed to be white. Of the female violators, 186 were white, 4 were black, and 1 Mexican. As far as place of birth, data for 123 of the women is unknown. Of the known women, 50 were born in the United States (73.5 percent) and 18 were foreign-born (26.4 percent)—the largest number from Italy (11) and France (3). When data for parents' place of birth is viewed, eleven of the fifty born in the United States had at least one parent born outside the country, a number that increases the number of women with an ethnic background to 29 (42.6 percent).

Marital status data is a bit more complicated. Data was found for 692 individuals—431 violators were married, 191 were single, 39 were widows or widowers, and 31 were divorced. For women, data was found for sixty-nine individuals, but it is difficult to truly assess whether a person is single, married, divorced, or widowed because census data is often years removed from when the individual was arrested. Taking the data at face value, forty-four women were married, ten were widowed, eight were divorced, and seven were single (of the 1535 males, marital status was determined for 622, of which 387 were married, 184 were single, 29 were widowed, and 22 were divorced). The data can be further expanded by adding women listed in newspapers with the prefix "Mrs." to the married data, bumping that number to eighty-three. Likewise, the category of "single" can be increased to eleven by including women referred to as "Miss" or "Ms."

Sanchez notes that most of the women in New Orleans who bootlegged fulltime were restaurant or grocery store operators and soft drink purveyors, with very few linked to prostitution.[10] Newspaper stories convey information about women arrested in Kern County. Sixty-three women were arrested at home, an indication that alcohol was sold as a home-based business. It is not inconceivable that many women peddled liquor to earn an income, but at least one husband disagreed with the actions of his wife. When Mrs. R. Cates was arrested in 1927, her husband said that he told her not to make wine and that she was on her own to take her punishment. Mrs. Cates paid a $250 fine. It is unknown if their marriage survived this incident.[11] Thirty-one women were arrested at businesses associated with the food and service industry—hotels, boarding houses, restaurants, roadhouses, soft drink parlors, and night clubs. Three women were identified in the *Bakersfield Californian* as women arrested in houses of ill repute, a slight verification that some women who bootlegged were involved in prostitution. And in an odd instance two women, Mrs. Mabel Jones and Mrs. Lena Walker, arrested in 1922, were both fined $350 and given a 180 day suspended sentence if they agreed to sell their belongings and leave town.[12]

Education level might correlate to willingness to violate Prohibition. Census data from this era notes whether a person can or cannot read or write. This data was found for 671 individuals, of which 632 individuals were able to read and 630 able to write, with 39 unable to read and 41 unable to write. With this data in mind, the overwhelming majority of the violators that data is available for, approximately 94 percent, were able to read and write. As an indicator of correlation between education level and the potential to violate Prohibition, the ability to read and write appears to be significant. That is, based on the available data the ability to violate Prohibition is dependent upon literacy. However, it is hard to imagine that education was a prerequisite for the ability to bootleg.

Ethnicity

Many scholars and temperance workers identified ethnicity as a factor for Prohibition violation. Athena Marmaroff, the director of WCTU work at Ellis Island, stated that the Eighteenth Amendment was commonly broken by foreigners, lamenting, "Let us see that the laws are obeyed and those who do not like them or obey them should be sent back to the country from which they came."[13] The struggle for Prohibition was seen as a conflict to preserve American values from invading cultures. At the WCTU national conference in 1928, Ella Boole stated,

> This is the United States of America, my country and I love it. From the towering Statue of Liberty to the sun-kissed Golden Gate, this is my country. It is all I have. It is the foundation and security for my property, home and

God. As my forefathers worked and struggled to build it, so will I work and struggle to maintain it unsoiled by foreign influences, uncontaminated by vicious mind poison. Its people are my people, its institutions are my institutions, its strength is my strength, its traditions are my traditions, its enemies are my enemies and its enemies shall not prevail.[14]

The fight against Prohibition violators was not only a struggle to create a "dry" nation, but it was also an expression of nativists' desires to maintain the cultural dominance of white Anglo-Saxon Protestants. In an exploration of the role ethnicity plays in the vice industry, Ivan Light notes that sociologists argue that vice is either something that is brought into the nation by immigrants—an argument rooted in xenophobia—or is domestic in origin—ethnic purveyors of vice supply what is demanded by the native population.[15] Light concludes that the best explanation the role ethnicity plays in the vice industry is a fusion between the demand of the American public for illicit goods and services and the extent to which the disadvantaged supplied those services; poor ethnics, subject to a harsh economic climate in the United States, sought to make a living by supplying a good that was scarce during Prohibition.[16]

References to ethnicity as a reason for resistance to Prohibition focus on the large eastern or mid-western metropolitan areas such as New York, Chicago, and Philadelphia. The question remains if ethnicity was a determinant in resistance to Prohibition in Kern County. In this study, 1726 names of people arrested for violating national, county or city Prohibition laws were collected from stories reported on in the *Los Angeles Times*, the *Bakersfield Californian*, or the *Morning Echo* from 1918 to 1933. Of that number, data indicating nation of birth was found for 692 people (40 percent). Although many questions remain concerning the individuals whose data cannot be found, some conclusions may be observed based on the available evidence.

The disproportionate number of violators who can be identified as ethnic, based on the best evidence available, lends credibility to the claim that ethnic groups were, on the whole, largely resistant to Prohibition. Of the 692 violators whose nation of birth status was identified, 431 (62.28 percent) were native-born. A large number of those individuals were born in California (111—25.75 percent). With this in mind, it is difficult to support the sociological argument that this form of vice (liquor) originated outside the nation and was a product of ethnicity. 261 (37.71 percent) of the individuals were foreign-born, with 118 (45.21 percent) born in Italy (Figure 17). If ethnic identity influenced whether a person was more apt to resist Prohibition laws, as some historians have insisted, then the number of ethnic violators should be sizeable, which it is not in the case in Kern County, that is, until violators with one or more parents who were foreign-born are added to the list. 352 violators (50.86 percent) have at least one parent born outside the United States. When these individuals are added to the number of foreign-born violators, the proportion of ethnics greatly increases to 613 (88.58 percent). This is a number that cannot be ignored or dismissed and it indicates that ethnic violators did make up a significant number of those reported arrested in Kern County. When compared to population figures from 1920, the percentage of foreign-born violators is not proportional to the number of foreign-born residents (45.21 percent of violators : 13.4 percent of the population). Native-born violators with at least one foreign-born parent are overrepresented even more when compared to their proportion of the 1920 population (50.86 percent of violators : 22.6 percent of the population). The combined total of foreign-born and native-born with foreign-born parentage further increases the representation of ethnic Prohibition violators (88.58 percent of violators : 36 percent of the population).[17]

Socioeconomic Status, Home Ownership, and Political Party Affiliation

Examining statistics on trade to reveal socioeconomic status is also informative in developing a profile of violators in Kern County. The trade of violators was found for 761 individuals through census data, city directories, and voter registration information.[18] Of the 761 violators in

Kern County that data is available for, 37 are classified as professionals. These are individuals who received advanced training, certification, or licensing. Included are teachers, nurses, law enforcement, firefighters, veterinarians, engineers, administrators, and government workers. Pharmacists were the largest number of professionals who were arrested, a total of five. It is not surprising that pharmacists were often involved in bootlegging. The temptation to sell alcohol without a prescription could be lucrative.

Unskilled (or entry-level) workers made up a sizeable number of violators—222 in all. These include drivers, waiters and waitresses, sheepherders, porters and packers, maids and other domestic workers, those identified as workers or helpers, and custodians. Also included in this classification are laborers, the largest number of unskilled workers who violated Prohibition—144 of the 222. Explaining why unskilled workers violated Prohibition is relatively straightforward—it was the opportunity to improve their socioeconomic status quickly, albeit illegally. Responding to the forces of supply and demand, individuals are willing to produce or supply alcohol because of the economic reward. The lure may have been strong because wage growth for the unskilled was stagnant or depressed during the 1920s. For example, the real average weekly earnings for selected unskilled workers was $22.28 in 1920; it was $22.47 in 1930. Even worse were the weekly earnings for farm laborers—$16.92 in 1920 and $13.26 in 1930.[19] Louie Labovitch, arrested in 1924, stated that he bought gin for $18 a case and then sold each bottle for $10.[20] T.P. Semple, a rum runner from San Francisco who was captured only after being shot in the arm after a car chase, planned on selling three cases of "Gordon's Gin" for $35 a case.[21] This could add up to lucrative, tax-free profits. Tax-free unless a violator was a person like Bill Hickman, arrested in 1921 for possession, given sixty days in the county jail, and taxed by the IRS $1064 for profit he made on moonshine.[22] According to the newspaper account, he was not the only person in jail who received a tax bill, but he was the person who received the largest bill. However, some individuals violated Prohibition out of economic necessity. William Jennings Gilmore was arrested in 1929 for transporting liquor. Gilmore explained that it was his first time doing this and only took the risk to earn $100 for a surgery his wife needed.[23]

The largest number of violators were skilled workers or tradesmen—a total of 501 of the 761 identified violators. This category includes a wide variety of careers—plumbers, butchers, miners, pipefitters, oil workers, railroad workers, contractors and construction trades, merchants and salespeople, farmers and ranchers, and owners of businesses. At least seventy violators from this category were proprietors of soft drink parlors, night clubs, or roadhouses.

Home ownership is another aspect of socioeconomic analysis of violators in Kern County.[24] The data for 465 out of the 1726 individuals was found in census records. What is interesting is that 212 violators (45.59 percent) owned their own home and 253 (54.40 percent) were renters, rates that are not outside of the norm. Between 1920 and 1930, home ownership in California ranged from 43.7 percent and 46.1 percent.[25] Violators, especially professionals and skilled workers, were often economically stable, reflected by home ownership. But a cursory examination of home ownership and trade does not reveal a consistent pattern—professionals, skilled workers and tradesmen, and unskilled workers are documented as both home owners and renters.

Political party affiliation was found for 380 of the 1726 individuals arrested in Kern County for violating Prohibition. As with data

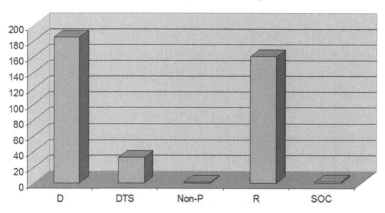

57. Violator's Political Party Affiliation

on trade, registration records for these individuals are not always found for the time period a person was arrested. 185 were registered Democrats, 160 were Republicans, 2 were registered as Socialists, 32 declined to state their affiliation, and 1 was registered nonpartisan. The fact that 48.68 percent of violators were Democrats and 42.10 percent were Republicans illustrates that potential to violate was not dependent upon how a person registered to vote.[26]

The Average Violator

Putting all of the analysis together, a portrait of the average violator of Prohibition in Kern County can be made. The violator is apt to live in or conduct business around Bakersfield, Delano, or the oil centers of Maricopa, McKittrick, Fellows, or Taft. They will be a literate white, married male in his thirties or early forties, native-born, but have at least one parent born outside of the United States—more than likely Italy, France, or Germany. They are likely to work in the hotel, restaurant or soft drink industry, are a farmer, or a laborer. He is more than likely a skilled worker or tradesman, it does not matter much if he is a Republican or Democrat, and it is slightly more likely that he will rent a home.

Regardless of this profile, individuals from all walks of life violated Prohibition laws. Men and women, either because of the challenge, economic potential, cultural imperative, or just the plain desire to have a drink made the choice to break the law. In towns, counties and states across the United States this was occurring. And law enforcement faced an uphill battle—understaffed and underfunded, they tried to bring a largely unwilling population into compliance with national laws. Something had to change.

5

Repeal of Prohibition

A War of Attrition

As people in Kern County and the United States continued to circumvent Prohibition restrictions, the "dry" years ticked by and the number of arrests continued to mount.[1] The longer Prohibition was the law of the land, the more difficulty officials seemed to have with enforcement. As individuals continued to largely ignore Prohibition laws, the more organized opposition to the Eighteenth Amendment became and the more realistic repeal appeared to be.

Law enforcement at the local, county, state and federal levels often revised tactics and policies to better deal with the realities of enforcement. The ASL admitted in 1927 that law enforcement officers could not handle the Prohibition situation and that more laws were needed.[2] In 1928, the Kern County Grand Jury issued a report to Judge Erwin W. Owen stating that law enforcement officials found it almost impossible to secure convictions by a jury in liquor cases.[3] To strengthen the evidentiary chain necessary to secure convictions, federal agents were authorized to "tip" informers anywhere between $5 and $200 for information leading to the arrest and seizure of alcohol and manufacturing apparatus. This program, scheduled to run until at least the end of June 1929, was based on programs funded by the WCTU and used by other law enforcement agencies.[4] The City of Taft revised its Prohibition ordinance to define a beverage as "intoxicating" if it contained over one-third of 1 percent alcohol—a stricter standard than the federal definition—in order to collect larger fines.[5] To broaden law enforcement capabilities in Bakersfield, the vice squad was disbanded and all members of the police department were expected to enforce "dry" laws.[6] Businesses that qualified as public nuisances because of repeat violations of Prohibition laws became subject to "padlock" orders.[7] The Chicken Inn, located three miles east of Bakersfield on Edison Highway, was padlocked by Deputy U.S. Marshall Sid Shannon for one year.[8] Another business, located at 102 East 6th Street, was padlocked by Shannon under the order that no person could enter the building or conduct business there for a year.[9] Prohibition enforcement

58. Judge Erwin W. Owen. *Courtesy of Kern County Museum. Used by permission*

was successful enough in Kern County that a former Chicago gangster involved in bootlegging supposedly stated that liquor smugglers

59. Number of Arrests in Kern County by Year

Year	Number of Arrests
1920	84
1921	273
1922	207
1923	194
1924	322
1925	141
1926	255
1927	89
1928	214
1929	130
1930	67
1931	110
1932	80
1933	11

from Chicago to New York and the Southland warned each other how tough the deputies and police in Kern County were—a reputation that apparently went far outside of Kern County but did little to stem the tide of illegal liquor traffic within the county itself.[10]

Regardless of successful arrests, enforcement of Prohibition laws became exceedingly difficult because of procedural restrictions and changes in policies. For example, the Assistant Secretary of the Treasury, Seymour Lowman, proclaimed that agents could not justify a search based on the smell of alcohol. They must obtain search warrants and must not destroy private property when conducting raids.[11] Many agents hoped to prosecute sellers of bottles, labels, barrels, and other equipment used to manufacture alcohol.[12] Unfortunately for agents, the Supreme Court ruled that agents must prove that the equipment was intended to be used for the manufacture and sale of liquor before it could be seized and individuals prosecuted.[13] And if raids and working undercover were not difficult enough, federal agents were ordered to place a metal shield

60. Director of Prohibition Bureau, Amos W.W. Woodcock (left), with sample of metal shield for autos. *Library of Congress*

measuring seventeen inches by twenty inches on the right door of their automobile in an effort to separate genuine federal agents from imposters.[14]

Complicating enforcement efforts, in August 1928, federal Prohibition agents were placed under the U.S. Civil Service Commission to weed corrupt and inept agents out of the Prohibition force. This new policy required agents, investigators and inspectors around the country to prove they were qualified by taking a competitive examination, even if agents were capable and effective at what they did—a

61. Bakersfield City Manager James Armstead Ogden. *Courtesy of Kern County Museum. Used by permission*

policy authorities projected to result in the replacement of 80 percent of federal liquor agents in Southern California.[15] Another policy designed to avoid corruption through familiarity, was the shifting of federal agents to different regions every year.[16] Additionally, the funds to adequately enforce Prohibition were never fully allocated by Congress. Republicans refused to appropriate $257,000,000 to enforce Prohibition, but eventually $24,000,000 extra—approximately 10 percent of the requested

62. Bakersfield City Attorney Walter
Osborne. *Courtesy of Kern County
Museum. Used by permission*

funds—was voted by the Senate, 50 to 27, to be used at the discretion of the President for enforcement.[17] At the local level, Bakersfield City Manager James Ogden and City Attorney Walter Osborne were more successful at acquiring extra funds, convincing the City Council to pass an emergency resolution allowing unlimited funds to be drawn from the city treasury for special investigatory work for the war on Prohibition and

vice.[18]

Not only did law enforcement face procedural, hiring, and funding obstacles, but they also experienced periodic difficulties doing their jobs because of lawsuits and internal conflict. C.A. Baumeister of Taft filed a suit for damages in the amount of $5000 against Constable E.J. McClintock and Prohibition Officers Paul Shannon and Maurice E. Tice. Baumeister stated that in the twenty minute search of his residence with a "John Doe" warrant listing no specific items to search,

63. Officer Paul Shannon.
*Courtesy of Kern County Museum.
Used by permission*

64. City Councilman Howard Carlock traded punches with the Chief of Police Font Webster over accusations of corruption in his department. *Courtesy of Kern County Museum. Used by permission*

officers damaged locks and furniture.[19] Officers Shannon, Thomas Nicely and Sergeant A.B. McCreary (former head of the Fresno police vice squad), in addition to other individuals, were accused of trying to "frame" federal Prohibition agent Paul Mathias, accusing him of taking liquor from government vaults for his own personal use. Dr. James Doran, Prohibition Commissioner, examined the evidence and completely exonerated Mathias, ordering an investigation into the motives of the accusation. Charged with conspiracy to "injure, oppress, threaten and intimidate" Mathias over a period of five months the accusers became defendants. In the end, the trio was acquitted of all charges and claimed that the clearing of Mathias was an attempt of the Civil Service Commission and the Prohibition Bureau to preserve their own reputations in Southern California.[20] In another case, federal agent Walter S. Patterson was charged with assaulting Henry D. Hoot, a disabled World War One veteran working as a taxi driver. According to reports, Hoot testified against Patterson at a hearing in front of a United States Commissioner earlier in the day. That afternoon, Patterson confronted Hoot and accused him of perjury. Hoot responded by introducing Patterson to the crowd as a prohibition agent, upon which Patterson proceeded to beat Hoot. On February 28, 1931, Patterson was acquitted of the charges, despite admitting the attack and multiple witnesses confirming the events.[21] And in February 1933, City Councilman Howard

Carlock and the Chief of Police, Font Weber, threw punches on the corner of 19th and L Streets. Carlock accused Weber of having officers who bootlegged on the side.[22] These issues were big news and raised questions about the quality and character of those paid to enforce Prohibition laws, contributing to the fact that many people who were neither for nor against Prohibition eventually joined the ranks of those calling for modification or repeal.

65. Officer Otto Heckman was accused of bootlegging under the watch of Police Chief Webster. An investigation did not verify the accusations. *Courtesy of Kern County Museum. Used by permission*

One of the main goals of Prohibition was to eliminate the consumption of liquor, producing a more industrious, efficient and thrifty, family-oriented and "Americanized" population. How effective the Eighteenth Amendment was at actually reducing the consumption of alcohol is debatable. Researchers Jeffrey A. Miron and Jeffrey Zwiebel wrote a study titled "Alcohol Consumption During Prohibition," in which they argued that at the beginning of Prohibition consumption fell to 30 percent of normal, but within a few years consumption had increased to approximately 60 or 70 percent of pre-Prohibition levels and remained at that level until Prohibition was repealed.[23] Despite the amount of money spent on enforcement—$6.3 million spent in 1921, $9.2 million in 1925, and $13.4 million in 1930— Miron and Zwiebel maintain that law enforcement had little to do with the decline in consumption.[24] The reduction in consumption had more to do with increased supply costs (associated with the risks of being caught) and the natural barriers to consumer access because of increased prices, questionable quality of liquor and the fear of being ripped off.[25]

Another researcher, J.C. Burnham, assessed Prohibition differently in "New Perspectives On The Prohibition 'Experiment' Of The 1920s." Burnham argued that Prohibition should be viewed as a reform movement, not an experiment, and that it should more aptly be assessed as a success, not a failure.[26] Success, according to Burnham, should not be judged on enforcement records which are inconsistent across the United States. Rather, the success of Prohibition lies in the reduction of alcohol consumption, an interesting perspective that relies on the same statistical information as the study by Miron and Zwiebel.[27] In fact, Burnham states that perhaps the greatest indicator of success is the decrease of alcohol consumption among workers, one of the main goals of the "drys."[28] Burnham further asserts that reports of crime waves were an invention of journalists, leading to the perception that Prohibition was a failure, and that the crisis of the Great Depression created a shift in public opinion to end Prohibition.[29] Regardless of whether Prohibition was a success or not, the fact remains that large numbers of Americans asked for modification or outright repeal of the Eighteenth Amendment by the end of the 1920s.

The Changing Tide

Many individuals at the beginning of the 1930s recognized the difficulties, but inevitability, of ending Prohibition. Public polls endorsed change. Some leading "drys," such as John D. Rockefeller, Jr., now favored repeal. The Republicans toyed with modifying their stance on Prohibition and the Democrats were for complete repeal. And there was the fact that Congress could effectively kill Prohibition by abolishing the Volstead Act.[30] No amendment to the Constitution had ever been repealed.[31] Repeal would be an uphill battle. The Seventy-second Congress—the Congress in session before the 1932 elections—was the "wettest" in the thirteen years of Prohibition, but 103 Representatives and 40 Senators had to switch to the "wet" side for a repeal amendment to be successful.[32] A repeal amendment was not expected to be proposed until 1934 or 1936, with a two year delay before it went into effect.[33] The prospects of repeal seemed insurmountable. Senator Morris Sheppard, one of the authors of the Eighteenth Amendment, predicted, "There is as much chance of repealing the Eighteenth Amendment as there is for a humming-bird to fly to the planet Mars with the Washington Monument tied to its tail."[34]

But that humming-bird seemed to be gaining strength the longer Prohibition was in effect. In an address before the Bakersfield Rotary Club, Attorney E.J. Emmons proclaimed that lack of respect for the "dry" laws was due to unequal law enforcement, and that Prohibition was an attack on liberty, as well as personal and states' rights.[35] In other words, the law was not consistently enforced across the nation, the national

66. Sen. Morris Shepherd, one of the authors of the Eighteenth Amendment. *Library of Congress*

government was trying to legislate morality (instead of trusting individuals), and many people believed that the liquor question was a state issue. This caused a large portion of Americans to lose respect for the law. Quoted in an interview appearing in the *Denver Morning Post*, Federal Judge John C. Pollock of Kansas opposed Prohibition on principle—it was leading the United States into slavery, narcotics, and disaster—but he believed it should be enforced because it was the law.[36] Superior Court Judge James L. Allen of Orange County declared the Jones Act (Increased Penalties Act), a federal law allowing fines up to $10,000 and or up to five years in prison, was not applicable to California, stating that the Wright Act's (state Prohibition law) provision that any changes to the Volstead Act would immediately apply to California was unconstitutional.[37]

In 1929, new President Herbert Hoover lectured the nation on the importance of law and order, urging Americans to obey the law.[38] However, even in state and federal government, increasing numbers of politicians began questioning the effectiveness, validity and necessity of the Eighteenth Amendment. On January 20, 1931, the Wickersham Commission on Law Enforcement (the National Commission on Law Observance and Enforcement), appointed by President Herbert Hoover, issued a report assessing Prohibition. The panel of eleven connected Prohibition with corruption in law enforcement, growth in the underground liquor industry, disrespect for the law, and the clogging of the justice system and prisons.[39] Two of the commissioners, Federal Judge William S. Kenyon and Chairman George W. Wickersham (former U.S. Attorney General), recommended immediate repeal of the Eighteenth Amendment.[40]

Across the United States, Americans circulated petitions for repeal. Working for the National Prohibition Referendum Association, Miss L.M. Bonner of San Francisco, along with a staff of seven, hoped to collect 25,000 signatures for repeal in Kern County. Within four days her staff collected over 1000 in Bakersfield alone.[41] At least thirteen states held referendums on Prohibition since 1920, some of them multiple times. Based on referendum results, only 43.7 percent of voters were "wet" before 1920, but that number had shifted to 59.8 percent since 1920.[42] In 1931, statistician Walter F. Wilcox attempted to measure public opinion about repealing the Eighteenth Amendment. His study, focused on two *Literary Digest* polls on Prohibition repeal (1922 and 1930), determined that the proportion of "wet" voters in every state increased between 1922 and 1930, and that thirty-seven of forty-eight

67. Pres. Herbert Hoover, George W. Wickersham, and William S. Kenyon. *Library of Congress*

states had respondents who favored repeal, one more than the three-quarters of states necessary to approve of an amendment for repeal.[43] An interesting aspect of these polls is the questions asked:

1. Do you favor the continuance and strict enforcement of the Eighteenth Amendment and Volstead Law?
2. Do you favor a modification of the Volstead Law to permit light wines and beers?
3. Do you favor a repeal of the Prohibition Amendment?[44]

Wilcox estimated that 97 percent of modification supporters would vote for repeal if the choice was just between maintaining Prohibition or repeal.[45] The *Bakersfield Californian* reported on April 5, 1930, that 843 ballots for the *Literary Digest* poll were received from Bakersfield—316 for repeal, 277 for modification, and 250 for enforcement.[46] By May 20, 1930, the returns from Bakersfield increased to 2125—848 for repeal, 696 for modification, and 581 for enforcement.[47] A third poll to measure public opinion on Prohibition was conducted by the *Literary Digest* in 1932, indicating that support for repeal increased from 61.5 percent in 1922 to 73.5 percent in 1932.[48] The 1932 poll asked for voters to choose solely between repeal and maintenance of Prohibition. Every county in California polled in favor of repeal, towns in California averaged 4 to 1 votes in favor of repeal, and Bakersfield polled 1392 to 330 in favor of repeal.[49] Forty of forty-eight states polled in favor of repeal. Only Kansas and North Carolina polled "dry."[50] As the decade of the 1920s edged to a close, straw ballots and polls translated into political action.

Several powerful organizations were created to place pressure on Congress for a measure to repeal Prohibition. The Association Against the Prohibition Amendment (AAPA), with an all-male membership, agitated for repeal.[51] Pauline Morton Sabin led a new, more effective anti-Prohibition group—one-million members strong—called the Women's Organization for National Prohibition Reform (WONPR).[52] Sabin, active in the Republican Party, was initially in favor of the Eighteenth

Amendment because she believed that it would produce a better world for her children.[53] The reality of Prohibition changed her perspective and she was not alone in her sentiment. Sabin testified before the House Judiciary Committee, stating:

> In preprohibition days, mothers had little fear in regard to the saloon as far as their children were concerned. A saloon keeper's license was revoked if he were caught selling liquor to minors. Today in any speakeasy in the United States you can find boys and girls in their teens drinking liquor, and this situation has become so acute that the mothers of the country feel something must be done to protect their children.[54]

That "something" would be the repeal of national Prohibition and a return of the issue to local and state legislatures.

It was apparent to most Americans that Prohibition was a failure. Support for repeal spread to a wide variety of organizations, including labor groups. The Carpenter's Union, Butcher's Union, and Oil Worker's Union in Bakersfield joined to form a local chapter of labor's National Committee for Modification of the Eighteenth Amendment. The chapter, led by Arthur Volk of the Carpenter's Union, invited all concerned citizens in Kern County who wished to modify the Volstead Act to join the movement. In explaining why activism was necessary, Volk stated that

> Labor wants modification because the present Volstead act, which destroys freedom, has brought the gangsters, racketeers, debauchery of youth and a revival of the ancient customs of state control of all personal conduct.

The group planned to sell buttons and membership cards for a small fee, keeping half of the proceeds for local campaigning and sending the other half to the national committee.[55]

Professional organizations and veterans groups also joined in the call for repeal. The American Bar Association called for change. Former President of the Association, Charles A. Boston, "denounced the Eighteenth amendment and the Volstead act as failures which had promoted violence, contempt for law and a spy system of law enforcement."[56] The American Legion also recognized the limited effectiveness of Prohibition and voted 1008 to 394 in support of a referendum to modify or repeal the Eighteenth Amendment.

Repeal Gains Momentum

As the new decade of the 1930s progressed and public opposition became more vocal, federal and local politicians and law enforcement officials responded. In August of 1930, the National Director of the Prohibition Bureau, Amos W.W. Woodcock, prohibited agents from raiding private home brewers without a search warrant or visual proof of a still in operation.[57] The California State Senate voted in May 1931 to keep the Wright Act, 35 to 5, but then voted 24 to 17 to consider a referendum bill, a step in the direction of real change in California.[58]

The potential for change was also reflected on the national political scene in 1931 when members of Congress pressed ahead to vote on Prohibition, despite the general congressional belief that economic issues (the Great Depression) should take precedence over the liquor issue. Proponents of repeal pushed for the vote to take place before the 1932 elections so the position of candidates for Congress would be placed on record for voters to see.[59] Only one vote concerning Prohibition was projected during that session of Congress; either a vote for a referendum on the Eighteenth Amendment or a vote to modify the Volstead Act to allow light wines and beer. Many representatives believed that the House

Judiciary Committee would not report in favor of either proposal, so a vote was only possible by bringing one of the issues—the most popular—to the floor through a petition of 145 members. "Wets" were in favor of either issue, but many "dry" leaders in both parties believed that Congress would opt for the referendum and accept it.[60] Republicans, typically seen as supporters of Prohibition, neared the 1932 elections in a less-than-unified fashion. Sixty-four "wet" Republicans in the House of

68. Many Californians moved to repeal Prohibition, including Rep. Florence Kahn. *Library of Congress*

Representatives, including Florence Kahn of California, formed a committee to organize for repeal of the Eighteenth Amendment, pledging to work with "wet" Democrats. As part of the "wet" strategy, it was believed that cooperation between the two parties aimed at a common goal could accomplish the task.[61]

To many reform advocates for change, amending the Volstead Act to allow the sale of light wines and beer seemed a more achievable task than complete repeal of the Eighteenth Amendment. In Senate Committee hearings on the beer issue, the vice president of the American Federation of Labor and president of the National Labor Committee to Modify the Volstead Act, Matthew Woll, testified that legalizing beer would reduce demand for hard liquor, take away power from organized crime, restore respect for the law, end political corruption, and stop the tyranny of the minority over the majority. Senator Warren Barbour, a Republican from New Jersey, argued that legalizing beer was a logical proposition. And in an interesting argument, the president of the

American Dental Association, Martin Dewey, asked for light wines and beer "in the interest of protecting and nourishing the health of expectant mothers and their unborn children," because "It has long been known that in certain types of malnutrition associated with pregnancy, the health of the mother can be greatly improved by adding a small quantity of beer or light wines to the diet;" alcohol was a stimulant, but it also aided in the digestion and absorption of nutrients.[62]

In March 1932, Representatives in the House cast votes to determine whether the states would be allowed to decide the issue of Prohibition. Despite efforts of the "wets," they were out-voted 227 to 187.[63] However, "wets" claimed that they would become the dominant faction in Congress with the elections in November, a factor that could make or break the Prohibition issue.[64] Papers for a state proposition were filed in April 1932 with the California Secretary of State Frank C. Jordan in anticipation that federal liquor laws would soon be modified. If 110,800 signatures of eligible voters were gathered in time, a proposition to repeal the Wright Act and allow the state to control the requirements of liquor licenses and regulate alcohol would be included on the November ballot.[65] With 111,311 signatures the proposition made it onto the ballot.[66] If voters approved of the proposition, state control would be allowed if the Volstead Act was modified.

Anti-Prohibition rhetoric and activity gained momentum as the election cycle of 1932 neared. Not only were numerous seats in Congress up for grabs, but so was the office of president. The Democratic Party candidate for president, Franklin Delano Roosevelt, offered a fresh optimism for economic recovery from the Great Depression, as well as a realistic potential to repeal the Eighteenth Amendment. In a letter to the Liberal Civic League Roosevelt writes,

> Please consider that I still maintain 100 per cent my earlier expressions of opinion favoring return of control of intoxicants to the several states...That is definite. I have on many occasions agreed with your statement that the time has come for definite action.[67]

Although apart from party leadership, a president has no real role in the Amendment process. But Roosevelt's outright support for repeal emboldened other politicians to take action. Several bipartisan bills were introduced in the Senate and House to legalize and tax beer containing 2.75 percent alcohol at .03 cents a pint, available in bottles and consumable outside the home in hotels, restaurants, and clubs.[68] Even though the bill was defeated 228 to 169 in the House and 55 to 26 in the Senate, it was a success in placing how representatives voted onto the record.[69]

The Republican Party, traditionally supportive of Prohibition, struggled with the issue in the coming election. In June 1932, the Republican resolutions committee adopted a plank on Prohibition that avoided taking a solid stand on the issue either way, declaring:

> We do not favor the submission of the Eighteenth amendment to the states for retention or repeal...[but they favored] submitting a substitute to the states which will retain the great gains already made under prohibition and which will protect the states in their desire to make prohibition laws and protect all people against the return of the saloon.[70]

What this stance actually meant was debatable and pushed many "wets" into the arms of the Democrats. But not all Republicans were as cryptic as the Republican leadership. Many of the California delegates to the Republican National Convention, especially Milton H. Esberg and William H. Crocker, were inspired by the proclamation by John D. Rockefeller, Jr. that Prohibition was a failure, and they hoped for complete repeal of the Eighteenth Amendment.[71] Even the incumbent president, Herbert Hoover, stated that he was in favor of changing federal law to allow the states to once again control liquor.[72] In anticipation of an end to or modification of the national "dry" laws, some enterprising individuals in Kern County hoped to get a jump on new business ventures. Mrs. Pete Gobil of Mojave applied to County Clerk Frank E. Smith, and the operator of the French Café at 1909 Chester Avenue, S.T. Andrews, applied to the city council for permits to sell light wine and beer.[73] Both applications were greeted with amusement and the applicants were told they had to wait.

As public support for Roosevelt and other "wet" politicians increased, so did Congress' willingness to reconsider "dry" measures. Republican Senator Bingham, from Connecticut, proposed a joint resolution to repeal the Eighteenth Amendment and return liquor control to the states and the control of interstate liquor traffic to the national government. Even many "drys," including California Senator Johnson, supported allowing the people of the states to vote on whether or not to keep Prohibition.[74] During the Democratic National Convention in Chicago, thirty-three of the forty-four delegates from California

69. Jackson Mahon (candidate in the 1932 House election who campaigned for repeal of Prohibition) and Bert E. Keithley, January 1939. *Courtesy of Kern County Museum. Used by permission*

voted in favor of the Democratic platform that included repeal of the Eighteenth Amendment.[75] Jackson Mahon, from Bakersfield, filed papers to run as a candidate for the House of Representatives in the new Tenth Congressional District. Included in his campaign platform was support for Prohibition repeal, not by referendum, but by the action of Congress.[76] Other candidates for the Tenth Congressional District echoed the sentiment for change. Adolph Zwirn, a Republican from

Ventura, favored light wines and 4 percent beer, and Arthur S. Crites, also a Republican, wanted the alcohol question to be referred to the states.[77] Justice S. Wardell, candidate for the U.S. Senate, called for a repeal amendment and early modification of the Volstead Act, citing that since 1920 more than $28 million was spent on unsuccessful enforcement efforts.[78] Both Mahon and Wardell, the strongest of the candidates for the House and Senate, received the endorsement of women against Prohibition.[79] By the end of the primary elections, voters in Kern County selected Crites as the Republican candidate and Mahon as the

70. House candidate Arthur Crites, campaigned on a platform to turn the liquor question over to the states. *Courtesy of Kern County Museum. Used by permission*

Democratic candidate for the House. Wardell lost the Democratic primary for Senate to William Gibbs McAdoo, former U.S. Secretary of the Treasury and a committed "dry."[80] Either way, voters chose candidates that favored change in federal liquor policy.[81]

The Ripple Effect of the Election of 1932

With the 1932 election, it was obvious that Americans overwhelmingly supported candidates who favored the repeal of Prohibition, especially Democratic candidates. Roosevelt defeated Hoover 472 electoral votes to 59. McAdoo won the Senate seat and Crites was defeated by the Democratic candidate for the House, H.E. Stubbs.[82] Along with the election for President, Representatives, and the Senate elections, a referendum in the State of California on the Wright Act was

110

placed on the ballot. Californians decidedly voted to repeal the Wright Act 1,342,114 to 609,608. Voters in Kern County supported repeal 17,422 to 7,567.[83] Additionally, voters approved of state regulation of liquor 1,185,629 to 680,621.[84] With these results, a slow but sure legislative domino effect began in California. Governor Rolph proposed that Wright Act prisoners held in jails across the state be released, a decision that had no effect in Kern County due to the fact that there were only city and federal violators in the jail.[85]

71. California Governor James Rolph responded to the political climate and moved to end Prohibition in the state. *Library of Congress*

Governor Rolph also toyed with the decision to pardon Jones Law violators—individuals who earned felony convictions for the possession of stills.[86] Indicating that the Governor was committed to actual change, Rolph followed through on his proposals, releasing 128 violators, including Jones Act violators, in December 1932 and 248 in January 1933.[87]

72. Bakersfield City Councilman Elmer Martin voted to repeal the city's Prohibition ordinances. *Courtesy of Nellane Croan Stussie*

Repealing the Wright Act began the process of questioning city and county "dry" ordinances throughout the state. The Bakersfield city council seemed poised to repeal the local liquor ordinance. Police Judge John W. Frye expressed his belief that it would be impossible to secure convictions now that the Wright Act was repealed.[88] Despite six of the seven council members agreeing that repeal of the local ordinance was necessary in light of election results their rhetoric was not backed with action. Councilman Howard Carlock presented a motion for repeal, but nobody seconded the motion. Another Councilman, Charles F. Johnson, stated he would second a future motion once Secretary of State Jordan certified Kern County's repeal vote on the Wright Act.[89] With Jordan's certification, the repeal vote succeeded, but not unanimously. Howard Carlock, Charles F. Johnson, Elmer Martin, and Ray I. Walters voted for repeal. F.S. Benson, Mayor Harry Headen, and Fred S. Boden opposed the change. As a result of the vote, City

73. Bakersfield City Councilmen Harry Headen (above) and 74. Fred S. Boden (below) both voted to keep Bakersfield's Prohibition ordinances. *Courtesy of Kern County Museum. Used by permission*

Ordinances No. 165 and No. 168 were no longer in effect.[90] The repeal went into effect December 28, and even though there were still two federal officers in Bakersfield, New Year's celebrants were safe; federal agents were only interested in arresting producers of liquor.[91]

Even though the Wright Act and many city ordinances were repealed, the Volstead Act and Eighteenth Amendment were still in effect, meaning liquor was still illegal by federal law. However, the 1932 election results were seen as a mandate for repeal. Both the Democrats and Republicans in Congress demanded a quick vote on the issue, and Speaker of the House John N. Garner scheduled it for December 5.[92] Of course, in order for a repeal amendment to move forward, two-thirds of the House and Senate needed to support it before it could move on to the states for ratification. In a close vote in the House, 272 to 144, the repeal amendment failed to win a 2/3 majority.[93] If a repeal amendment could not be secured quickly, there was another way to enact change—modification of the Volstead Act.

The House Ways and Means Committee proposed bills to allow beer with 3.2 percent alcohol by content and wine with an unlimited percent of alcohol. Beer would be taxed $5 per barrel and brewers were to be charged $1000 for a license.[94] Grape growers in California, including those in Kern County, were greatly interested in legalizing wine to broaden their economic potential.[95] The beer bill—called the Collier Bill—was easier to support than the one on wine. It was

75. Bakersfield City Councilman Charles F. Johnson supported repeal of Bakersfield's Prohibition ordinances. *Courtesy of Kern County Museum. Used by permission*

argued that the legalization of 3.2 percent beer would create jobs, generate tax revenue, and was constitutional; whereas the bill on wine—the Lea Bill—would violate the Eighteenth Amendment. Despite the fact that the Volstead Act allowed for naturally fermented wines, it was possible for wine to be fermented with as much as 14 percent alcohol by content, producing a beverage that was surely "intoxicating." In a disappointing move for the wine bloc, it appeared that legalization of beer necessitated denial of the same thing for wine. Representative Lea of California, leading proponent for the wine interests, stated that beer proponents "acted for their own interests without much regard to our interests in California," and that "naturally fermented wine is permitted for home use under section 29 of the Volstead Act. We only asked that this principle be extended to apply to the public sale of wine for table use in restaurants and hotels."[96]

After the Collier Beer Bill was passed in the House, 230 to 165, the measure was sent on to the Senate. Many "wets" hoped that a national law would allow the sale of beer by Christmas, but the process was slower than expected, largely because Senators argued over the legality of 3.2 percent beer.[97] The California State Assembly, wishing to show support for a repeal amendment (not just modification of the Volstead Act), voted 54 to 21 to urge Congress to repeal the Eighteenth Amendment.[98] And once again, in anticipation of a change to national liquor laws, two individuals, John Parenti and Jess Switzer, submitted written applications to the Kern County Board of Supervisors for permits to sell light wines and beer.[99]

Ironically, a measure to submit repeal of the Eighteenth Amendment to the states passed in Congress before modification of the Volstead Act. The Senate Judiciary Committee voted 10 to 4 to submit a repeal amendment, allowing for protection of "dry" states and prevention of saloons, to the Senate. If approved of by two-thirds of both Houses of Congress, state conventions had seven years to ratify the amendment.[100] The Senate approved the measure, 63 to 23.[101] In a vote of 289 to 121, the House of Representatives approved of the amendment. Instead of ratification by the states, ratification had to be accomplished through state conventions.[102] In the meantime, the Director of the Prohibition Bureau, Amos W.W. Woodcock, ordered agents not to raid speakeasies, and funds to purchase evidence were not included in the appropriations bill for the Justice Department for the next fiscal year.[103]

In March 1933, President Franklin Roosevelt sent a surprising message to Congress:

> I recommend to Congress the passage of legislation for the immediate modification of the Volstead Act, in order to legalize the manufacture and sale of beer and other beverages of such alcoholic content as is permissible under the constitution; and to provide through the manufacture and sale, by substantial taxes, a proper and much needed revenue for the government. I deem action at this time to be of the highest importance.[104]

Now, under the guidance of Presidential leadership, Congressional squabbling eased and modification became a reality. After several minor modifications in both the House and Senate, the Cullen Beer-For-Revenue Bill passed and was sent on to the President. Roosevelt signed the bill, legalizing 3.2 percent beer, wine and other beverages where it was allowed by state law. It also mandated that it was illegal to sale to patrons under the age of sixteen. On April 7, 1933, the new national law went into effect.[105]

In preparation for the coming of beer and wine, Bakersfield became the distribution center for the Southern San Joaquin Valley. It was planned for Bakersfield to receive beer from Los Angeles breweries almost exclusively; towns to the north would more than likely receive beer from San Francisco breweries.[106] Now that beer was legal, the State of California moved to regulate the beverage, passing a bill with seven provisions:

1. A state license fee of $100 for manufacturers.
2. State tax of 2 cents a gallon. (This section is similar to the tax measure already enacted and in effect).
3. Governing bodies of counties and cities may grant licenses for "on sale" and "off sale."

4. Limitation of local license fee for "on sale" to $50 and for "off sale" to $10.

5. Beer may be sold only with bona fide meals.

6. Limitation of local tax to 50 cents a barrel.

7. Reserving the right of local option to cities and counties.[107]

Governor Rolph signed this Peterson Beer Regulatory Measure on April 28, 1933, opening the way for communities to regulate licensing.[108]

Beer and Wine Returns to Kern County

In Bakersfield sixteen applications were filed with the City Clerk. However, the Clerk, Vance Van Riper, maintained that he could not issue licenses because no ordinance authorized them. W.D. Clarke, Bakersfield City Manager, declared that until an amendment concerning a city licensing ordinance is passed, the sale of beer would be covered under the Soft Drink Ordinance. Essentially, 3.2 percent beverages were to be

considered soft drinks.[109] A similar application request was made to the County Board of Supervisors to sell beer and light wines under soft drink licenses in the county, but no action was scheduled on them until the next meeting.[110]

76. Bakersfield City Clerk Vance Van Riper. *Courtesy of Kern County Museum. Used by permission*

77. List of County Applicants for Licenses (March 27, 1933)

Name	Location
James F. Hart	North of Cantil
W.W. Tate	Fellows
Claude J. Griffin	Fruitvale
W.W. Moses	Wasco
Mrs. J.E. Matthews	Wasco
L.L. Krauss	Keene
Peter Giovannetti	910 Union Avenue
W.T. Oliver	Kernville
R.L. Gordon	Inyokern
C.O. White	Shafter
James W. O'Brien	Kernville
Tom Zarker	Tropical Inn
Gino Pera	Buttonwillow

The return of beer was greatly anticipated in Bakersfield. Redlick's Store prominently displayed beer steins, mugs and glassware in a front window.[111] Described as "Probably the widest open city in the state as far as the unrestricted sale of beer is concerned," 3.2 percent beer was welcomed back into Bakersfield on April 7, 1933. Just one brand, Valley Brew from Stockton, was available by 7:00 am, delivered by a driver from the Coca-Cola Bottling Works. Only a few places offered draft beer on tap, but the beverage could be purchased at soft drink establishments for .15 cents a bottle or .10 cents a glass. Unfortunately for hotels and restaurants, they were still waiting for supplies.[112] The desire for beer did have one tragic consequence—a truck headed to Bakersfield laden with beer hit an automobile near McFarland, killing an unknown hitchhiker.[113]

For the city of Taft, repeal of the Wright Act mattered little—the city voted itself "dry" in April 1918 with a vote of 686 to 412. A vote to repeal local option was needed to implement change. Unincorporated McKittrick remained "dry" until the county "dry" ordinance was repealed; however, the city of Maricopa became "wet" with the repeal of the Wright Act due to their 1918 local option vote to remain

78. Taft Mayor Clarence Williams called for an election to repeal Taft's "dry" status. *Courtesy of West Kern Oil Museum*

"wet."[114] Within three months Taft planned to hold a vote to repeal their local option law.[115] Taft Mayor Clarence Williams, speaking before the West Side Business Men's Club, called for repeal of local option. Until then, beer was not allowed in Taft, but a crafty citizen could get it in "wet" South Taft, Taft Heights, Ford City, Fellows, or Maricopa.[116] George

Fiester ushered in the change with a big celebration. On a ranch outside of Maricopa on the Santa Maria Highway, Fiester scheduled a load of beer to be shipped from Northern California on April 9. He arranged to have enough beef and beer for 4000 people, and three old-time bartenders and several cashiers; an event surely to be remembered.[117] The barbeque was so successful that Fiester planned another gathering with a beer judging contest. Free samples of Budweiser, Blue Ribbon, Schlitz, Lemps, Blatz, Tacoma, Rainier, East Side, Valley Brew and other brands would be available—a creative advertising gimmick, to say the least.[118]

Held on April 28, 1933, voters in Taft turned out to the firehouse to cast their ballots in front of the all-female, save one male, election board. By a vote of 603 to 62 (10 to 1 in favor), residents in Taft voted to end their "dry" spell. The city council amended Ordinance No. 137 to allow the sale of beer with an alcohol content of 3.2 percent by weight or 4 percent by volume.[119] Taft, and the majority of the West side of the County, was now "wet."

Delano was in the same boat as Taft—initially "dry." In a meeting held at the Kern Hotel, the Delano City Council took the issue up and voted to allow 3.2 percent beverages, although the sentiment among leaders was not

79. Kern County Supervisor W.R. Woollomes (circa 1936) worked with others to try and figure out a uniform policy on beer. *Courtesy of Kern County Museum. Used by permission*

unanimous. The Delano Commerce Directors were afraid that legalization would lead to minors gaining access to alcohol. George W. McClintock and Leslie Adams, members of the City Council, opposed

119

80. Jonathan Bush, Benjamin Bush, Sarah A. Bush, Carrie Hart, and John O. Hart
at the Cliff House in San Francisco, 1912. John Hart, as Kern County
Supervisor, encouraged cities in Kern County to contribute ideas to formulate
a uniform beer policy. *Courtesy of Kern County Museum. Used by permission*

legalization as well. Regardless, 3.2 beer and light wine would be allowed
in Delano.[120]

The Kern County Board of Supervisors, Bakersfield City
Councilmen and representatives from cities around Kern County met
May 5, 1933, at the County Courthouse to discuss a uniform policy on the
sale of beer and the necessity for regulation. Based on a proposal by the
City of Delano that mirrored the guidelines of the state Assembly, the
group considered charging wholesalers $50 a year for a license, retailers
$50 a year for a license to sell beer to be consumed at their place of
business, and other businesses $10 a year for a license to sell beer not to
be consumed at their place of business. Supervisor Roy Woollomes
indicated that he had heard that for beer to be sold on-site a business had
to serve a meal; a meal being "anything equal to or greater than a sandwich
in gastronomic value." The group joked that "they could have rubber
sandwiches...and nail them to the plate so no one could carry them
away." Some questioned having regulations at all, citing that Bakersfield
was getting along just fine without defined regulations. Chairman Perry

Brite responded, "We must have some regulation so the police and sheriff's office will be protected. If they cinch down too tight on them in the city they go on the outskirts and if they cinch down on them in the outskirts they come back to the city." Uniformity in regulations would avoid that. Supervisor J.O. Hart recommended each city prepare ordinances and then the group would meet again to review developments.[121] Three days later W.A. McGinn, Deputy District Attorney for Kern County, met with representatives of cities in Kern County—including Attorney A.G. Baron from Taft, Walter Osborne from Bakersfield, and Attorney Palmer from Delano—to determine the general regulations all would follow. It was imperative to find a balance between charging too much and too little for a license to sell beer in order to encourage people to follow the law and discourage bootlegging. State regulations set the maximum license fee at $50, and cities in the county could tax a maximum of .50 cents a barrel for beer, but if a tax was levied it had to be the same amount in the whole county. It was also mandated that only reputable individuals would be issued licenses, proposing that applicants must have good morals and possess no criminal record since the legalization of beer, a stipulation that potentially opened the door for business opportunities to many Prohibition violators.[122] In the end, the Kern County Board of Supervisors did not pass a uniform beer regulation law before the Eighteenth Amendment was repealed.

81. Louis Banducci portrait for the first Frontier Days, 1934. Louis was arrested two times for violating Prohibition (1923, 1931) and enter the legal liquor trade with the repeal of Prohibition. *Courtesy of Kern County Museum. Used by permission*

82. Sample of Violators Involved in the Legal Liquor Trade in Bakersfield, 1934.

Name	Business
Mike Alvarez	233 East 8th Street
Frank Amestoy	Cesmat Hotel, 622 East 21st Street
Guilo Antongiovanni	Lucca Café
Louis Banducci	Europe Café
Mary Belluomini	Belluomini and Pasquini, 2101 L Street
Mrs. Emma Burubeltz (relative)	619 Sumner
Joseph Cinelli	Lido Café
Daniel Costello	Princeton Bar
Richard Fanucchi	Soft Drinks, 814 Kern Street
Gaston Gastoni	1001 19th Street
Peter Grimaud	1207 19th Street
Fred Harvey	1501 F Street
George Helm	Beverages, 1823 Chester Avenue
Charles Lane	324 Lakeview Avenue
Joe Lemucchi	Grocery, 725 East 19th Street
Joseph Moretti	1808 K Street

83. View of Hotel El Tejon looking southeast, 5/7/1926. Kern grape growers and businessmen met here to promote acceptance of naturally fermented light wines. *Courtesy of Kern County Museum. Used by permission*

Since March 1933 the focus of the nation, including Kern County, was on 3.2 percent beer. Wine was also allowed if it remained at or below 3.2 percent alcohol. But the wine industry was not as excited about the new changes as the beer interests were. For many in the wine industry, producing 3.2 percent wine was more trouble than it was worth. Wine

84. Agricultural Commissioner Lewis Andrew Burtch (third from left) pushed for naturally light wines. *Courtesy of Kern County Museum. Used by permission*

85. M.A. Lindsay (left) and 86. Secretary of the Chamber of Commerce Lawrence B. Nourse (right) also pledged to support naturally light wines. *Courtesy of Kern County Museum. Used by permission*

grape growers in Kern County joined a larger effort led by the State Grape Growers' Association to replace 3.2 percent with light natural wine.[123] Many of the major vintners in California decided not to produce wine with their approximately 20,000,000 gallons of prime grape juice, choosing instead to wait for the legal right to produce wine that was naturally around 10 percent alcohol.[124] In a meeting held at the Hotel El Tejon in Bakersfield, twenty-one Kern grape growers and businessmen gathered to support the legalization of naturally fermented light wine and to press Congress to adopt such a measure. With 17,500 acres of wine grapes in the

87. Hugh S. Allen, circa 1910. *Courtesy of Kern County Museum. Used by permission*

124

88. Hotel Padre at H and 18th Streets, late 1920s. Chairman of the Agricultural Commission, Hugh Allen, urged the Bakersfield Chamber of Commerce to endorse a 10 percent wine bill at a meeting held here. *Courtesy of Kern County Museum. Used by permission*

County, the health of California's $350,000,000 grape industry was of a paramount concern.[125] In another meeting held at the Hotel Padre, Hugh Allen, Chairman of the Agricultural Commission, urged the Bakersfield Chamber of Commerce to endorse a 10 percent wine bill.[126] With its lobbying, the State Grape Growers Association and other supporters of natural wine might have achieved a new bill supporting their position, but it was not needed. With the impending repeal of the Eighteenth Amendment wineries planned to produce naturally fermented light wine with no worry. An $85,000 winery was planned on the Walter J. Wallace ranch near Delano and potentially run by the head of the California Grape Products Company, A. Perelli-Minetti.[127]

89. Growers and Businessmen Who Met at Hotel El Tejon to Support Naturally Fermented Light Wines

Name	Vocation
Alfred Harrell (Speaker)	Bakersfield Publisher
Harry W. Mellen (Speaker)	Delano Grower
F.W. Brewster (Speaker)	Arvin-Weedpatch District Grower
Arthur Hoagland (Speaker)	Realtor and Farmer, President of the Kern County Chamber of Commerce
W.L. Landsborough (Speaker)	Secretary of the Bakersfield Chamber of Commerce
T.N. Harvey (Speaker)	Former Superior Court Judge
A.A. Sprehn (Speaker)	Vineland Grower
Harry A. Caddow (Speaker)	Secretary of the Grape Growers League of California
W.R. Woollomes (Speaker)	County Supervisor
David L. Wishon	Bakersfield Manager of the San Joaquin Light and Power Corporation, Lerdo District Grower
Arthur Theile	Power Company Official, Lerdo District Grower
Ned Barlow	Arvin Grower
Lloyd Frick	Weed Patch Grower
Buford Fox	Chief Deputy Agricultural Commissioner
T.E. Day	Weed Patch Grower
Ollie Harris	Southern Pacific Railroad Agent

90. Arthur Hoagland.
     Courtesy of Marji Turner.

91. Arthur Theile. *Courtesy
     of his granddaughter,
     Nancy Fitch*

92. Alfred Harrell, circa 1923. *Courtesy of
     Kern County Museum. Used by permission*

93. Adolph A. Sprehn
     (11/22/1944). *Courtesy of
     Kern County Museum. Used by
     permission*

94. Buford Fox (1937). Arrested
     once for violating Prohibition
     (1923). *Courtesy of Kern County
     Museum. Used by permission*

"Drys" Refuse to Give Up

But not all Americans were in favor of repeal. In 1931, "dry" groups began to see a general movement to repeal Prohibition, prompting them to increase their efforts to convince fellow citizens of the virtues of a nation "free" of alcohol. At least fifty-five statements from the WCTU or stories on their activities appeared in the *Bakersfield Californian* between 1931 and the repeal of Prohibition in December 1933.[128] In response to statements that the Eighteenth Amendment infringed upon states' rights, Mrs. Elizabeth Ballagh, vice-president of the Frances E. Willard Union of the WCTU, writes:

> People are sick of this continued talk about state's rights, for it is no more than a transparent smoke screen intended to mask a returning to a sordid trafficking in liquor. This smoke screen has been used by liquorites since the Whiskey Rebellion in George Washington's time. When he [Governor Ritchie of Maryland] says that each state can be trusted to settle the liquor question so as to promote temperance, he is mistaken.[129]

95. First Christian Church, circa 1940s. *Courtesy of Kern County Museum. Used by permission*

The Flying Squadron, speaking on behalf of the National Conference of Organizations Supporting the Eighteenth Amendment traveled to churches, including some in Bakersfield, to organize local "dry" societies. At the First Christian Church, 250 Prohibition supporters met to form a board of strategy. Their goal was to generate support to keep the California Wright Act from being repealed. Listening to two main speakers—Mrs. Eva C. Wheeler, the California State President of the WCTU, and C.W. Gawthrop, Superintendent of the Northern Division of the ASL—the group selected potential officers of the board,

96. Rev. J.D. Page, Executive Secretary of the "Dry" Board of Strategy, hoped to keep Prohibition in Kern County. *Courtesy of Betty Page Brackenridge*

urged that a third political party be formed to counter the Democrat and Republican repeal/modification agenda in the 1932 Presidential Election, and that defense of the Wright Act should not be linked to the defense of Prohibition.[130] On the eve of the election the group published refutations to arguments proposed by those favoring repeal of the Eighteenth Amendment, claiming that the majority of Americans supported Prohibition, alcohol consumption had actually decreased, bootlegging was less of a problem than the saloon, the youth of America were not being corrupted, lawlessness had not increased, Prohibition was not sprung upon the public because of the Great War, and Prohibition was not responsible for creating unemployment.[131] Even after Roosevelt was elected, "dry" activists continued the push for residents in Kern County to continue their support against liquor with several organized activities.

Members of the WCTU continued their annual picnic on May 23 at Beale Park, with speakers, an invocation, posters from students, and a display of food worth $3.10—the amount of food that could be bought for a glass a beer a day at .05 cents a glass for 62 days.[132] And in October 1933, after California voted to repeal the Eighteenth Amendment, Miss Ethel Hubler, editor and publisher of the *National Voice*, planned to visit the First Methodist Episcopal Church of Bakersfield to continue Prohibition advocacy.[133]

Writers for the WCTU continued to assail Roosevelt's desire to modify the Volstead Act to allow for real beer, claiming that the public will continue to homebrew due to the added-on taxes that will increase the cost of legal beer—an increase of approximately $4.50 per five gallons.[134] As the ratification of the Twenty-First Amendment progressed and appeared to be successful, the WCTU changed the focus of some of their statements—promoting the concept of not drinking and driving, advocating that alcohol had zero medicinal purposes, and that individuals should pursue abstinence because alcohol is a poison that destroys the body.[135] Expanding upon the belief that alcohol was a poison, anti-alcohol

97. First Methodist Episcopal Church, 1920s. *Courtesy of Kern County Museum. Used by permission*

advocates planned to continue temperance education in the schools, stressing the negative effects of alcohol on the body and brain, promoting the idea that voluntary abstinence was superior to that of legislative Prohibition, and focusing on studies based on science.[136] Others wrote of the difficulties repeal will bring, especially the threat that saloons would make a return.[137]

In response to an apparent mandate for change reflected in the Presidential Election of 1932 and the potential revenue repeal promised, the Twenty-First Amendment was submitted to state conventions for ratification. California planned an election to choose delegates to its ratification convention in June, but many "drys" in the state refused to accept change quietly. Opponents of repeal petitioned the California State Supreme Court to block the repeal vote in California. Four Los Angeles prohibitionists, including the son of Bishop James Cannon, Richard M. Cannon, argued that the issue should be voted on during the State primary election in 1934 and the names of "wet" and "dry" candidates should be removed from the ballot, stating:

> ...Congress has failed to prescribe how the issue shall be voted upon, that the Legislature is still in session and might enact a new statute, and that the measure does not become effective until 90 days after the legislature adjourns, thus invalidating names at this time.[138]

Their petition attempt was unsuccessful, but they did threaten to appeal California's potential repeal vote to the U.S. Supreme Court.[139] Regardless, Californians voted on delegates to the convention. It was estimated that 2,582,173 eligible voters would decide California's position, possibly favoring "wet" delegates and ratification of the Twenty-First Amendment by a majority of 3 to 1. A veteran leader of the WCTU in California, Mrs. W.C. Hamilton of San Mateo, was forced out of the organization because of her new stance favoring repeal of the Eighteenth Amendment, an indication that the pending issue fractured not just the undecided.[140] As results came in, voters in Kern County and California were on track to support a slew of delegates who supported ratification. It was reported on June 28 that 11,801 in Kern County voted for repeal and 3429 against. On a broader scale, 885,983 Californians voted against the Eighteenth Amendment and 282,534 to keep Prohibition.[141] The twenty-two delegates elected to the convention, all of whom were in favor of repeal, were tentatively scheduled to meet on July 24 to cast their formal ballots. However, proponents of Prohibition continued to craft resistance to the convention. E. Neal Ames, an attorney from Los Angeles, stated that he would appeal the validity of California's repeal election to the U.S. Supreme Court if necessary, prompting Secretary of State Frank C. Jordan to hold off on certification of the repeal vote.[142] The challenge to the repeal vote from Los Angeles was subsequently dismissed, allowing for the delegates to meet and formerly vote unanimously for repeal.[143]

A Return to Business as Usual

The writing was clearly on the wall. Attorney General Cummings announced the closure of more than one hundred federal Prohibition

98. Emma and Paul Derkum with unidentified women in a car by the Clock Tower. *Courtesy of Kern County Museum. Used by permission*

enforcement offices across the country, including the Bakersfield office. The room in the basement of the Post Office was abandoned, the telephone line disconnected, and it was generally believed that without federal, state and local law enforcement Bakersfield would be a "wide-open" town as in the past. Agents operating out of Fresno were now in the business of investigating major offenders, such as racketeers, gangsters, bootleggers, and commercial violators.[144]

Businesses, especially those involved in the beer industry, prepared to expand their interests. The Kern County Beer Distributor's Association was formed at a meeting held at the Hotel Padre, selecting Paul Derkum (representative of Sierra Brewing Company) as the President, Al Hammel (representative of Acme Brewing Company) as the Vice-President, and George Higgins (distributor for Maier Brewing Company) as Secretary.[145] It was announced that a new $150,000 Bakersfield Brewery was to be constructed. With a potential market from Taft to Visalia, the Brewery was to be built on the Agnetti Property on T Street near Truxtun, incorporate in California, and offer shares of stock for $10.[146] Beer companies, such as Pilsner and Sierra, not only advertised the supposed health advantages of beer and where their products could be purchased, but also how brewing in California was aiding the revitalization of the economy during the Great Depression.

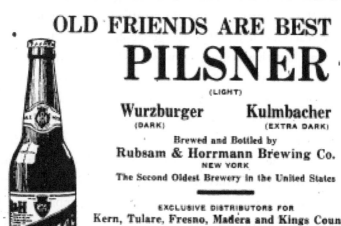

99. "Pilsner Beer Advertisement," *Bakersfield Californian,* June 17, 1933, 2. Notice how the Rubsam and Horrmann Brewing Co. are billed as "The Second Oldest Brewery in the United States, a status that could appeal to the consumer's sense of tradition and desire for a quality product.

100. "Sierra Beer Advertisement," *Bakersfield Californian*, June 19, 1933, 5. Focusing on the multiplier effect of a brewery opening in Fresno, Sierra Beer pushed the notion that consuming their beer contributed to the economic health of the San Joaquin Valley.

101. "Sierra Beer Advertisement," *Bakersfield Californian*, June 19, 1933, 5. As seen in this advertisement, Sierra Beer was available in several locations in Kern County. Notice the variety of establishments where beer could be purchased (pool halls, cafes, cigar stores, drug stores, lunch counters, and bars).

Increasing numbers of state conventions ratified the Twenty-First Amendment. By early November 1933, it was reported that over 14,000,000 voted to repeal the Eighteenth Amendment and only 5,000,000 to keep it.[147] In that same time-frame enough states ratified the Twenty-First Amendment to add it to the Constitution; the states of Ohio, Pennsylvania, and Utah, making thirty-six states, tipped the scales for repeal.[148] California's new liquor law went into effect in December 1933. Many individuals were confused as to what they could or could not do as far as liquor laws went, but the United Press was kind enough to list the restrictions which were mainly enacted upon the sellers of alcohol, not the consumers. It was up to proprietors to abide by restrictions and take responsibility for their patrons. What consumers were allowed to do was pretty far reaching:

> [You Can]
> Drink wine and beer with meals.
> Drink 3.2 beer over the bar without restriction.
> Drink any kind of liquor any place except at a public bar or in a public dining room. (Wine and beer only permitted in public dining rooms).
> Drink hard liquor over the bar of a private club, provided it is your own liquor. The bartender may keep it for you, or you may carry it in, or leave it in your club locker and have the bartender mix your drinks, using your own liquor. (This privilege will be extended only to bona fide, nonprofit clubs of which each member owns a share).
> Buy any kind of liquor in bottles at a retail liquor store.
> Purchase as much as 5 gallons at a time.[149]

It is almost as if being released from the restrictions of federal Prohibition created the atmosphere for a free-for-all. Opponents of Prohibition reveled in new found freedom; proponents cringed at the thought of going backwards.

On December 5, 1933, the Twenty-First Amendment was ratified, repealing the Eighteenth Amendment and beginning the age of liquor regulation. This "noble experiment," facing great opposition from the start, finally had the constitutional permission to end. As an editorial in the *Bakersfield Californian* on December 5, 1933, states:

> The control legislation, which will take the place of the Prohibition law, allows the states to decide on the question of prohibition, and provides for supporting any such state that prefers to continue or to adopt prohibition. But as a national principle the citizens of the United States have decided that the experiment has failed.

> Adoption of the Prohibition amendment indicated that the liquor question was one that concerned the American people, and at the time; it was considered this was the best means of overcoming its dangers. But the very decision to remove it as a temptation, made it doubly so, and through lack of enforcement and the evasion of the law by bootleggers, the amendment brought on wholesale disregard of the law. It fostered gangsters and racketeers, and made the use of liquor an adventure for youth. Its fundamental failure was that it interfered in the moral judgments of the citizens, and was thus fell as a curb on their liberty. This they asserted by defying the law until it was more honored in the breach than in the observance.[150]

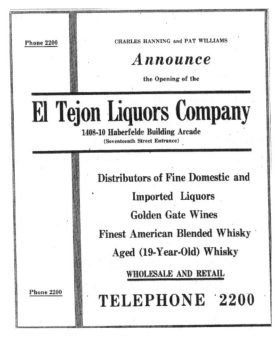

Phone 2200

CHARLES HANNING and PAT WILLIAMS

Announce

the Opening of the

El Tejon Liquors Company

1408-10 Haberfelde Building Arcade
(Seventeenth Street Entrance)

Distributors of Fine Domestic and

Imported Liquors

Golden Gate Wines

Finest American Blended Whisky

Aged (19-Year-Old) Whisky

WHOLESALE AND RETAIL

Phone 2200

TELEPHONE 2200

102. "El Tejon Liquors Company Advertisement," *Bakersfield Californian*, December 6, 1933, 8.

Beginning on December 6, many states allowed the sale of alcohol if the correct application process and regulations were followed. President Franklin Roosevelt stated that "The policy of the government will be more to see to it that the social and political evils that have existed in the preprohibition era shall not be revived nor permitted again to exist." He also advised Americans to abide by regulations and pursue true temperance.[151] In California, license applications were available from police and sheriff's offices, and the license itself was issued from the State Board of Equalization.[152] Since Bakersfield had no bonded warehouses, fast cars transported liquor from Los Angeles and San Francisco to vendors who possessed a permit.[153] Pat Williams and Charles Hanning announced that they were opening a retail and wholesale liquor store, operating under the name El Tejon Liquors Company, in the Haberfelde Building arcade on 17th Street.[154]

The general reaction to the repeal of Prohibition was not excessive revelry, but calmness. A contemporary assessment of repeal appeared in the *Bakersfield Californian* on December 9, 1933. The writer contemplated the reasons for the sensible response to the Twenty-First Amendment, declaring:

Several reasons are given for this. One of them is that liquor is not the main subject and object of the majority of Americans. It was a question to be faced, and they faced it, after which they went about their various businesses. Another cause of the calm reception for the repeal was that it was made possible by citizens who are temperate, and was an assertion of their belief that legislation to regulate morals is an infringement of the right of personal judgment and liberty. They removed the Prohibition amendment because of this, and without them it would not have been repealed. It was not the liking for liquor, but the love of liberty that prompted their action. To these are to be added the people of temperate habits who saw in the Prohibition law a stimulus to general disrespect of the law, and an encouragement to crime and vice. Thus, the repeal of the Eighteenth amendment was not approval of the liquor traffic, but a deep desire that this business should be put under regulation for the promotion of real temperance.[155]

For thirteen years, from 1920 to 1933, Prohibition was a national policy; a policy over one-hundred years in the making. As a moral cause, an economic and efficiency cause, and an Americanization cause the issue was pushed forward by individuals and organizations. Communities and states enacted their own liquor laws when possible. It was not until the momentum created during the Progressive Era, coupled with the pressure politics of the ASL and perceived wartime necessity, that prohibition became "Prohibition"—a national policy codified by the Eighteenth Amendment. Eventually, it was pressure politics and agitation by "wet" organizations that swung the pendulum to repeal. Of course, change would not be easy and the issue would not die easily in many areas of the nation. Will Rogers, ever the observant sage, noted on December 6, 1933:

Talk about the "noble experiment." "The noble experiment," is just starting. Every state is in doubt as to how their liquor will be handled. Say it's not how the state will handle its liquor, it's how the folks will handle theirs. States are going to have scandal over the sale of it, and politicians will fight over the taxes of it. But anyhow, the first week will be the hardest.

Yours. WILL ROGERS.[156]

One era ended and another began. However, the legacy of Prohibition lingers today as a topic of movies and documentaries. It remains in the nation's memory of the 1920s. As a comparison to current governmental policies, Prohibition is compared to laws regulating and prohibiting drugs. Prohibition continues, not as a footnote in history, but as a statement on ethnicity and culture, law, special interest politics, and democracy itself. Movements come and movements go; the American taste for liquor proved to be enduring, the ingenuity at providing it lucrative, and the drive to acquire it unquenchable.

Appendix

Reported Name of Individuals (with variation in spelling) and Year or Years Arrested

Ackis (Actis)	Domick (Dominic) (Domenico)	1928, 1928, 1930
Actie	Demonlen	1926
Actis	B.	1921
Actis	Joe	1924, 1932
Actis	Robert	1928
Actis	Teresa	1928
Actus (Actas)	D.	1926, 1927
Adair	H. James	1925
Adam	Bill	1924
Adams	William	1923
Adcock	Charlie (Charles A.)	1929
Addie	George	1925
Agmatti	G.	1931
Aguello (Aguelo) (Agualio)	Y.	1921, 1923
Aitken	Sid	1925
Aitken	William T. (Walter)	1925
Akers	W.J.	1921
Albrittan (Albbrittan?)	Gene (Eugene O.)	1923, 1926, 1929
Albritton	Francis	1929
Allen	D.T.	1922
Allen	Lawrence Dow	1924
Allen	William Ira	1925
Allen	C.A.	1926, 1926
Allen	Clayton	1926
Allon	William	1923
Alvarez	Mike	1928

143

Amell	Charles (W.)	1928
Amestoy	Frank	1926, 1932
Amor (Armour) (Amour)	August (Augustine)	1920, 1921, 1928
Anderson	Katherine	1922
Anderson	E.L.	1923
Anderson	C.E.	1927
Anderson	Ben	1932
Anderson (?)	Frank (L?)	1921
Andrade	Rosie	1924
Andrews	Eli	1921
Andrews	K.	1926
Andrews	T.	1926
Androelli	Augustine	1925
Androus	Harold	1923
Angeles (Angelos)	Peter	1921
Angone	Nick	1930
Annie	"Jew"	1924
Ansolebhere	Mike (Michael)	1920
Anthony	Walter	1922
Antionia (Anton)	(J.) Julius	1929
Antongiovanni	Julius	1926, 1932
Antongiovanni	Susie (Suzy A.)	1929
Antongiovanni	Pola (Paolo)	1931
Antongiovanni (Antongiovann)	Giulio (Guilio) (Guillo) (Guilo)	1920, 1921, 1924, 1925, 1926
Antongioveni (Antongiovani)	Luigi (Louis)	1923
Antongivani (Antongiovanni)	Joe	1924
Arnold	Carl	1925

Arnow	David	1928
Arnow	Walter	1928
Arriat (Iriart)	Grace	1928
Arriat (Iriart)	Jack	1928
Assenmacker	J.K.	1922
Assenmasher	J.D.	1923
Assenmasher (Assenmacher)	Jake (J.A.) (Joseph H.)	1921, 1922
Augello	Carl	1931
Austin	Eljie (L.G.) (L.J.)	1932
Auzerine	Mr. A.	1921
Auzerine	Mrs. A.	1921
Avilo	Dick	1924
Azevedo	William	1928
Bacon	Robert	1931
Badger	H.	1921
Bailaz	Thomas	1928
Bailey	Alia Mae	1932
Baird	William (J?)	1924
Baker	M.C.	1923
Baker	Frank	1927
Baker	Percy	1928, 1929
Ballestone	G.	1926
Ballestone	Mary	1926
Bandettinni (Bandetini)	A. (Aliprando) (S.)	1921, 1924, 1924
Bandoni	George	1924
Banducci	F.H. (Frank?)	1921
Banducci	William	1922
Banducci	L. (L.A.) (Louis)	1923, 1931

Banducci	Pasquale (Pascal)	1924, 1924
Banducci	Fred	1927
Banducci	John	1928
Banducci	Joseph	1928
Bannister	Mike	1925
Banulzan	Henry	1923
Barbaich (Barvich?)	John	1921
Barber	J.	1920
Barbie (Barble?)	Edgar	1928
Bares	Pedro	1921
Barnes	J.A.	1920
Barnes	Louis	1926
Barnes	Arthur	1932
Barnes	Margaret	1932
Barnes	Walter	1932
Barnett	Harry	1922, 1923
Barnett	Charles	1928
Barnett	James M.	1928
Barney	George (P)	1926
Barr	James H.	1922
Barrett	J.C.	1927
Barros	Nebol (Mabol) (Nabal) (Nebar)	1921, 1927
Barry	Joe	1930
Barsotti	George	1921, 1921, 1922, 1924
Barsotti	Joe	1923
Barsotti	Frank	1924
Barsotti	Crento	1929
Barton	C.J. (Caleb?)	1932
Bateman	Lewis L.	1921
Bateman	Raymond B.	1923

Bateman	R.C. (R.S.) (Ray S.)	1924, 1929
Battlace (Battiston) (Battlase)	Grace (G.)	1926, 1926
Baty	Horace	1928
Baujaudus	George	1922
Baum	William J.	1924
Baum	Ed F. (Edward)	1932
Bauman	Fritz	1923
Baumeister	C.A. (Clifford)	1928
Baumgartner (Jr.)	Joseph	1921
Baumgartner, Jr.	John	1919
Baxtel (Bextel?)	William A. (W.A.?)	1924
Baxter	Grover Cleveland "Babe"	1921
Beagle	R.M.	1923
Beal	(Jesse?) W.	1924
Beall	Gus	1922
Beasley	Wile	1931
Beatty	John H.	1924
Beaty	E.J.	1928
Beaustrom (Beaustrum)	Andy	1921, 1922
Becker	Chris	1921, 1921
Becker	Max	1923
Bedini	Nello	1926
Bell	Carl	1926
Belle	Ante	1921
Bellumoni	Joe	1926
Belluomini	Dena	1921
Belluomini	G.	1921, 1922
Belluomini	Dan	1922

Belluomini	Mary	1928
Belluominly (Belluomini?)	N. (Nello?)	1920, 1924, 1924
Bemis	W.E.	1922
Bendecchio	Frank	1926
Bennett	B.C.	1923
Bennett	F.	1925
Bennett	E.E. (Edward B.?)	1926
Bennett	Marguerite	1928, 1928
Benso	J.L.	1923
Benso	Mrs. J.L.	1923
Bentley	E.	1925
Berchtol (Berchtold)	J. (Joseph?)	1920
Bergez (Burges)	Frank	1920
Bernacchi	Victor	1922, 1923
Bernsberg	George	1930
Berry	Mildred	1931
Bertolucci	Guilio	1921, ?
Bertolucci	Lewis (Louis)	1924
Bertram (Bertrand)	Arthur	1924
Bestitatoe	John	1926
Beveright (Deversright?)	Lewis	1925
Bewley	Mrs. S.	1926
Bewley	Carl	1929
Bextel	William (W.A.?)	1920
Bianchetti	Lawrence	1930
Bianchi	A.	1921
Bibson	Ernest	1928
Bibson	Olivio	1928
Bidabe	N. (Nick?)	1924

148

Bimat	Mrs. Melvina (Malvina?)	1923
Bimendoffer (Bemenderfer)	William H.	1921
Bird	Floyd	1930
Black	J.L.	1927
Blacker	J.H. (James H.)	1923
Blacker	D.H.	1924
Blackwell	D.E.	1924
Blackwell	George (G.W.?)	1924, 1924, 1925
Blackwell	May	1924
Bliss	J.D.	1924
Blizzard	Art	1924
Blye	Sam	1921
Bockling	D.F.	1924
Bocquet	George	1923
Boehner	Dan W.	1921
Bohlmer	D.W.	1928
Boles	Frank (C.)	1928
Bon	Manuel	1922
Boni	Julian	1928
Boni (Buoni?)	Mario	1928
Boni (Buoni?)	Jennie	1929
Booe	L.E.	1924
Booth	James (E?)	1924
Borda	Bapitiste	1928
Borda	Dominguez (Domingo)	1928
Boros	Herman	1921
Bosustow	Jesse	1923
Botking	Daniel	1931
Boust	Fred (Aka Freddie	1924

	Lane)	
Bowley	Charles	1931
Bowman	Edith (Mae)	1931
Boyd	J.H. (John H.?)	1931
Brady	Juanita	1928
Brassfield	Micky	1923
Bratton	Dorothy	1921
Brent	George	1923
Brewer	Bill	1925
Briones	Severo (Severano)	1928
Briscoe	Mike	1921
Britt (Britz?)	Nick	1921
Broland	Arthur	1924
Brooks	Lionel L.	1924
Brooks	Bertha	1925
Brooks	Georgia	1926
Brown	P.H.	1921
Brown	J.W.	1922
Brown	Paul	1922
Brown	James	1923
Brown	Walt	1924
Brown	C.P.	1926
Brown	Thomas Calvin	1927
Brown	C.H.	1928
Brown	Hiram (J.)	1928
Brown	John W. (William)	1929
Brown	Harold	1930
Brown	J.F.	1930
Brown	Phil	1930, 1931
Brown	Frank	1931
Brownell	Charles	1924
Bruce	E.	1924
Bruize	H.C.	1924

Brunero (Bernero)	John	1921
Bryant	Laurel (Lawrel)	1922, 1922
Bryant	Charles (E.)	1923
Bryden	R. (Robert S.)	1925
Bryson	Mrs. M.L. (Mary L.)	1924
Buchanan	Mike "Buck"	1925
Buck	O.T. (Oscar)	1922, 1922
Buckland	Alonzo	1928
Bucquet	George	1923
Bumach	Pete	1921
Burger	Frank (O.?)	1921
Burich	Frank	1925
Burke	Frank	1928
Burkhart	E.L.	1929, 1929
Burnacchi	Victor	1922
Burnes	M.J.	1925
Burns	H.O.	1921
Burright	L.C. (Lew or Lewis)	1924, 1924
Burright (Burrite?)	C.M.	1925, 1925, 1926
Burton	Ernest E.	1921
Burton	John Doe	1931
Burubeltz	P. (Paul?)	1921
Buskard	V.M. (Vernon?)	1921, 1921, 1921, 1922, 1922
Bustos	Lottie	1925, 1925
Butler	Andy (Andrew M.)	1921
Butts	V.R.	1926
Byrne	William F.	1921
Cabona	Louis	1928
Callahan	Owen	1920, 1922, 1927

Callahan	J.	1924
Cambra (Cambro)	Tony	1921
Campbell	Clyde	1924, 1925
Campbell	R.E.	1924
Cantrell	Birdie	1926, 1926
Canup	F.O. (C.)	1932
Cape	George	1927
Capps	A.H.	1921
Cardoni	Joe	1924
Carega	John	1931
Carey	Joe (Joseph)	1924
Carey	Mark	1925
Carico	A.J. (Alexander)	1922
Carlson	Fred	1920
Carlson	Gus	1928
Carmignani	A. (Agide)	1925
Carmignani	Frank	1925
Carpenter	Fred	1921
Carpenter	Henry (H.)	1921
Carr	Anna	1921
Carroll	Mrs. Mabel	1931
Carson	Edward	1927
Carson	Charles B. (D)	1928
Caruthers	S.O. (Shelley O.)	1921
Casper	J.C.	1929
Castle	Marion	1927
Cates	Mrs. R.	1927
Catton	George A.	1928
Cauzzo (Cauzza)	C. (Casere)	1921
Cauzzo (Cauzza)	Mrs. Madeline (Maddalena)	1921

Cavez (Chavez?)	M.C.	1927
Cayce	E.N. (Edgar U?)	1921
Ceburn?	Frank	1925
Cecchine (Cecchini)	Faustina	1925, 1926, 1927
Cecchine (Cecchini)	Joe	1927
Cecchini	Gildo	1928
Ceccrelli (Ceccarelli)	Fadio (Fabio)	1928
Cemo	Frank	1931
Chamberlain	G.B.	1923
Charletti	F.	1924
Chauvet	Louis	1920, 1922, 1924, 1925, 1925
Cheney	Jack	1920
Cheney	Albert	1925
Chicca (Chicci)	Albert	1928, 1930, 1933
Chicca (Chicci) (Cicca)	John	1924, 1929
Chicorelli (Ceccarelli?)	Steve	1924
Chieca (Chicca)	Tony	1932
Childers	Beo	1929
Chinburg	A.	1924
Chittenden	A.M.	1922
Chong (Fong)	Fong (Chong)	1925
Christoful (Christofel)	Myron (Moran)	1932
Church	E.E. (Fred E.?)	1921, 1922

Cima	John	1921
Cinelli	Mrs. Elvine	1921
Cinelli	Joe	1921, 1925, 1927, 1928
Cipriano	Mary	1923
Cipriano	Mary's son— 17 years old	1923
Clark	George	1921
Clark	Dan	1922, 1925
Clarke	D.H.	1923
Clarke	Mrs. L.H.	1926
Clarke (Clark)	Norris J.	1928
Claudino	Frank	1921
Clauser (Clausen)	Fred	1930
Clay	Alonza (Alonzo)	1930
Clayton	Victor	1931
Clements	James (G.?)	1920
Clough	William (aka W.E. Brodie)	1921
Coburn	Stanley	1933
Cocco (Coco)	John	1919, 1924, 1927
Cochran	E.W.	1929
Coday	Lowell D.	1923
Coe	A.B. (Alvin B.?)	1925
Cognaccio	Isabella	1921
Coleman	Frank	1929, 1930
Collett	C.C. (Charles C.?)	1924
Collins	Walter (D.?)	1922
Collins	G.A. (G. Albert)	1925

Colombo (Columbo)	Joe	1928, 1929, 1931
Colomiana	G.	1924
Columbo	Louis	1928
Comestock	Joe	1931
Compher	E.B. (Earnest)	1927
Compton	A.R.	1930
Concannon	William	1921
Conley	Archie	1931
Connely (Conley)	Lindon	1926
Connon	Harry (P?)	1924
Converso (Couverso) (Convirso)	Carlo	1920, 1921, 1922, 1926
Conway	Pete	1924, 1925
Cook	A.	1920
Cook	Pete (Peter H?)	1924, 1925
Cook	Ralph (C?)	1924
Cook	Leon (G?)	1925
Cooper	A.H.	1922
Cooper	Joe	1931, 1931
Cordoni	Joe	1924
Cortez	Antonio	1924
Corti	Clements	1930
Costa	Louise	1923
Costello	Dante P.	1923
Costello	Dan	1925
Cougars (Cogar)	Braxton	1923
Coughron	V.O.	1923
Cousins	E.W. (Edward) (Eddie)	1921, 1922, 1924
Cousins	Suzane (Susanne)	1924

Cowley	Harry (Harrison)	1922
Cox	James	1921
Cox	T.	1925
Crabtree	Melville	1929
Craig	Jack	1929
Craig	Mary	1929
Creason (Creasin)	Linn (Lynn) (Lem)	1925, 1925, 1926, 1929, 1929
Crockett	J.D.	1926
Crockett	M.L.	1926
Crockett	W.J.	1926
Crookshank	S.C. (Sherman?)	1920, 1921
Crosbie	J.W.	1924
Croslin	B. (Buck)	1927
Cross	Samuel J.	1928
Cross (Gross)	C.	1924
Crow	Herman	1924
Crum	F.O.	1925
Cruz	G.	1929
Cuarez	Lois	1921
Cudeback	Jesse	1920
Cummings	Ben	1930
Cummins	Mrs. L.	1920
Cupp	L.W. (Lon)	1926
Curry	John (T.)	1928
Daiz	John	1923
Dale	William	1933
Dalparto	F.	1921
Dalphino (Delfino)	M. (Marsio)	1926
Dami	Ernest	1921

Daniels	Tom (Thomas)	1929
Darling	Mrs. C.C.	1926
Davis	R.L.	1921
Davis	Cliff	1923
Davis	E.O.	1924
Davis	W. "Blackie"	1924, 1924
Davis	H.J.	1926
Davis	Jack	1927
Davis	T.	1927
Davis	M.J.	1928
Davis	Charlie	1930
Davis	Jim	1930
Dawes	Jack	1930
Day	Fred (Alfred?)	1920
Day	Jesse	1923, 1924, 1924
Day	Anna	1928
Dazatun	Gus	1924
De Bene (Di Bena) (Di Bene)	Domingo (D.J.)	1920, 1921
De La Cruz	Phillip	1922
De Leon	Eddie (T.)	1931
De Line	Charles	1923
De Maria	John B.	1924
De Pois	George	1925
Deal	John Doe (John's brother—Charles M.)	1923
Deal	"Doc"	1924
Deal	John (H.)	1923, 1924
Dealo	Fred	1922
Dean (Deane)	George	1929
Del Carlo (Delcarlo)	Louis (Luiz)	1928, 1932, 1933

	(Luis)	
Del Frate	P. (Pellegrino?)	1927
Del Port	G.	1922
Delfinisi (Dalfonsi)	Henry	1920
Delfrate (Del Frate)	Mrs. Marie	1928
Delich	Gus	1921
Delporto	George	1921, 1921
Delporto	P.	1921
Delporto	O.	1927
Demas (Damas) (Demos) (Dumas)	Gus	1920, 1921, 1922, 1923
Demas (Deman) (Demar)	John	1919, 1921, 1921, 1923
Deming	F.W.	1922
Deming (Denning)	Mrs. Bertha	1929
Depedrazzi	Tom	1928
Deruccia	Mr.	1925
Deruccia	Mrs.	1925
Devoti (Devoto?)	Henry (J?)	1924
Dexter	George	1930
Di Martini	Sam	1931
Diaz	Florensio (Florencio)	1922
Diaz	Frank (Francisco)	1926
Diaz	J.H.	1926
Diaz	John	1926
Dickson	D.E.	1924
Diement	Harry	1928

Dierlam	Marjorie (wife) (Nettie f.)	1925
Dierlam (aka-Ed Davis)	C.J. (Calvin G.?)	1922, 1925, 1928
Diez	John	1926
Dillereal	Crescencio	1927
Dillon (Dillow)	H.T. (Harry?)	1920, 1921, 1921
Dilzer (Dilger?)	W.B.	1924
Diodall	A.	1924
Dixon	J.	1920
Dodd	Jack	1927
Dodd	J.O.	1932
Doll	Frank (E)	1921, 1921, 1922, 1925
Domingo	Margaret	1929
Don Carlo	Luis (L.)	1931
Donahow (Donahoe)	G.A. (Gilbert)	1925
Doran (Duran)	George	1922
Dorr (Door)	Charles A.	1926, 1928, 1928
Dorstewitcz (Dorstewitz)	Charles (W.)	1922
Doty	Foster (R.)	1928
Douglas (Douglass)	Roger (M.)	1928
Dove	H.J.	1921
Downing	James (E.)	1924
Downs	John	1924
Downs	William	1924
Drake	C.H.	1924
Dresser	C.E. (Charles E.)	1924
Drinkwater	Herman	1927

Duccett (Duckett)	Olive	1932
Duden (Dudgeon)	Arthur	1920
Dudley	Harvey	1924
Duiseree (Dusserre)	August	1921, 1922
Dunkel	John	1924
Dunn	J. (Jay) (Ernest?)	1921, 1922
Dunn	Roy	1925
Dunn	Peter	1930
Dunn	Jack	1931
Duran	Pasqual (Pascual)	1925
Dussere (Dusserre)	John	1920
Dustin	E. (Elderkin)	1923
Dye	James	1925
Dyerlam	C.C.	1925
Dylerlan(m)	Mrs. C.C.	1926
Ealli	Natalie	1929
Eaton	Fred (Earl)	1926
Edmunds	C.W.	1924
Edwards	William	1920
Edwards	James	1922
Edwards	Paul (aka Paul Hibbs)	1932
Edwards (Allbrittan)	Jack	1923
Eggerson	John	1927
Eienhoefer	Fred	1921
Eierlan	Calvin G.	1928
Elb	J.F.	1921

Elder	W.F.	1932
Elicalde (Elezalde)	John	1931
Elke	W.G.	1923
Ellis	J.	1930
Ellis	Myrtle	1931
Ellits	Mrs. M.	1931
Ely	A.O.	1924
Entatron	Charles S.	1929
Erickson	Edward	1921
Erwin	Annie	1924
Escallier	Andre (Andrew)	1921, 1921, 1921
Espitalier	E.	1928
Espitallier	Joe	1920, 1920, 1921
Espitallier	Henry	1923, 1923
Espitallier	Jean	1924
Espitallier	Frank	1932, 1932
Estes	T.H.	1922
Estey (Espey?) (Espy)	Pauline	1928, 1928
Estribou	J.B.	1921, 1922
Etchegary (Etchegaray)	Ramon	1928
Evans	Ed	1923
Eyraud	E.L. (E.F.?)	1924
Faber	Corbett J. (Corbit)	1928
Fachin	Peter (Pete)	1926
Fagan	W.G. (William B.) (D.?)	1923
Falaschi	Guy	1927

Fanucchi	D. (Dick)	1920, 1924, 1926, 1929, 1929, 1931
Fanucchi	Joseph	1932
Farchani (Forchini)	James	1922
Farchine (Forchini?)	Mrs. J. (Sarah?)	1921
Farrel	Mike	1923
Farrel	W.F.	1924
Fasce	Angelo	1924
Faure	L. (Leon) (Leron)	1924
Favilla	Guiseppi	1924
Feagan	Walter S.	1928
Feather	Troy O.	1922
Ferear (Frear)	Albert	1920
Fernandez	E.S.	1921
Fernandez	Joe (Jose)	1921
Fernandez	Aveline (Avalino)	1926
Fernandez	Manuel	1928
Fery	Joe	1923
Field	J.B.	1921
Field	John (R.)	1924, 1924
Field	Ward	1928
Field	Robert E.	1932
Finley	Robert	1931
Finnabach (Fininbaugh) (Fenenback)	Morris	1923
Fisher	C.W.	1922
Fisher	L.H.	1922
Fisher	Mrs. Bernice	1931
Fitzgerald	A.	1924
Fitzgerald	E.J.	1924

	(Edward J.)	
Fitzgerald	William	1926
Fleming	Jesse	1922
Flores	Marino	1923
Flores	D. (Demetrio)	1924
Flynn	Clarence	1921
Flynn	Tom	1928
Foote	John Doe	1923
Foote	B.L. (Dallas L.)	1924, 1931
Foote	Della	1931
Forchini	James	1928
Ford	Raymond	1930
Forester	W.J.	1928
Forman (Foreman)	Dennis (Denis W.)	1928
Formonack	L.	1921
Foulk	J.E. (J.C?)	1922
Fouvela	G.	1924
Fox	James (D.)	1921
Fox	Burford (Buford I. or L.)	1923
Fox	Minnie	1924
Fraley	Robert F.	1929
Franklin	James	1921, 1921, 1922
Frantonf	Mrs. Hortease	1928
Fraser	Al	1924
Fraser	George (H.)	1929
Fraser	Howard	1932
Fresalli (Frassella?) (Freseli?) (Freselli) (Frassilli)	Ernest (Ernesto?)	1922, 1929, 1932

Frever (Frover)	H.C.	1926
Froelich	Octavian (Carl)	1932
Frost	Frank	1929
Fugett	Grover	1928
Fujii	S.	1926
Fulton	Fred (G.)	1924
Fultz	C.H. (Charlie H.)	1924
Funderburk	W. (William?)	1922
Furrier	J.E.	1926
Gaestas	Ora	1931
Gale	Willis	1925, 1926, 1926
Gale	Arthur	1929
Gale	Henry	1929
Galey	Otto	1932
Galiapules	Peter	1921
Galindo	Massilino	1925
Galindo (Golinda)	Mike	1925
Gallagher	Jack	1924
Galli	G. (Giacomo)	1921, 1921
Galli	Charles	1931
Galliducci	J.	1925
Galligan	Tom	1923
Gannon	Steve (Stephen)	1922
Garcia	Irene	1929
Gardner	G.	1921
Garner	A.G. (August)	1921, 1929, 1932
Garner	J.E.	1923
Garner	Gus	1931

Garnis	Desue	1926
Garrett	George C.	1921
Garrett	U.J. (U.C.)	1924
Garrett	Della (M.)	1926, 1927
Garzelli	Salvadore (Salvatore)	1923
Gastoni	Gaston (Gastone)	1926
Gaul	Herman	1923
Gayce	E.N.	1920, 1927
Gazioli	Giolonde	1923
Gearing	John M.	1923
Geesman (Gessman)	West R.	1930
Geiger	August	1932
Geiger	Howard T.	1932
George	Henry V.	1925, 1925
Gestner (Gester)	Louise C. (Louis)	1926, 1928
Gfeller	Christ	1929
Gharckery	P.	1924
Ghilarducci	Beneth	1920
Ghilarducci	A. (Amato)	1923, 1924, 1928
Giamiani (Giminiani)	Mike (Mik)	1924
Gianelli	Albert	1928
Gianelli	Mrs. Lena	1928
Gianiani	Mike	1923
Giboney	R.F. (A.F.?) (Alonzo?)	1921
Gibson	Mrs. Ernest (Earnest)	1928
Giffen	Mrs. T.R.	1926
Giffing	H.D.	1924
Gilbert	Loren	1930

Gill	H. (aka James Reagan)	1921
Gillespie (Gillispie)	Betty (aka Marie Walters)	1928, 1929, 1931
Gilliducci	J.D.	1921
Gillum	Marrietta	1928
Gilmore	William Jennings	1929
Ginnilli (Giannella)	Albert	1929
Giovanetti	Ricardo (Renny)	1922
Giovanni	Julius	1931
Giovanni	Ralph A.	1933
Giovanni (Giovani)	Anton	1929
Giraud	Jean P.	1922
Gish	Charlie	1924
Gish	Jim	1924
Gitzel	August	1928
Gleeson	R.M.	1922
Glerille	Albert	1927
Glouis	Bessie	1924
Godinez	Louis	1922
Godner	Joe	1921
Golzman	Max	1926
Gomez	Pete	1922
Gonzales	Rafael	1923
Gonzales	Mrs. A.	1924
Gonzales	Pete	1927
Goodwin	Jack	1923
Goodwin	J.E. (Joe E.)	1923
Goos	H.W.	1924
Goos	W.C.	1924

166

Gordon	Grover	1924
Goss	Henry	1921
Gould	Elmer	1930
Grace	Al	1922
Graf (Graff)	Mrs. Marie	1927
Graham	C.A.	1922
Grahame (Graham)	Harry C.	1921
Gram	Otto	1929
Granville	A.	1932
Grauf	Mrs. John (Eva Mary)	1923, 1924
Gray	Dave (David M.)	1921
Gray	Charles	1931
Greatrex	William Stewart	1931
Green	Claire	1926
Gregory	J.	1920, 1922, 1927
Gregory	R.F. (Robert?)	1926
Griffin	Ed	1925
Griffin	Gilbert Lee	1933
Griffin (Giffin)	Mrs. Gertrude	1926
Griffith	George	1928
Grijalva	Ella (F.)	1922
Grijalvo	John	1921
Grimaud	Peter (?)	1920, 1921, 1921, 1923
Grimaud	M. (Marios)	1921
Grimaud	V. (Ambrose V.?)	1921, 1921, 1921
Groff	Charles (C.)	1924
Grol	Joe	1924

(Groi?)	(Joseph)	
Grouten	Eisle	1928
Grovanetti (Giovanetti)	Pete	1930
Gualco	Peter	1920
Gualco	Mrs. P. (Rosa)	1924
Guera	A.C.	1924
Guerrerro	Mary	1923
Guerrerro (Guererro)	Lupe	1923
Guitirrez	Mariano	1928
Gunther	Robert	1931
Gusti	F. (Fanny?)	1921
Gusti	G. (Gus?)	1921
Gusti	George	1928
Guthrie	Edward	1919
Guthrie	A.H.	1924
Guthrie	S.W.	1924
Haas	Mrs. Blanche (M.)	1924
Hack	Emil D.	1928
Hadden	Leona	1927
Hagen	A.H. (Albert H.?)	1921, 1922
Hale	William	1924
Hale	E.V. (Epham V.?)	1925
Hall	W.P.	1923
Hall	L.	1925
Hall	John	1928
Hall	George	1929
Hall	W.A.	1921, 1921, 1922
Haller	George	1922
Halley	E.A.	1920

Hamilton	James	1921, 1921, 1921, 1921
Hamilton	Barney	1924
Hamlin	R.F.	1922
Hanley	T.E. (Tom F.?)	1920
Hannagan	William (T.)	1928
Hanning	Dan (Don L.)	1930
Hansen	Haris?	1923
Hardestry	T.L.	1932
Harding	William	1928
Hargraves	Mira	1931
Harrara	Al	1924
Harrelson	John W.	1927, 1928
Harrington	J.S. (J.L.)	1927
Harrington	Dan	1928
Harris	Perry J.	1924
Harris	Sam	1922
Harrison	Alice	1922
Harrison	John	1922
Harrison	Jack	1924
Hart	Ed	1923, 1924
Hart	G.	1925
Hart	Ben (Benjamin H.?)	1922
Hart (Hunt)	William	1922
Harter	Harry	1928
Hartford	John	1922
Harvey	Fred	1923, 1924, 1926, 1926, 1929, 1931, 1931
Hastings	C.E. (Charles E.)	1924
Hawker	Ray (C.)	1926

Hawley	Thomas	1927
Hayes	Guy Emery	1928
Head	D.C.	1923
Heckman	Emil E.	1928
Heine	C.A.	1922
Helm	George (G.W.?)	1921
Helm	Charles	1932
Helm	Henry A.	1932, 1932
Henley	George	1929
Herman	F.W.	1920
Herman	Mrs. F.W.	1920
Hern	George	1929
Hernandez	C. (Catarino?)	1920
Hernandez	Joe	1921
Hernandez	Rose	1922, 1923, 1923, 1932
Hernandez	A.	1924
Hernandez	Mike	1929
Hess	George	1927
Hickman	Bill (William)	1921
Higgens	Jack	1926
Hill	Howard	1928
Hilyard	Julia	1926
Hing	Tom Mow	1923
Hing	Wong (Yee Hing Wong?)	1924
Hinnant	T.J.	1924
Hoage (Hogg)	B.B. (Bob)	1926
Hoff	Nels	1925
Hoffman	Leo (G.)	1925
Hoffman	Eddie (G.)	1929, 1930
Hogan	R. (N.?)	1921

Hogan	Floyd (S.)	1928
Hogan	Ben (Benjamin F.)	1931
Holden	(D.S.) Dewey J. (G.)	1929, 1932
Holl	Nels	1925
Holland	T.M. (Thomas M.)	1924
Holland	James	1929, 1930
Holley	H. (Herman)	1924
Holloway (Halloway)	Grant	1928
Holmes	J.L.	1921
Holmes	J.F. (John)	1922, 1923
Honan	Mike	1925
Hood	William E.	1923
Hooper	Frank	1925
Hopper	Abram (G.)	1922
Hornbeck	W.	1922
Horton	E.K	1931
House	Ernest (D.) (B.?)	1924
Howard	F.E.	1929
Howard	Ray E.	1930
Hoy	C.A.	1922
Hudson	Irene	1923
Hudson	Charles	1930
Huerta	Pasqual (Pasquale)	1927
Huey	J. Hong	1928
Hughes	Clarence (D.)	1922, 1923
Hughes	Joe	1926
Hughes	John	1926
Hunter	Howard	1926
Huntington	J.	1921

	(Jay?)	
Hutchinson	H.H.	1926
Hynes	A.	1928
Ildo	J.D.	1921
Iribarne	John	1921
Irouliguy (Irouleguy)	Dominique	1921
Iroz	John	1928
Irwin	Anna	1924
Isom	Orphie (Orphle) (Archie?)	1921
Isugi	I.	1923
Ivener	Sam	1924, 1926
Jacks	Sam	1921
Jackson	Rufus	1923
Jackson	W.R. (William)	1923, 1924
Jackson	Ruth (A.)	1924
Jackson	L.	1925
Jacobsen	Ollie	1926
Jarrar	H.J.	1925
Jarsaud (Jaussaud?)	Mrs. Martin	1926
Jarvis	James (E.)	1923
Jarvis	Ed	1926
Jasper	Joe	1929
Jassaud (Jaussaud)	Jean	1920, 1923
Jaussand (Jaussard) (Jassaud)	Martin	1921, 1921, 1924, 1925, 1926, 1927
Jenkins	J.A.	1927
Jenkins	James P.	1928
Jensen	Jack K.	1929
Jensen	E.W.	1923
Jensen (Johnson)	Loren (Soren)	1931, 1932

Jewett	Bert (Burt L.?)	1924
Jimitale	J.	1927
Jimitola	Julio	1929
Joe	Ah	1921
Joel	Ed (E. Manuel?)	1924
Joel	Mrs. Sarah (M.)	1924
Johnson	Arthur (J.)	1921
Johnson	John	1921, 1923, 1928
Johnson	James	1922
Johnson	Sam	1922
Johnson	S.F. ("Slim") (S.T.) (Sim)	1922, 1923, 1924, 1924, 1928, 1928
Johnson	Julius	1923
Johnson	Clyde	1927
Johnson	Fred	1927
Johnson	C.	1928
Johnson	Lena	1928
Johnson	Al (A.L.)	1930
Johnson	Lankford (Lakeford)	1932
Johnston	Sam	1922
Jones	G.F. (George F.?)	1921
Jones	Mabel	1922
Jones	Robert	1922
Jones	W.C. (William?)	1922
Jones	B.O. (D.O.)	1924
Jones	H.H.	1924
Jones	O.D. (David O.)	1924

Jones	Rosie	1926
Jones	Ormond	1928
Jones	J.W.	1930
Jones	J.O.	1932
Juan	Jim Hong	1928
Kaliapules (Kaluepulos)	Peter	1921
Kaman	Henry	1921
Kanjed	M.J.	1925
Kanoch (Kanoth?)	Charles (aka Charlie Brown)	1924
Karleskint	Lawrence	1932
Kazasa	Louis	1921
Kee	Jew Shunk (Sam?)	1931
Keeler	Belle	1931
Keenan	William	1922
Keiper	H.	1924
Keith	Charles L.	1924
Kelly	Tom (Thomas F.)	1923, 1925
Kelly	Miss Francis E.	1927
Kelm	Theodore	1918
Kennedy	Blackie	1925
Kerney (Kearney)	Ben	1931
Killian	Walter	1929
Kim	Charlie	1922
Kimball	G.L.	1923
Kimball	J.D.	1930
Kimble	George	1924
Kindred	M.B. (Marion B.)	1923
King	L.W. (Louis?)	1921, 1922, 1923, 1923, 1924
King	Clarence	1931

King	Mabel	1931, 1931
Kirby	James (B.W.)	1923, 1924
Klethley (Kiethley)	William	1921
Klimper	C.L.	1925
Knapp	Amador	1928
Knoth	George (H.)	1926
Knowles	Eva	1930
Koehn	William	1923
Kohal	Mabel	1928, 1931
Koleopulas (Kolepoulos?)	Alec (Alex)	1922, 1923
Kolevis	Nick	1921
Kooken	D.T.	1930
Koutroulos (Koutroulis) (Koutroules)	Gus	1921
Krause	Fred	1922
Kurtz	C. "Mike"	1923
LaCosta (Lacoste?)	Tom	1922, 1922
La Martini (Di Martini)	Sam	1931
Labovitch	Louie (aka Labow)	1924
Lacumbery	Pete	1924
Ladanway	Virgil	1928
Lair	Ora	1928
Laiva (Leiva)	John	1931
Lambero (Lamberg)	Fabian	1921
Lamley	Charles (H?)	1922
Landis	Ben	1928
Landon	D.W.	1924
Landucci	Annie	1921

175

Landucci	Angelo	1926
Landwehr (Lanwehr)	Charles	1923
Lane	C.F.	1922
Lane	Fred	1922
Lane	Charles	1928
Lapardo (Lopardo?)	Antonio	1921
Laselve (La Selva?)	Walter	1921, 1922
Lastin	Antonio	1921
Lattemar (Lattimer)	Viola	1926
Lawrence	Val (Vall)	1921
Lawyer	W.F.	1926, 1926
Lazarena (Lazzerino) (Lazzerini)	Mike	1929
Leach	Thomas	1929
Lean	W.H. (William H.)	1921, 1922, 1922
Lecaralio	Joe	1926
Ledoux	Ms. Babe	1922
Lemucchi	A.L.	1920
Lemucchi	Dick	1920
Lemucchi	Joe	1924, 1926, 1926, 1928
Lemucchi	Mrs. C.L. (Carmelina?)	1925
Lemucchi	Amador (Amerideo?)	1926
Lemucchi	Amado (Amadeo)	1929
Lemuchi	A.	1920
Leonard	Frank	1922
Leonard	Charles	1925
Leonard	Mrs. L.E.	1926, 1926

Leonard	William	1926
Lepori	Gino (Guino)	1927
Lewis	J.L.	1922
Lewis	Charlie	1932
Lewis	George	1932
Liebe	F.P.	1921
Lima	D.	1922
Limi	D.	1922
Limi	Domick	1930
Limi	Joe	1930
Lockwood	Frank (E.)	1925
Loeffel	J.D.	1921
Logan	R.	1921
Long	Jack	1925
Long	Robert (F.)	1926, 1926, 1929
Long	Dallas (M.)	1929
Lopez	Marie	1924
Lord	Horace A.W. (Harry)	1921
Lorenzi	Leopardo	1921
Lorenzi	P. (Paul?)	1921
Lorenzi	Cino	1927
Love	James (M?) (Jim)	1922, 1922, 1924, 1924
Love	Tom (Tommy)	1922, 1925, 1928
Love	Tony	1924
Love	Anna L.	1929
Love	F.S. (Floyd Scott)	1929
Love	Thomas E.	1929
Loveall	George	1932
Lowe	Louis (Lewis?) (I or L)	1924

177

Lukiniv	Mrs. Mary	1923
Lundeen	Elmer	1921, 1924
Lundquist	Clarence (R.)	1922
Lynch	P.A.	1925
Lyons	Ralph	1920, 1921
Lyons	Joseph	1921
Mack	William	1921
Mackey	Joe	1920
Mackey	John	1921
Magardill	G.	1925
Magginonoi (Magginoni)	Lorenzo (Loreno)	1932
Maggneti (Maggenti)	Frank	1923, 1924
Maiconi (Malconi?)	Joe	1922
Majors	L.A. (Louis Alfred)	1930
Malator (Malatore)	Giovannia (Giovanna)	1931
Malatore (Malitore?)	George	1923
Malavitz (Malvitch?)	Nick	1920
Malcome	Hugh	1924
Malinengo (Molinengo)	Joe	1925
Mallanacci	L.	1924
Malotore (Malatore)	Antone (Antonio)	1928
Malovitch	Nick	1921
Mandeburn (Mendibulo)	G. (Gregorio)	1924
Mandich	Obren G.	1923
Mandy	George (P.)	1924
Maney	Ed	1922
Mangles	George	1922
Mankins	Ed	1924

	(Fred)	
Manly	J.H.	1924
Manney	E.	1921, 1922
Manny	Alfred	1924
Manny	Isadore	1929
Maraccini	Guerico	1925
Marble	R.	1930
Marchetti	Harry (Henry)	1928
Marconi	Joe	1923
Margantini	John	1928
Margarinni	D.	1926
Marichelar	Manuel	1927
Marino	Catrino	1924
Marins	A.	1922
Martin	Albert	1921, 1921, 1921, 1922, 1923, 1924, 1924
Martin	Alfred (D.)	1923
Martin	J.R.	1924
Martin	Marie	1925
Martin	Marjorie	1925
Martin	Alice M.	1929
Martine	Albert	1921
Martinez	E.	1922
Martini	Umberto	1921, 1923
Martino (Martinto)	John	1920
Marugg	Nick	1924
Masconi	Tony	1924, 1928, 1928, 1931
Masocca	Joseph	1927
Mason	Pat (Patrick)	1925, 1927
Mason	Frank	1929
Mason	Mrs.	1931
Masoni	L.	1926, 1926

Massoni	Louis	1928
Massozza	Joe	1926
Mathews	C.C. (Charley C.)	1924
Mattel	Henry	1931
Matthews	S.J. (Al?)	1921
Matthieson	F.M. (E.M.) (Ernest M.)	1923, 1924
Maulia	Pete	1924
Mavis	Antonio	1920
Mayfield	Voney	1932
Maynard	H.G. (Harry)	1923
Maynard	Mrs. H.G.	1923
Mazza	R. (Ralph R.)	1924
McAfee	Walter (W.)	1927
McAntyre (McAintyre)	Jack	1922
McCain	Billy (William Lee)	1923
McCarthy	W.J.	1921
McCool	Lon	1925
McCord	Grace	1932
McCormack (McCormick)	Robert (A.) (Bob)	1924, 1924, 1928
McCourt	Grace	1928
McCoy	Blanche	1926
McCoy	Barney	1930
McCready	J.E.	1924
McDonald	J.P.	1921
McDonald	Joe	1928
McDonald	Maude	1928
McDonald	Charles	1929
McDonald	James T.	1929

McDonald	Bert	1931
McDonald	Dan	1931
McDonald	John	1931
McGarigol (McGarigle)	Charles	1925
McGeorge	John (R.)	1924
McGraw	Lynn E.	1927, 1928, 1929
McGraw	Elsie	1929
McIntyre	Cecil	1931
McIntyre	Herbert	1931
McKay	J.R.	1926
McLaughlin	J.D.	1925
McManins (McMains)	Vera	1931
McMellon	Lee	1923
McMullin	C.R.	1927
McPherson	Miss Gladys	1921
McQuaid	E.R. (E.B.)	1925
McQueen	E.H.	1923
McQuerney	George	1922
McSwain	Gus	1930
Mead	Charles Matt	1927, 1928, 1928
Meany	Ed (Edward)	1928
Meek	Thomas	1929
Meeks	Walter	1929
Melendrez	Tomaso	1922
Mellen	A.F.	1922
Melone	Alexandro (Alessandro) (Alexander)	1932
Melton	C.R.	1924, 1924
Melville	Sam	1921, 1924

Melville	T.H. (Thomas?) (Thomas A.)	1922, 1924, 1928, 1928, 1929
Menzoni	E. (Ermenegildo?)	1922
Merideth	Tom	1925
Mertzman	B.H. (Bernard H.)	1922
Metzer	Frank	1924
Meyers	O.S.	1924
Meyers	May	1931
Mickey	Mrs. J.D.	1921
Migueltoreno	Gracian	1923, 1924
Millage	Marion	1931
Miller	Joseph	1922
Miller	Frank	1924
Miller	Louis	1924
Miller	Bill	1925
Miller	Herman (F.)	1933
Miller	Chester (C.)	1922
Millerweiz	Albert	1921
Minter	Ray Jackson	1928
Missoni (Massoni)	Aliso (Alesio)	1920
Missoni (Massoni)	Andiola	1920
Mitchell	Bettie	1922
Mitchell	C.	1927
Miwa	S. (Sodalro)	1925
Molinengo	Joe	1923
Molingo (Moringo)	Joe	1921, 1928
Monfort	J.C.	1926, 1927
Mongrum	Nomi (Naomi) (Neomi)	1931

Monroe	George	1930
Montana	C.	1926
Montana (Montanna)	A.F. (Agapito F.)	1925, 1927
Montie (Montey)	Olga (A.)	1931
Moon	Ira C.	1928
Moore	Jim	1922
Moore	Bob (Robert S.?)	1929
Moorman	T.A.	1931
Moran	James	1928, 1929
Moreno	C. (Charles)	1926
Moretti	Joe	1920
Morgan	Harry P.	1924
Morgantini	John	1930
Morino	Betty	1923
Morris	G.E.	1920
Morris	J.T.	1924
Morris	Charles	1926
Morris	G. (George A.)	1931
Morrison	Eliza Eleanor	1929
Morrow	J.L. (John L.)	1921
Mott	Julius	1921
Moulia	Jean (Baptiste) (Juan?)	1922
Mulford	N.	1924
Mullen	J.W.	1921
Munger	Sam (Samuel)	1923, 1924
Murphy	William	1922
Murphy	Joe	1923
Murphy	Dan	1928, 1929
Murray	S.J.	1924
Murray	A.J.	1927

Murry	John	1924
Musselman	John F.	1926
Myers	H.R.	1926
Myers (Meyers)	David	1922
Myston	Ed	1926
Nance	Mrs. N.E. (Eleanor)	1922, 1922, 1922
Naponelli (Naponilli)	E.	1921
Nardelli	A.J.	1923
Nardelli	T.P.	1923
Nash	F.L.	1921
Navarrio (Navario?)	Juanita	1928
Neal	Doc	1924
Neal	Elmer E.	1931
Neeley	A.	1922
Nevis	Tony	1920, 1927
Newman	W.J. (William) (W.F.)	1923, 1925, 1925
Newman	Edward (J.)	1931
Nicely	Sam	1920
Nicholas	M.	1924
Nomoto	Alka	1932
Nonella	C.	1924
Nord	Delma (M.)	1932
Noriega	F.M. (Faustino?)	1920
Norris	May	1923
North	J.L.	1926
Novice	A.S.	1922
Nunally (Nunelly)	H.	1920, 1927
Nunley	George	1931
O'Boyle	Don	1929
O'Brien	P.J.	1924

	(J.P.)	
O'Brien	J.F.	1926
O'Connor	L. (Lawrence)	1924
O'Davis	Ernest	1924
Odom	Clifton	1928
Odom	R.S.	1928
Ogden	Henry	1928
Ogden	Louise	1928
Ohomato	F.	1925
Okley	Jack	1927
Oldham	E. (Elodie?)	1923
Oldham	Earl (E.)	1928
Olivieri (Olivera?)	Antonio	1920, 1922, 1922, 1923
Olsen	Martin	1924
O'Meara	Joe	1931
O'Neill	E.J.	1924
O'Rourke	Pete (Peter E.)	1924
Ortez	Paul	1924
Ostrosky (Ostrowski)	G. (Gordon)	1924, 1924, 1925
Otero	A.	1924
Owalve	J.	1925
Owens	B.E. "Midnight"	1927
Ozenne	Robert (C.)	1921
Ozenne	O.A.	1924
Pace	Harry (Henry W.)	1929
Pacini	Albert	1924, 1932
Packer	Charles (M)	1924, 1925, 1926
Packer	John	1924
Pacuzzi	C.	1921
Paddock	Charlie (James?)	1923

185

Padella	Fred	1922
Paheco (Pacheco?)	Joseph	1922
Paladino	Salvadore	1929, 1930
Palmer	E.C. (Ernest C.)	1922
Palmer	Ed	1923
Palmer	A.B.	1924
Palmer	A.K.	1924, 1925, 1926
Palos	S.	1922
Panes	Gus	1922
Pappas	George	1924
Pardini	Arturo	1926, 1932
Pardini	Mrs. Anna	1927
Parenti	Rafaella (Raphal?)	1921, 1921, 1930
Parker	L.A.	1921
Parker	J.C.	1923
Parker	John	1924
Parker	Charles	1925
Parker	Fred	1929
Parry	Joe	1926
Pasquini	D.J. (Dante J.)	1921, 1927
Pasquini	Joe (Joseph)	1925, 1926, 1929
Pasquini	Baute (Dante?)	1926
Pasquini	E. (Egdio) (Hedio) (Egidio) (Egevio)	1927, 1928, 1929, 1932
Pasquini	J.B.	1927
Pasquini	Pasquino	1929
Pasuzzo (Pascuzzo)	Carlo	1921

Patch	William (J.)	1924
Patterson	Ruth (E.?)	1922
Patterson	William	1929
Patton	J.C. (Judson C.)	1921
Payan	M.	1922, 1923
Payne	Harry	1927
Payne	Frank	1928
Payne	John	1926, 1928
Payner	August	1924
Pearlman	Lewis	1925
Peck	M.D.	1923
Pecka	Alonzo	1925
Pena	Leonidas	1923
Pena	Lawrence	1925
Pena	Victor	1927
Peorrouchke	S.	1924
Pera	Gino (Geno?)	1922
Perez	Manuel	1927
Perretto	Paolo	1921
Perretto (Peretto) (Peretta)	Victor	1921
Perrucci	Luigi	1923
Perrucci	V.	1923
Perry	C.P	1925
Perry	M. (Marion L.)	1932
Perucci	Fernillo	1932
Perucci	Joe	1932
Peterson	J.W.	1921
Petruchi	Jaspine	1926
Pettin	Mary	1928
Petty	George	1932
Phillipps	J.L.	1926
Phillipps (Phillip)	Jean	1920

Phillips	W. (Billy)	1920
Phillips	George M.	1923, 1923, 1924
Piccone	Frank	1932
Picket	G.E.	1924
Pierucci	A.	1921, 1923
Pierucci	Antone (Anton)	1921
Pierucci	Marcisco (Narcisco)	1921, 1931, 1932
Pierucci	N.	1921
Pierucci	Julia	1929
Pierucci	Fiernello	1931
Pierucci (Pierrucci)	Vinecenzo (Vincent?)	1921
Pifer	D.H. (David H.)	1924
Pike	W.E.	1924
Pikos	Gus	1922
Pina	Vincente	1926
Pippi (Domenico)	Domenico (Pippi R.)	1926
Pirto	M.	1924
Plantier	M. (Marius)	1920
Polston	C.J.	1921, 1922, 1924
Poncet	Mrs. S.	1923
Ponton	Lee	1927
Pope	John (N.)	1927
Pope (Popes?)	J.R. (Julian?)	1924, 1931, 1932
Pope (Popes?)	Tennie	1925, 1931
Porigeaini	Angelo	1921
Porter	Elija	1928
Porter	James	1928

Potter	Ray	1924
Powers	Ada	1928, 1928, 1928
Poy	Charles	1929
Prati	Tom	1924
Prati	B. (Battista?)	1926
Prati (Pratti)	Robert	1927, 1928, 1929
Pratl	M.	1923
Prenitti	Sam	1929
Price	Paul	1920, 1921
Pucci	Rudy	1933
Quong	Charlie	1922
Rabbit	Burr (Bure)	1922
Racagni (Racagnie)	Edward	1924
Radar (Rader)	C.C.	1931
Rafell (Rafeli)	Arretia	1921
Ragan	Richard (R.)	1921
Raineri	P.	1920
Ramey	George L.	1921, 1924
Ramos	Benito	1924
Ramos	Pedro	1925
Ramos	Santos	1925
Ramos	Mrs. Carman (Carmen)	1932
Randall	Dean (M.)	1928, 1929
Rapoli	A.	1923
Rapoli	Mrs. A.	1923
Rascoe	George Cornelius	1924
Raymond	John B.	1923
Reader	W.E. (William E.)	1931

Reagan	C.A.	1922
Reagan	J.R. (T.R.?)	1924
Rechou	Bert	1920
Rechow	Ethel	1928
Reed	Fred	1921
Reed (Redd)	Tom (Thomas)	1922
Renaud	Eli	1921
Rentrerias	Pasqual	1925
Restituto	John	1926
Reynaud	P.	1921
Reynolds	Fred	1920
Reynolds	F. (Fred)	1923
Reynolds	John (W.?)	1923
Reynolds	Harry (D.?)	1924
Rhoades	Dean	1928
Rhyan	E.	1924
Ribas	Juan	1923
Ricci	Lee	1928
Riccomini	C.	1925
Rich	William	1922
Richards	(Marie?) Louise	1928
Richards	Walter G.	1928
Richardson	W.W. (Walter W.)	1929, 1930
Richey	Clyde	1922
Rickman	Paul (R.?)	1928
Ricon	Mrs. Jules (Sidonie)	1932
Ricotti	S.	1929
Ridgeway	Mary	1931, 1932
Riffle	Calvin (H.?)	1930
Riley	Don	1922
Riley	John	1922
Rincou	J.	1925

Ring	R.	1923
Rini	John	1933
Rioz	John	1928
Ripoli	A. (Amerigo)	1922, 1929, 1931
Robb	J. (James M.)	1926
Robbins	Finley (E.)	1924
Robbins	Pete	1928, 1930
Roberts	H.D.	1921
Roberts	Hiraham (Hiram)	1922
Robins	Frank	1931
Robinson	B.F. (Frank) (Benjamin Franklin)	1926, 1929
Robinson	Clara	1931
Robinson	Henry	1931
Robinson	Ruby	1931
Robinson	Tom	1932
Rodriguez	Pedro	1923
Rodriguez	Ricardo	1924
Rogers	E.F.	1923
Romero	Ed	1932
Rosa	Steve	1929
Rose	Joe	1924
Rose	Edmund C.	1928
Rose	Henry (Harry)	1929
Rose	Tom (Thomas R.?)	1931
Ross	Edna	1922
Rossetti (Rossetto)	John	1921
Rossi	Fred	1922
Rossi	Albert	1928
Rossi	Steve	1929

Roth	Merrill P. (Merle P.)	1928
Roth	Pete	1928
Roustelous	Gus	1921
Rouzi (Ruozi) (Ruosi)	A. (Alfonzo) (Alphonso)	1920, 1925, 1928
Rowray	George	1920
Rubin	Isaac	1920
Ruby	W.P.	1921
Rucker	Roy A.	1923
Rudneck (Rudnick)	Morris	1922
Rueno	Sarah	1923, 1923, 1924
Ruozi	Mrs. Beatrice	1926
Rupich (Ruprich)	S. (Sam)	1922, 1924, 1924
Rush	Clarence E. (F.)	1929
Russick (Rusick) (Bussick)	M.J.	1922
Ryan	Tom	1929
Saddachi (Sadacchi) (Sadoecki)	Mrs. Julia	1921
Sadocchi	Joe	1921
Sadwin (Sadivin?)	Leonard S.	1921
Sakamoto	J.	1927
Sakamoto	Takehichi	1928
Salas	Gracia	1922
Salcido (Saleido)	Frank	1921, 1928, 1931
Salmargun	John	1928
Salyonie	G.	1922
Sanchez	A.	1924, 1924
Sanchez	S.	1924

Sanders	W.C.	1924
Sanders	John (D.?)	1927
Sanders	Charles	1930, 1930
Sandrini	Dick	1924
Sandrini	F. (Fermino?)	1924
Sandrini	George	1924
Sangchi	F.	1924
Santiago	Simon	1924
Santini	Pasquale	1930
Sanucchi	D.	1926
Sartiat	Peter	1920
Sassello (Sasselli)	V. (Victor C.?)	1922
Sather	Al	1923
Saunders	Mrs. W.C.	1923
Saunders	W.C.	1923
Scantina	Frank	1920
Scaramellini	Frank	1923, 1927
Scarpetito (Scartpito)	Frank	1921, 1925, 1928, 1930
Scateno (Scatina) (Scatena)	Sabatino (Sabatina)	1928, 1929
Scattania	Frank	1920
Schafer (Schearf) (Scharef) (Schaerf)	Ernest	1929, 1930
Scheidt	F.J.	1923
Schimada	K.	1930
Schmidt	A.	1928
Schmitz	J.D	1924
Schonefeld	August (C.)	1925
Schuster	Fielding	1931
Schuttenholm	Harry	1924, 1924
Scott	Kenneth	1930

Secor	T.M.	1921
Secunza	M. (Manuel)	1920
Segolvia	M.	1922
Semple	T.P.	1924
Sentena (Saetena) (Seatna?)	S. (Sabascatino?)	1921
Sepulveda	Frank (L.)	1932
Setina	Salomi	1931
Shackleford	Nick (Mick)	1925, 1928
Shafer	Mrs. Edna	1923
Shafer	Thelma	1923
Shafter (Shaffer) (Shafer)	William (H.)	1928, 1929
Sharp	Henry B.	1920
Sheaf (Shonf?)	John	1928
Sheeley	Rose	1928
Shemie	Ms. Jessie	1922
Shepman	Joe	1928
Sherman	Mrs. Lucy	1924
Sherman	Eugene	1929
Sherwood	Ed	1923
Shore	Annie	1922
Shore (Schorr)	Nettie	1924
Shry	C. Wilbur (Chester W.?)	1922, 1924
Siemens	J.J. (Jacob J.)	1924
Sierra (Sierras)	Jim	1921
Silva	G.	1923
Silva	Manuel	1928

Simmons	D.S. (Dempsey S.)	1924
Simson	Lee J.	1924
Sing	Charles	1922
Sisneros	Jesus	1932
Slack	Elmer	1931
Sloan	Mrs. Abby	1921, 1928
Slusser	Benjamin H.	1931
Smartt	Mrs. L. (Lulu?)	1920
Smith	C.L. "Tex"	1921
Smith	Bill	1923
Smith	Mrs. Bill	1923
Smith	C.C.	1923, 1925
Smith	Thomas J.	1923
Smith	Andy	1924
Smith	C.	1924
Smith	E.	1924
Smith	George	1924, 1925
Smith	M.C.	1924
Smith	Mrs. Birnice	1925
Smith	Forrest B. (F.B.)	1925
Smith	Mrs. Rose	1925
Smith	Sam	1925
Smith	G.E.	1926
Smith	Glen A.	1926
Smith	Glenn	1926
Smith	H.D. (D.H.)	1927, 1928
Smith	Albert G.	1928
Smith	Mrs. D.H.	1928
Smith	Homer	1928
Smith	Harry R.	1929
Smith	Jack	1931
Smith	Mable	1931
Smith	W.M.	1931

Smith	J.H.	1921
Sneed	E.L. (Evertt)	1926
Snyder	D.L.	1922
Sockness	Oscar (S.)	1928
Soehnel (Suehnel)	Ernest	1924
Soto	Frank	1923, 1924, 1926, 1928
Souza	Joseph	1933
Spaulding (Snyder)	N.E.	1932
Spear	Clyde	1931
Speas	Bill (William M.?)	1923
Speller	Joe	1921
Spencer	Robert	1924
Spore	Ranson (E.)	1929
Spratt	George	1924
Springer	Charles	1927
Sprout	Jack	1924
Stallard	Charles (H.?)	1931
Stas	Charley (Charles J.)	1928
Steele	David (M.)	1924
Steinborn	Cliff	1927
Stephens	Charles (L.?)	1928
Sterling	Donald B.	1928
Stevens	Grover C.	1929
Stevenson	John	1929
Stevenson	Tom	1929
Stewart	G.C.	1921
Stewart	A.	1924
Stickler	Harry	1924
Stidham	Fred	1921
Stokes	George	1921, 1930

Stoler	R.W.	1924
Stone	Eddie (Edward)	1930
Stoner	Dick	1922, 1922, 1923, 1923
Storms	Robert	1929
Stout	Jack (E.?)	1924
Strauss	Ben (L.?)	1929
Street	William (R.)	1923, 1924
Street	Al	1924
Stubblefield	Jesse	1922
Stubblefield	Leroy M.	1926
Stubbs	L.E. (Lonnie E.?)	1925
Suey	Fong Kay	1932
Sullivan	Tim	1920
Summers	Dan H.	1926
Sumner	Morris	1921
Supira (Supera)	Bernard	1926
Sutherland	William	1921
Swartz	Rodney	1931
Sweet	Emory	1928
Sweetland	R.W.	1923, 1924
Swett	J.L. (John L.?)	1920, 1921
Takas	Joe	1922
Takemoto	Tom	1924
Talamantes	Jack	1924
Talamantes	Lizzie	1924
Tapple	S.	1920
Taylor	Ed (Edward)	1922
Taylor	Robert	1928
Tazuoli	Joe	1928
Teague	A.L.	1920
Temple	William	1921

Ternetti	Sam	1928
Tesse	Norazo	1920
Thackeray (Thackery)	Al	1924, 1924
Thackery	A.L. (Aubrey L.?)	1932
Thatcher	Charles E.	1929
Thom	Chris	1925
Thom	Herbert	1926
Thomas	Zoe	1923, 1924
Thomas	L.	1926, 1926
Thomas	Sidney	1927
Thomas	Henry	1931
Thomey (Thome?)	Alexander	1923
Thompson	George E.	1924
Thompson	Harry	1924, 1928
Thompson	H.C.	1926
Thompson	J.G.	1926
Thompson	J.R.	1927
Thorne	Charles (L.?)	1928
Thorne	Horton	1928
Thrasher	B.F. (Benjamin Frank)	1924
Tinney	C.E.	1924
Titenix (Teutimez)	Ben	1925
Tobisch	John	1929
Toldo (Toaldo)	Tony	1923
Tonatie (Tonetti)	Frank	1920
Toomey	C.W.	1926
Topper	Joseph	1922
Tosche (Toshey) (Tosci) (Toschi)	Joe	1922, 1924

Toti	Mrs. G. (Gismonda)	1921
Totl (Toti)	Amelia (Emilio)	1923
Toziola	Joe	1926
Tracy	T.A.	1926
Trammell	Dennis	1928
Trask (Traft)	Cyril P. (Clifford G.)	1921, 1926, 1927
True	F.B.	1924
Tullos	John	1926
Tullos	Mrs. William (Louise)	1926
Tullos (Tulles)	William (H.) (W.H.)	1924, 1924, 1925, 1926
Tuziolleri	R.R.	1921
Tweed	C.O.	1923
Ueba	Matago	1928
Urisalki (Urizalqui)	Lawrence (Laureano)	1931
Urlarte (Uriarte)	F. (Fabian?)	1923
Ursetta	Albert	1931
Usher	Dave	1922, 1922, 1928, 1931
Uyeno	Frank	1921
Val	Mrs. Wayne	1922
Valdez	L. (Librado)	1925
Valenti	Mike	1930
Valentino	Mike	1926
Valle	Paul	1921
Vallie	Natiali	1929
Van Bezel	Frank	1922
Van De Luvster (Van de Lyster) (Van De Luster)	J. (John)	1923, 1925

Van Derventer (Deventer)	Mary (Marjorie)	1930
Van Sant	Dr. J.E. (James E.)	1923
Van Scyoe	C.	1922
Vander Goor	Tom	1923
Vanducci	Pasqual	1924
Vanego (Vandanega)	G.	1923
Vanella	C.	1923
Varis	A.	1924
Vaughn	H.N.	1921
Venick	Robert	1921
Verde (Vardy)	Frank	1928
Verdecchio	Frank	1923
Verdier	Jean (G.?)	1923
Vergano	John	1927
Vernacci	Victor	1921
Vido	Al (Albert)	1921
Vieux (Vieu)	Andrew (Andre)	1924
Vigna	Mrs. M.	1923
Vivian	Joseph	1921
Wahner	Tom	1925
Walker	Lena	1922
Walker	Henry	1924
Wallace	J.D.	1922
Wallace	Jack	1923
Wallace	Joseph E.	1930
Wallaman	Frank (Franks?)	1927
Walls	A.	*1921*
Walsh	David (L.?)	1921
Walsh	L.	1932
Walters	John	1922
Walters	J.F.	1923
Walters	E.E.	1928

200

	(Ervin E.?)	
Walton	B.	1920
Wannaker	W. (Will)	1932, 1932
Ward	"Grip"	1921
Ward	I.H. (Iva H.?)	1921
Ward	John	1923
Ward	Harry P.	1927
Ward	J.	1927
Warner	E.	1923
Warren	G.A. (Gilbert A.?)	1924
Washington	Henry	1929
Watson	A.G.	1922
Wayne	F.B.	1922
Weaver	A.W. (Augustus?)	1922
Webb	David (L.)	1927, 1932
Wedgewood	A.L. (A.C.?)	1925
Weeks	Willie	1929
Weir	James (Jim)	1927
Weldon	G.W.	1923
Weldon	J.W. (John W.)	1923
Wells	Mattie	1929
West	Charles J.	1928
West	Fay (Craig)	1932
West	William	1933
West	R.	1925
Weston	D.P.	1921
Wheat	David (Davis)	1929
Wheat	Gaines D.	1929
Wheeler	R.E.	1921

Wheeler	D.	1930
Wheeler	Harry (L.?)	1932
White	Sidney	1921
White	Frank (W.?)	1922
White	C.W. (Charles W.?)	1924
White	Howard E.	1928
White	G.A. (Gilbert?)	1929, 1929
Wiles?	J.W.	1925
Williams	Bennie	1921
Williams	Nellie	1921
Williams	Joseph	1923
Williams	A.A.	1924
Williams	A.E.	1924
Williams	L.	1924
Williams	John	1930
Williamson	Joe	1926
Williford	D.W. (Daniel W.)	1922
Willis	Charles	1931
Willoby	Jack W.	1928
Wills	G.	1921
Wilson	Albert	1920
Wilson	W.E.	1921
Wilson	Mrs. Blanche	1922
Wilson	Joe	1922, 1922
Wilson	W.H.	1924
Wilson	G.N.	1925
Wilson	Wilbur J.	1928, 1929, 1929
Wilson	W.J.	1929
Wilson	Gertrude	1932
Wingfield	James (R.)	1926
Wirth	Henry A.	1923
Womack	C.J.	1924
Wood	Thomas C.	1921

Wood	E.	1925
Wood	O.L.	1926
Wood	E.G.	1931
Wood	William Allen	1931
Wood	Joe	1932
Woods	James	1922
Woods	Bill (William L.)	1924
Woods	Marion	1924
Woods	O.L.	1926
Woods	Elmer	1930, 1930
Woodward	Vernon (Aka Vern Howard)	1931
Wormer	P.F.	1921
Wueringer (Weringer)	Joseph	1928
Wylie	Marion (Marlon)	1928
Yano	H. (Hidelaro)	1928
Ybanez	M.Y.	1930
Ybarra	Carrie	1929
Ybarria (Ybarra)	Harry	1928
York	Mrs. J.	1922
Young	A.E.	1925
Young	Al	1932
Yowell	Charles (F.)	1921
Zakos	Sam	1921
Zimmerman	M.R. (Mark R.)	1922
Zimmerman	Frank	1929
Zink	C.L.	1921

Notes

Introduction

[1] Edward Behr, *Prohibition: Thirteen Years That Changed America* (New York: Arcade Publishing, 2011), 127.

[2] This period of reform, lasting from 1890 to the beginning of the 1920s, was a movement by members of the Democratic and Republican Party to create legislation to reform politics, economics, and society. See Michael Martin and Leonard Gelber, *Dictionary of American History* (Philosophical Library, Inc., 1978), 512.

[3] Joseph R. Gusfield, *Symbolic Crusade: Status Politics and the American Temperance Movement* (Urbana: University of Illinois Press, 1963), 6-8.

[4] The Eighteenth Amendment to the United States Constitution states, "The sale or manufacture of intoxicating liquors is forbidden;" however, what was to be considered "intoxicating liquor" was left undefined. The National Prohibition Act, or Volstead Act, determined that the production, distribution, transportation, possession, and consumption of anything over 1/2 of 1% alcohol would be illegal.

[5] For an overview of the sociological aspects of the Prohibition movement see Gusfield, *Symbolic Crusade*; John Kobler, *Ardent Spirits: The Rise and Fall of Prohibition* (New York: G. P. Putnam's Sons, 1973); Sean Dennis Cashman, *Prohibition: The Lie of the Land* (New York: The Free Press, 1981); S.J. Mennell, "Prohibition: A Sociological View," *Journal of American Studies* 3, no. 2 (December 1969): 159-175; Ira M. Wasserman, "Prohibition and Ethnocultural Conflict: The Missouri Prohibition Referendum of 1918," *Social Science Quarterly* 70, no. 4 (December 1989): 886-901; Jeanie M. Wayne, "Caging the Blind Tiger: Race, Class, and Family in the Battle for Prohibition in Small Town Arkansas," *The Arkansas Historical* Quarterly LXXI, no. 1 (Spring 2012): 44-60; Elliott West, "Cleansing the Queen City: Prohibition and Urban Reform in Denver," *Arizona and the West* 14, no. 4 (Winter 1972): 331-346; J.C. Burnham, "New Perspectives on the Prohibition "Experiment" of the 1920s," *Journal of Social History* 2, no. no. 1 (Autumn 1968): 51-68; and Mark Edward Lender, *Drinking in America: A History* (New York: The Frees Press, 1982). For Prohibition as a gender issue, see Mary Murphy, "Bootlegging Mothers and Drinking Daughters: Gender and Prohibition in Butte, Montana," *American Quarterly* 46, no. 2 (1994): 174-194; Tanya Marie Sanchez, "The Feminine Side of Bootlegging," *Louisiana History: The Journal of the Louisiana Historical Association* 41, no. 4 (Autumn 2000): 403-433; Joseph R. Gusfield, "Social Structure and Moral Reform: A Study of the Woman's Christian Temperance Union," *The American Journal of Sociology* 61, no. 3 (1955): 221-232; K. Austin Kerr, "Organizing for Reform: The Anti-Saloon League and Innovation in Politics," *American Quarterly* 32, no. 1 (1980): 37-53; David E. Kyvig, "Women Against Prohibition," *American Quarterly* 28, no. 4 (1976): 465-482. An urban-rural assessment of prohibition can be found in Charles W. Eagles, "Congressional Voting in the 1920s: A Test of Urban-Rural Conflict," *The Journal of American History* 76, no. 2 (1989): 528-534; Michael Lewis, "Access to Saloons, Wet Voter Turnout and Statewide Prohibition Referenda, 1907-1919," *Social Science Review* 32, no. 3 (Fall 2008): 373-404; and Walter F. Wilcox, "An Attempt to Measure Public Opinion About Repealing the Eighteenth Amendment," *Journal of the American Statistical*

Association 26, no. 175 (1931): 243-261. For analysis of Prohibition as an economic issue see Ivan Light, "The Ethnic Vice Industry, 1880-1944," *American Sociological Review* 42, no. 3 (1977): 464-479. Prohibition as public policy is explored by Mark Lawrence Schrad, "Constitutional Blemishes: American Alcohol Prohibition and Repeal as Policy Punctuation," *The Policy Studies Journal* 35, no. 3 (2007): 437-463; Paul A. Carter, "Prohibition and Democracy: The Noble Experiment Reassessed," *The Wisconsin Magazine of History* 56, no. 3 (Spring 1973): 189-201); Gregory G, Brunk, "Freshmen vs. Incumbents: Congressional Voting Patterns on Prohibition Legislation during the Progressive Era," *Journal of American Studies* 24, no. 2 (August 1990): 235-242. As a comparative study with modern drug policy see Harry G. Levine and Craig Reinarman, "From Prohibition to Regulation: Lessons from Alcohol Policy for Drug Policy," *The Milbank Quarterly* 69, no. 3: Confronting Drug Policy: Part 1 (1991): 461-494.

[6] The difference between those who supported a "wet" or "dry" country generally centered on place of birth: foreign-born Americans tended to oppose the regulation and outlawing of liquor, whereas native-born white Anglo-Saxon Protestants were more apt to be in favor of Prohibition to safeguard middleclass values. See; Gusfield, 6, 50-51, and 57; and Ira M. Wasserman, "Prohibition and Ethnocultural Conflict: The Missouri Prohibition Referendum of 1918," *Social Science Quarterly* 70, no. 4 (December 1989): 886 and 898.

[7] Paul A. Carter, "Prohibition and Democracy: The Noble Experiment Reassessed," *The Wisconsin Magazine of History* 56, no. 3 (Spring 1973): 196-197.

[8] As will be revealed in later chapters, violators of Prohibition in Kern County are found in all regions of the County. At the time of Prohibition, the following towns were incorporated in Kern County: Bakersfield (1898); Delano (1913); Fellows (1910); Maricopa (1911); McKittrick (1911); and Taft (1910). See William Harland Boyd, *Lower Kern River Country 1850-1950: Wilderness To Empire* (Bakersfield, CA: Kern County Historical Society, Inc., 1997), 68, 72, 75, 77, 97, and 141.

Chapter 1

[1] Pietism, focusing on faith based on the Bible and manifested in intense emotional experiences, include the Presbyterian, Methodist, Baptist, and Pentecostal churches. Many of these pietistic organizations believe that alcohol interferes with the religious experience and intensifies the sin of humans. Also, followers of Pietistic churches tend to have roots in Northern and Western Europe. Liturgical religious organizations include the Roman Catholic Church, Eastern Orthodox Church, Oriental Orthodox church, the Episcopal Church, and the Lutherans. Many members of liturgical churches hailed from Southern and Eastern Europe, and tended to oppose Prohibition because alcohol was used in certain ceremonies, and the closing of drinking establishments would eliminate centers of social activity. See Wasserman: 889-890.

[2] Gusfield, *Symbolic Crusade*, 2.

[3] Gilman Marston Ostrander argues in *The Prohibition Movement* that California, in reference to prohibition, can be divided in half at the Tehachapi Mountains. North of the Tehachapis, California was largely cosmopolitan, immigrant, and Catholic. San Francisco represented all that was modern in California, including the proliferation of strong drink. Temperance movements, although present, had difficulty taking root. Native-born Protestant Americans, largely a result of Protestant migration from the Midwest, on the other hand, dominated Southern California. The heart of Southern California, Los Angeles, was the backbone of temperance, the Prohibition Party, and Progressivism in California. Bakersfield and Kern County lies in the "borderland" between these two regions. See Gilman Marston Ostrander, *The Prohibition Movement in California, 1848-1933* (Berkeley: University of California Press, 1957), v. and 94.

[4] Joseph R. Gusfield, "Social Structure and Moral Reform: A Study of the Woman's Christian Temperance Union," *The American Journal of Sociology* 61, no. 3 (1955): 222-225.

[5] Ostrander, 45.

[6] Ibid., 58.

[7] Mrs. Leavitt, as an integral member of the "Round-the-World Missionaries," was Honorary President of the World Women's Christian Temperance Union since 1891. Tirelessly promoting the cause of temperance in South America, Mexico, the Hawaiian Islands and the Pacific Coast, Mrs. Leavitt settled in Southern California. A Mrs. Foster was also scheduled to speak, but information on who she was has not been found. See Frances Willard, "Address Before The Second Biennial Convention Of The World's Woman's Christian Temperance Union," Accessed January 26, 2013, http://gos.sbc.edu/w/willard.html.

[8] Mary Alderman Garbutt, *Victories of Four Decades: A History of the Women's Christian Temperance Union of Southern California, 1883-1924* (Women's Christian Temperance Union, 1924), 80.

[9] Ibid.

[10] The new County officers elected at the convention were: President, Mrs. S. S. Hunter (Bakersfield); Vice-President, Mrs. Henri P. Anderson (Spottswood); Corresponding Secretary, Mrs. Melvin Baker (Bakersfield); Recording Secretary, Mrs. S. M. Morse (Delano); and Treasurer, Mrs. M. K. Adams (Rosedale). See Garbutt, 81.

[11] Ibid., 81.

[12] Gusfield, "Social Structure and Moral Reform," 222.

[13] In 1887, the California State Legislature passed the Scientific Temperance Instruction Law. School texts, such as the high school text *Hygienic Physiology*, attempted to scare children into sobriety. See Ostrander, 60.

[14] Garbutt, 82. Who this trustee was and how active they were in promoting temperance is unclear. The following women served successive terms as the President of the Kern County WCTU: Mrs. A. W. Brown; Mrs. S. S. Hunter; Mrs. Henri Anderson; Mrs. Alice Robinson; Mrs. Miranda Bradford; Mrs. Henri Anderson; Mrs. C. N. Miller; Mrs. Ada E. Harmon; Mrs. Anna Bohna; Mrs. Huldah S. Nelson; Mrs. Georgia Robison; Mrs. Anna Colver; Mrs. Mary Collins; Mrs. Sara Nixon; Mrs. Anna Colver; Mrs. Effie Loomis; and Mrs. Henri Anderson. See Garbutt, 159.

[15] Ibid.

[16] With Hiram Johnson's election as Governor of California, the Progressive agenda, including women's suffrage, the initiative, referendum and recall, and other social reforms were championed. In Nov. 1911, California voters approved of suffrage for women, giving women new opportunities for political activism. See Ostrander, 116-117.

[17] Ella A. Boole, *Give Prohibition Its Chance* (Evanston: National Women's Temperance Union Publishing House, 1929), 61-68.

[18] Ibid., 80.

[19] Boole, 86-88. These two petitions will be discussed further in Chapter 2: The Passage of National Prohibition.

[20] Frances Willard promoted the idea that every aspect of social reform had components that were tied to temperance. In essence, temperance would be a three-pronged attack against white slavery (prostitution), slavery of workers, and slavery to alcohol. As a social reform movement, temperance was a component of larger social changes and improvements. See "Address Before The Second Biennial Convention," accessed January 26, 2013, http://gos.sbc.edu/w/willard.html.

[21] K. Austin Kerr, "Organizing for Reform: The Anti-Saloon League and Innovation in Politics," *American Quarterly* 32, no. 1 (1980): 37 and "History of the Anti-Saloon League," accessed January 26, 2013,
http://www.wpl.lib.oh.us/AntiSaloon/history/.

[22] The leadership of men was probably the result of the fact that only men could vote, be elected and serve in political positions, and were the leaders in religious organizations. As was stated, the work of women was integral to the success of temperance organizations, but the leadership of men gave the movement a sense of "legitimacy."

[23] Kerr, 40.

[24] Ibid.

[25] Michael Lewis, "Access to Saloons, Wet Voter Turnout and Statewide Prohibition Referenda, 1907-1919," *Social Science History* 32, no. 3 (Fall 2008): 374.

[26] Kerr, 43.

[27] Ostrander, 71.

[28] Compiled from "Table No. 323: Distilled Spirits, Wines, and Malt Liquors: Quantities Consumed and Average Annual Consumption Per Capita in the United States, 1850 To 1920," United States Census (1920), 561. Although data indicating the amount of beer, wine, and distilled spirits consumed in Bakersfield is not known to me at this point, some considered consumption a socially common and economically beneficial venture, while others viewed it as a threat to middle-class values.

[29] The decline in alcohol consumption from 1914 to 1915 is probably due to the beginning of the Great War (World War One) in Europe and the allocation of grains and other farm products used in distillation and brewing to be sold to the Allied Powers.

[30] "The Anti-Saloon Men Hold First Meeting," *Bakersfield Californian*, March 22, 1906, 3.

[31] Perhaps inspired by the WCTU, the Home Protective Association advocated against tobacco and alcohol. This would lend credence to the belief that the WCTU's ideas reached beyond organized women.

[32] "Formed A Law And Order League," *Bakersfield Californian*, March 28, 1906, 3. The "Law and Order League" was not against all saloons, just those of "low character" associated with dance halls and brothels.

[33] "Rev. Shaw Discusses Work Of Law An Order League," *Bakersfield Californian*, April 5, 1906, 3.

[34] "Bakersfield's Regeneration," *Los Angeles Times*, March 29, 1906, sec. J7.

[35] Kenneth D. Rose, "Wettest in the West: San Francisco & Prohibition in 1924," *California History* 65, no. 4 (December 1986): 285.

[36] "Editorial: Our Neighbors," *Bakersfield Californian*, March 28, 1906, 2.

[37] "Bakersfield's Regeneration."

[38] Other areas of Kern County experienced controversy over saloons. For example, the Southern Pacific Railroad Company was sued by property owners in Taft for $20,000 when the Company allowed saloonkeepers to open up business on those properties in violation of the property lease. See "Railroad Has No Means To Drive Out Saloons," *Bakersfield Californian*, January 3, 1913, 8.

[39] "Chairman Jastro Takes Stand Against Local Option Petition," *Bakersfield Californian*, July 14, 1908, 1. Jastro believed that the proposed ordinance was illegal because it bound future members of the Board of Supervisors to more stringent regulatory measures. In order for a saloon to open, the businessman had to gain the consent of the majority of property owners within a five mile radius; the new ordinance would require a two-thirds consent.

[40] "Guns Trained On Saloons," *Los Angeles Times*, February 12, 1910, sec. JJ10

[41] "Anti's To Wage War On Saloons," *Bakersfield Californian*, February 9, 1910, 1.

[42] "Would Limit Saloon Hours," *Bakersfield Californian*, January 23, 1911, 1.

[43] "Women Start With Petitions," *Bakersfield Californian*, January 28, 1911, 4. At that time, Bakersfield had one saloon for every two hundred residents.

[44] Ibid.

[45] S.E. Nicholson, "The Local-Option Movement," *Annals of the American Academy of Political and Social Science* 32, Regulation of the Liquor Traffic (November 1908): 471, 475.

[46] The bar in a saloon is the counter at which patrons could be served drinks. Some reformers believed that establishments that served alcohol to patrons at tables, and did not have a bar, were more reputable and of a higher class than the saloon.

[47] Russell Macnaghten, "Local Option and After," *The North American Review* 190, no. 648 (November 1909): 630-641.

[48] "Local Option Bill Goes To Governor," *Bakersfield Californian*, March 16, 1911, 1.

[49] Ostrander, 88-89. "High-license" refers to the tactic of limiting the number of drinking establishments by charging a high fee for a license to operate said establishment.

[50] "Anti-Saloon League Declares for General Local Option Elections," *Bakersfield Californian*, May 6, 1911, 1, 6 and "Call Read For Local Option Convention," *Bakersfield Californian*, May 8, 1911, 1.

[51] "Anti-Saloonists Organized By Precincts," *Bakersfield Californian*, May 18, 1911, 1.

[52] "Temperance Speaker Has Praise for the Trustees' Cleaning Up Activities," *Bakersfield Californian*, July 24, 1911, 1.

[53] "Will Enforce Regulations," *Los Angeles Times*, July 3, 1911, sec. J17.

[54] "Dry Petition Filed With Clerk," *Bakersfield Californian*, August 23, 1911, 1. Signatures from twenty-five percent of the voters in each district were necessary. 126 signatures were needed in District 1; 173 were collected. 522 were needed in District 4 were needed; 800 were collected. 107 were needed in District 5; 170 were collected. The tally from District 3 was not stated in the story.

[55] "Petition For 'Dry' Election Filed Today," *Bakersfield Californian*, August 29, 1911, 1.

[56] See "Who's Who On 'Dry' Petition," *Bakersfield Californian*, September 1,1911, 1, 4 and "Anti-Saloon League Reassures Timid Ones," *Bakersfield Californian*, September 2, 1911, 6.

[57] Ostrander, 115.

[58] Ibid., 107 and 109.

[59] Using the list of names published in the *Bakersfield Californian*, a representative sample was created. Starting at the beginning of the list, which was not organized alphabetically, every tenth name was added to the sample list. If the tenth name was illegible, the next name was taken as a substitute. Using this methodology, seventy-two names were generated as a test sample. Political party affiliation was determined, when possible, by searching the "Index of Registration: Kern County, 1912," *Great Register of Vote, 1900-1944* (Sacramento: California State Library, 1986).

[60] Five of the people from the sample declined to state their political party affiliation. Twenty-seven people were not found on the 1912 registration, but occupational information was compiled for twelve of the twenty-seven using the *Bakersfield City Directory, 1911* (San Francisco: The Polk-Husted Directory Co., 1911). This leaves fifteen individuals who were not accounted for.

[61] The 1908 presidential election serves as a comparison of voter registration. An examination of election results the day after the election reveals that the Democratic candidate, William Jennings Bryan, received 752 votes; the Republican candidate, William Howard Taft, received 658 votes; and the Socialist candidate, Eugene V. Debs, received 103 votes. If this accurately represents voter registration in Bakersfield, 49.7 percent of voters were Democratic, 43.5 percent were Republicans, and 6.8 percent were Socialists. A complete analysis of political party affiliation for signers of the local option petition may reveal percentages that more closely match the 1908 election results.

[62] "Merchants Did Not Sign 'Dry' Petition," *Bakersfield Californian*, September 2, 1911, 6.

[63] Ostrander, 100.

[64] Ibid.

[65] Ibid., 101.

[66] "Warns Gin Dispensers," *Los Angeles Times*, June 15, 1911, sec. J13.

[67] "Minors Must Keep Out of Saloons," *Bakersfield Californian*, August 11, 1911, 2.

[68] "Sixty Saloons To Close At 1 Tonight," *Bakersfield Californian*, July 13, 1911, 1 and "Bakersfield Virtue Spasm," *Los Angeles Times*, July 15, 1911, sec. J15.

[69] "No Liquor From One To Six Is Ordinance," *Bakersfield Californian*, October 3, 1911, 4.

[70] "Regulation VS. Prohibition," *Los Angeles Times*, October 20, 1911, sec. I13.

[71] The W.O.W. is a fraternal organization dedicated to helping their fellow members, especially by offering simple term insurance providing members with death and monument benefits. See "History: Woodmen of the World's Storied History. Accessed January 26, 2013, http://www.woodmen.org/about/history.cfm

[72] "Local Women Take Hand In Dry Fight," *Bakersfield Californian*, September 11, 1911, 1.

[73] "Women Organize To Fight Wets," *Bakersfield Californian*, September 14, 1911, 1.

[74] "Drys Hold Good Meeting," *Bakersfield Californian*, September 18, 1911, 1.

[75] "Rally Of Drys On Sunday," *Bakersfield Californian*, October 9, 1911, 4.

[76] "Wylie to Speak Twice Sunday," *Bakersfield Californian*, October 14, 1911, 6 and "Wylie Spoke---To Tour Through County," *Bakersfield Californian*, October 16, 1911, 1.

[77] "Hundred Women Register Today With Clerk," *Bakersfield Californian*, October 16, 1911, 1 and "Three Hundred Women Register," *Bakersfield Californian*, October 18, 1911, 1.

[78] "Drive Nails In Saloon Coffin,'" *Bakersfield Californian*, October 19, 1911, 3.

[79] "Dry To Have Street Meetings," *Bakersfield Californian*, October 26, 1911, 2.

[80] Advertisement, "Crime Is Mostly Due To Booze," *Bakersfield Morning Echo*, October 22, 1911, 16.

[81] Ibid.

[82] Advertisement, "I Am Still Strong For The Boy," *Bakersfield Morning Echo*, October 29, 1911, 16.

[83] This is probably due to the fact that most Protestant churches actively promoted the "dry" cause and offered their facilities to be used for gatherings. The daily existence of saloons and saloon patrons acted as informal promotion of the "wet" vote.

[84] "Meetings By The Wets and Drys," *Bakersfield Californian*, October 21, 1911, 1.

[85] "Minister Opposed To Prohibition," *Bakersfield Californian*, October 25, 1911, 2.

[86] Ibid.

[87] "Colored Voters Express Opposition To Prohibition," *Bakersfield Californian*, October 26, 1911, 4.

[88] Advertisement, "Come And Hear The Other Side," *Bakersfield Californian*, October 21, 1911, 3.

[89] Advertisement, "This Is The Way To Vote Wet," *Bakersfield Morning Echo*, October 31, 1911, 6.

[90] Advertisement, "Wet or Dry," *Bakersfield Californian*, October 28, 1911, 6.

[91] "Business Men Protest Against Prohibition," *Bakersfield Californian*, October 21, 1911, 1.

[92] Many in the business sector, especially businesses that complimented or were associated with drinking, opposed anything related to prohibition, including local option due to the belief that restricting drink would hurt their own business and that if laws restricting liquor could be passed, laws regulating or restricting their businesses could be passed, too. See J.C. Burnham, "New Perspectives on the

Prohibition "Experiment" of the 1920s," *Journal of Social History* 2, no. 1 (Autumn 1968): 54.

[93] In addition to the 101 individual names listed on the petition, 10 businesses were listed as opposing local option. To compile political party affiliation the names of individuals were checked against the "Index of Registration: Kern County," *Great Register of Vote, 1900-1944* (Sacramento: California State Library, 1986).

[94] Population numbers and the data compiled for Table 4 were taken from "Table III: Composition And Characteristics Of The Population, For Cities of 10,000 To 25,000: 1910," United States Census (1910), 182. Statistics for Americans of Asian or American Indian ancestry are not included due to the fact that this demographic is not widely included as a "problem" as either proprietors or patrons of saloons on a national basis.

[95] Statistical data for Table 5 was compiled using information from the University of Virginia, "Historical Census Browser," accessed January 27, 2013, http://mapserver.lib.virginia.edu/.

[96] "Greater Bakersfield's Vote May Exceed 3000," *Bakersfield Californian*, October 31, 1911, 1.

[97] "Registration In City Is 6348," *Bakersfield Californian*, October 24, 1911, 4.

[98] "Election Auto Runs Down Woman," *Bakersfield Californian*, October 31, 1911, 1. A Mrs. Emma Rinehart appears in a 1916 voter registration list for Los Angeles County, leading to the belief that Mrs. Rinehart survived her injuries.

[99] "Both Sides Claim Victory At Close Of Long Campaign," *Bakersfield Californian*, October 28, 1911, 1 and "Wet Or Dry Campaign In Kern County Near End With Both Sides Confident," *Bakersfield Morning Echo*, October 29, 1911, 1.

[100] The *Bakersfield Californian* reported a "wet" majority of 1,134. See "Bakersfield Votes Wet By Majority of 1,134," *Bakersfield Californian*, November 1, 1911, 1. The *Bakersfield Morning Echo* reported that "drys" lost by 1158 votes. See "Drys Lose in City by 1158 Majority," *Bakersfield Morning Echo*, November 1, 1911, 1.

[101] "Extent Of The Majority A Surprise," *Bakersfield Californian*, November 1, 1911, 1.

[102] "Two Districts Are Dry And Three Wet," *Bakersfield Californian*, November 1, 1911, 1 and "More Votes For Wet And Dry," *Bakersfield Californian*, November 2, 1911, 1. Seven years later, in 1918, the towns of Maricopa, Taft, and McKittrick also held local option elections, with Taft voting itself "dry." See "Liquor Elections Planned On West Side," *Bakersfield Californian*, February 2, 1918, 7, "Wet and Dry Issue on West Side Today," *Bakersfield Californian*, April 8, 1918, 7 and "Taft Goes Dry; Maricopa, McKittrick Stay Wet," *Bakersfield Californian*, April 9, 1918, 7.

[103] Delano, Petroleum, Sumner, Fairfax, McFarland, Fruitvale, Stockdale, South Bakersfield, Oil, Linn's Valley, Keene, Wasco, Rosedale, Buttonwillow, Adobe, Canfield, Panama, Tejon, Tejon Canyon, Maricopa 1, Midway 1, and Piute Precincts voted "dry." Randsburg, Goler, Johannesburg, Amalie, Weldon, Havilah, Hot Springs, Kernville, Caliente, Rosamond, Mojave, Old Town, Cummings Valley, San Emidio, Lake, Poso, Antelope, Maricopa 2, Midway 2, Asphalto, Paleto, Lost Hills, Fellows, and Famosa Precincts voted "wet."

Chapter 2

[1] Andrew Sinclair, *Era of Excess: A Social History of the Prohibition Movement* (New York: Harper Colophon Books, 1964), 154.

[2] Ibid.

[3] Floyd W. Tomkins, "Prohibition," *Annals of the American Academy of Political and Social Science* 109, Prohibition and Its Enforcement (September 1923): 15.

[4] Paul A. Carter, "Prohibition and Democracy: The Noble Experiment Reassessed," *The Wisconsin Magazine of History* 56, no. 3 (Spring 1973): 192-193.

[5] Sinclair, 155.

[6] L. Ames Brown, "Prohibition," *The North American Review* 202, no. 720 (November 1915): 719.

[7] Sinclair, 156.

[8] David M. Kennedy, *Over Here: The First World War and American Society* (Oxford: Oxford University Press, 1980), 116.

[9] Ibid.

[10] "Great Increase In Production Aim Of Farm Bureau," *Bakersfield Californian*, January 1, 1918, 1.

[11] "Food Pledge Card Total To Date Is 5,300," *Bakersfield Californian*, November 3, 1917, 1.

[12] "Look In The Woodpile," Editorial, *Bakersfield Californian*, January 7, 1918, 6.

[13] "A Patriotic Duty," Editorial, *Bakersfield Californian*, January 26, 1918, 12.

[14] "Record of Political Events," *Political Science Quarterly* 34, no. 3, Supplemental (1919): 75.

[15] Sinclair, 122.

[16] "Alcohol In Beer To Be Reduced To 3 Per Cent," *Bakersfield Californian*, November 27, 1917, 7. Even if whiskey supplies had been depleted, Americans with money could still purchase imported distilled spirits. See "Distilled Spirits May Be Imported Is Ruling," *Bakersfield Californian*, October 22, 1917, 5.

[17] Sinclair, 101.

[18] Daniel Okrent, *Last Call. The Rise and Fall of Prohibition* (New York: Scribner, 2010), 54.

[19] "Liquor And Cigars Being Listed For Taxes Here," *Bakersfield Californian*, October 5, 1917, 1.

[20] "5,000 Dealers Fail To Report Liquor Stock," *Bakersfield Californian*, March 20, 1918, 1.

[21] "Soldiers May Have Liquor In Homes," *Bakersfield Californian*, February 20, 1918, 1.

[22] "Bars Are Ordered To Close When Troops Arrive," *Bakersfield Californian*, October 4, 1917, 6.

[23] "Mojave Saloonman Has Hearing On Serious Charge," *Bakersfield Californian*, January 8, 1918, 6.

[24] "New Licenses May Be Revoked At Any Time," *Bakersfield Californian*, January 9, 1918, 6.

[25] See "Saloons Are Charged by Defense Council," *Bakersfield Californian*, April 1, 1918, 6, "Council Cites Two Saloon Men To Appear Monday," *Bakersfield Californian*, April 2, 1918, 6, and "Saloonmen Before Council Get Coat Of Whitewash," *Bakersfield Californian*, April 9, 1918, 6.

[26] "Action On Liquor Licenses set For Wednesday," *Bakersfield Californian*, January 7, 1918, 6.

[27] "New Licenses May Be Revoked At Any Time," 6.

[28] "Grand Jury Would Close Bars July 1st," *Bakersfield Californian*, February 10, 1918, 1.

[29] "Saloon Closing As War Measure," *Bakersfield Californian*, February 13, 1918, 1. Along the same line of argument citing efficiency, directors of the Kern County Farm Bureau proposed to the Bakersfield City Council, the Kern County Board of Supervisors, and the Kern County Council of Defense the closing of saloons for the duration of the harvest season to maintain efficient laborers. See "Farmers Want Kern Saloons Closed," *Bakersfield Californian*, April 27, 1918, 1.

[30] "Grand Jury Files Its Report and Adjourns," *Bakersfield Californian*, April 24, 1918, 7.

[31] "Council Declines To Raise Saloon License Charge," *Bakersfield Californian*, February 26, 1918, 6.

[32] Councilman Frost, Hougham and Baughman voted for the proposition; Willow, Taylor and Howard voted against it; and Councilman James was absent.

[33] Gilman Marston Ostrander, *The Prohibition Movement In California, 1848-1957* (Berkeley: University of California Press, 1957), 142.

[34] Ibid., 143.

[35] Ibid., 145.

[36] "Pro-German Forced To Kiss U.S. Flag," *Bakersfield Californian*, December 4, 1917, 6.

[37] "Man Arrested Here Under Espionage Law Clause," *Bakersfield Californian*, December 5, 1917, 1.

[38] "Bar German Study From Schools Of Kern County," *Bakersfield Californian*, April 11, 1918, 1.

[39] "German Intrigue Is Suspected In Placards," *Bakersfield Californian*, January 3, 1918, 7.

[40] "Kern County Organizes To Fight Pro-Germans," *Los Angeles Times*, September 1, 1918, 14.

[41] "New German Spy System Broken Up," *Bakersfield Californian*, January 10, 1918, 1.

[42] "Woman Arrested as Spy at Hanford," *Bakersfield Californian*, January 11, 1918, 1 and "Man Held As Agent Of Germany At Visalia," *Bakersfield Californian*, January 12, 1918, 2.

[43] "Ex-Bakersfield Man Seized As German Spy In Tucson," *Bakersfield Californian*, January 14, 1918, 1.

[44] "Alien Enemies To Be Registered Feb. 4 To 9," *Bakersfield Californian*, January 24, 1918, 4, "Registration Of German Aliens Next Monday," *Bakersfield Californian*, February 2, 1918, 6 and "German Arrested For Failure To Register," *Bakersfield Californian*, February 21, 1918, 6.

[45] A basic search of the words "saloon, German agents" was conducted in the digitized database of the *Bakersfield Californian* through the Los Angeles Public Library. "Newspaper Archive," accessed February 7, 2013, http://access.newspaperarchive.com.ezproxy.lapl.org/.

[46] "To Test 'Dry' Law On Beer," *Los Angeles Times*, July 10, 1919, I11, "Set Date To Hear Beer Test Case," *Los Angeles Times*, July 26, 1919, I15 and ""Holds Fate Of War-Time Beer," *Los Angeles Times*, August 5, 1919, I11.

[47] "Bartenders Aid Shelter Fund," *Bakersfield Californian*, January 9, 1918, 1.

[48] "Local Lodge, Wet Ass'n, Gives $100 To Shelter," *Bakersfield Californian*, January 10, 1918, 1.

[49] "Bartenders Entertain at Informal Dance," *Bakersfield Californian*, January 29, 1918, 6.

[50] "Mothers-Parent-Teachers Elect," *Los Angeles Times*, May 26, 1917, 14.

[51] "W.C.T.U. Prepares For War Relief Drive Here," *Bakersfield Californian*, January 22, 1918, 2, "W.C.T.U. Now Aims To Buy Trench Kitchen," *Bakersfield Californian*, February 14, 1918, 2 and "W.C.T.U. Would Raise $2000 In The County For War Activity Fund," *Bakersfield Californian*, March 14, 1918, 5.

[52] "Bakersfield Lands W.C.T.U. State Convention," *Bakersfield Californian*, March 23, 1918, 4.

[53] John R. Meers, "The California Wine and Grape Industry and Prohibition," *California Historical Society Quarterly* 46, no. 1 (March 1967): 20-21.

[54] Ibid., 23.

[55] "Petitions Started On Rominger Bill," *Bakersfield Californian*, October 8, 1917, 7, "Rominger Petitions For Signers Here," *Bakersfield Californian*, October 11, 1917, 3 and "Wants Names Here To Put Rominger Bill On Ballot," *Bakersfield Californian*, November 19, 1917, 2.

[56] "The Grape Men," Editorial, *Bakersfield Californian*, February 13, 1918, 2.

[57] "Close Bars, Serve Beer Sans Meals Brewers' Plan," *Bakersfield Californian*, February 9, 1918, 9.

[58] "Wet Federation In Annual Meeting Decides To Oppose Rominger Bill," *Bakersfield Californian*, March 7, 1918, 7. According to the 1910 Census, Fred Gunther was born in New York, had parents born in Germany, and worked as a wholesale liquor dealer.

[59] Sinclair, 113.

[60] Ibid., 115.

[61] While the Anti-Saloon League aimed to destroy the saloon, but not necessarily prohibit individuals from drinking in the privacy of their homes, the Prohibition Party's ultimate goal was nationwide prohibition. The Anti-Saloon League's willingness to compromise with wets to close saloons was unacceptable to many members of the Prohibition Party.

[62] "Prohibition Party Is Defeated At Convention," *Bakersfield Californian*, February 6, 1918, 9.

[63] "A Big Question In 1918," Editorial, *Bakersfield Californian*, February 7, 1918, 10.

[64] "House Passes 'Dry' Measure 282 To 128," *Bakersfield Californian*, December 17, 1917, 1 and "Senate Also Approves U.S. Dry Measure," *Bakersfield Californian*, December 18, 1917, 1.

[65] Ibid.

[66] "Prohibition Party Asks Nation Wide Temperance For Duration Of War," *Bakersfield Californian*, March 5, 1918, 2.

[67] "Record of Political Events," 76.

[68] Lindsay Rogers, "American Government and Politics," *The American Political Science Review* 14, no. 1 (1920): 79.

[69] "Record of Political Events," 76.

[70] Meers, 25.

[71] Rogers, 79.

[72] Meers, 26.

[73] Sinclair, 161-162.

[74] Ibid., 163.

[75] Gregory G. Brunk, "Freshmen vs. Incumbents: Congressional Voting Patterns on Prohibition Legislation during the Progressive Era," *Journal of American Studies* 24, no. 2 (August 1990): 236.

[76] Ibid., 239.

[77] Ibid., 241.

[78] It is necessary to note that with the passage of the Eighteenth Amendment in Congress I will refer to "prohibition" as "Prohibition" and the "amendment" as the "Amendment" to illustrate the transition from agenda to policy.

[79] Michael Lewis, "Access to Saloons, Wet Voter Turnout, and Statewide Prohibition Referenda, 1907-1919," *Social Science History* 32, no. 3 (Fall 2008): 373.

[80] A basic search for the word "prohibition" on the digitized database of the *Bakersfield Californian* through the Los Angeles Public Library reveals that the word "prohibition" turns up 1,267 times. "Newspaper Archive," accessed February 7, 2013, http://access.newspaperarchive.com.ezproxy.lapl.org/.

[81] Mark Lawrence Schrad, "Constitutional Blemishes: American Alcohol Prohibition and Repeal as Policy Punctuation," *The Policy Studies Journal* 35, no. 3 (2007): 445-449. Repeal of Prohibition is also an expression of punctuation politics

[82] Ostrander, 147.

[83] Ibid., 164.

[84] Ibid., 141.

[85] Will Rogers, *Rogers-Isms: The Cowboy Philosopher on Prohibition* (Stillwater: Oklahoma State University Press, 1975), 22, 38.

[86] Ostrander, 142, 153.

[87] Ibid., 159.

[88] Schrad, 448.

[89] Between 1889 and 1937, thirteen bills were vetoed due to questions over constitutionality. Only two, both dealing with the control of liquor (Webb-Kenyon Act and the Volstead Act, were overridden. See Katherine A. Towle, "The Presidential Veto Since 1889," *The American Political Science Review* 31, no. 1 (1937): 51-56.

[90] "Must Report Cellar Stock 10 Days From January 17," *Bakersfield Californian*, January 1, 1920, 1.

[91] "Organize Forces to Clasp Screws to Bone-Dry Lid," *Bakersfield Californian*, January 3, 1920, 1.

[92] Ostrander, 147.

[93] "Put Limit On Highway Fund," *Los Angeles Times*, March 22, 1919, I3.

[94] Ostrander, 147, 154, 159. The Wright Act of California stipulated that a beverage was to be considered "intoxicating" if it contained over one-third of one percent alcohol. Further discussion of this measure will be in Chapter 3.

[95] "Wood Alcohol," Letter To The Editor, *Bakersfield Californian*, January 3, 1920, 12.

[96] "Use of Bootleg Warned Against," *Bakersfield Californian*, January 7, 1920, 4.

[97] "2.75 Beer Is Held Illegal," *Bakersfield Californian*, January 5, 1920, 1.

[98] Associate Justices Day, Vanderventer, Clark and McReynolds dissented. McReynolds, in his dissenting opinion, asserted that the war emergency had passed and that national prohibition was no longer needed.

[99] "Liquor Interests to Renew Battle Against Dry Act," *Bakersfield Californian*, January 6, 1920, 1.

[100] "Ask Injunction To Stop Prohibition Enforcement," *Bakersfield Californian*, January 8, 1920, 1.

[101] "CA Wine Men To Intervene in R.I.," *Bakersfield Californian*, January 9, 1920, 5.

[102] "Legislature Cannot Repeal Ratification," *Bakersfield Californian*, January 13, 1920, 2.

[103] "Says Revolution Likely To Follow US Prohibition," *Bakersfield Californian*, January 9, 1920, 2.

[104] Schrad, 437, 439.

[105] "Whiskey Valued at $10,000 Is Burglars' Prize," *Bakersfield Californian*, January 8, 1920, 1.

[106] "Big Force To Be Used To Guard Liquor," *Bakersfield Californian*, January 15, 1920, 2.

[107] "Officers Discover 'Moonshiners' On East Side," *Bakersfield Californian*, January 8, 1920, 8.

[108] The men arrested were Henry Delfinisi, Aliso and Andiola Missoni, Beneth Ghilarducci and Fred Carlson. Chapter 4 will analyze the role ethnicity, place of birth, socio-economic status, and political orientation placed in prohibition support and violation.

[109] "M. Plantier Fined $150 in Los Angeles," *Bakersfield Californian*, January 15, 1920, 8.

[110] "New Ruling On Sale of Wine Found By Seizure," *Bakersfield Californian*, January 7, 1920, 1.

[111] Big Shipments of Liquor On Way," *Bakersfield Californian*, January 7, 1920, 1, "US Whiskey Moving Out Over Border," *Bakersfield Californian*, January 13, 1920, 1, "Liquor Worth Million Sent Into Mexico," *Bakersfield Californian*, January 14, 1920, 4, "Last Chance to Move Liquor Supply," *Bakersfield Californian*, January 15, 1920, 1 and "1,500,000 Gallons Of Wine Exported From Fresno," *Bakersfield Californian*, January 15, 1920, 1.

[112] "Zero Hour For John Barleycorn To Be Struck At Midnight, Jan 16," *Bakersfield Californian*, January 15, 1920, 12.

Chapter 3

[1] All of the statistics and local examples used are tallied from data collected from the *Bakersfield Californian*, *Bakersfield Morning Echo*, and the *Los Angeles Times* between 1919 and 1933.

[2] A basic search on http://search.ancestry.com/search/db.aspx?dbid=2469 of the digitized version of the *Bakersfield City Directory* published by the Polk-Husted Directory Company of the term "soft drink" reveals the number of soft drink parlors between the years 1921-1925: seventeen in 1921; nine in 1922; ten in 1923; eleven in 1924; and thirteen in 1925. The number of saloons reopened as soft drink parlors in other communities throughout Kern County is unclear.

[3] *Bakersfield City Directory, 1920* (San Francisco: The Polk-Husted Directory Co., 1920). For the disappearance of the Bakersfield Brewing Company see the *Bakersfield City Directory* for the years 1920 to 1926.

[4] *Bakersfield City Directory, 1919* (San Francisco: The Polk-Husted Directory Co., 1919).

[5] See "County Officials In Open Revolt Against Revenue Men Trying To Enforce Dry Law," *Bakersfield Californian*, February 23, 1920, 1 and "Prohibition Controversy In Michigan Still Heated," *Bakersfield Californian*, February 25, 1920, 2, "Peace Conference in Liquor Rebellion," *Bakersfield Californian*, February 27, 1920, 2, "1 Dead, 3 Injured, Result Federal Raid," *Bakersfield Californian*, March 9, 1920, Part 2, 2, "Police Raid N.Y. Café; Seize Booze," *Bakersfield Californian*, April 7, 1920, Part 2, 2 and "Agents Unable to Stop 'Moonshining'," *Bakersfield Californian*, April 29, 1920, 1.

[6] "Gov. Edwards of N.Y. Is Fighting Prohibition Act Along Two Lines," *Bakersfield Californian*, February 14, 1920, 5.

[7] "Prohibition Act Violates States Rights Claim Of R.I.," *Bakersfield Californian*, March 1, 1920, 2.

[8] See "Distillers Also File Brief on Dry Act," *Bakersfield Californian*, March 6, 1920, 1, "Legalize 2.75 Per Cent Beer in N.Y.," *Bakersfield Californian*, April 24, 1920, 1 and "Colorado Going After Wine and Beer," *Bakersfield Californian*, April 29, 1920, 2.

[9] Unbeknownst to them at the time, the grape industry would greatly prosper during prohibition. This is discussed later in Chapter 3.

[10] "Hope to Prevent Vineyardists' Loss," *Bakersfield Californian*, January 24, 1920, 4.

[11] "Grape Growers to Seek New Markets; Stop 'Dry' Battle," *Bakersfield Californian*, February 24, 1920, 2.

[12] "To Make Syrup From Wine Grapes," *Bakersfield Californian*, February 28, 1920, 2.

[13] "'Wet and Dry' Is New Kolb and Dill Vehicle Here Next Wed. and Thurs.; 'Up In Mabel's Room' Coming Monday Night," *Bakersfield Californian*, January 24, 1920, 3.

[14] "'The Bootlegger' Without A Kick," *Bakersfield Californian*, April 22, 1920, 7.

[15] "Can Horse Drink Champagne Under New Amendment," *Bakersfield Californian*, April 1, 1920, 1.

[16] "Drink Book Gets Official Kibosh," *Bakersfield Californian*, April 16, 1920, 5.

[17] "Special Officers Search City for Illicit Liquor," *Bakersfield Californian*, March 19, 1920, 1.

[18] "$7500 Total Fines Under City Dry Act In 5 Weeks," *Bakersfield Californian*, December 21, 1920, 1.

[19] Chief Stone was the Chief of Bakersfield Police from July 15, 1919 to July 31, 1923.

[20] "Alleged Blind Pig Raided Here," *Bakersfield Californian*, May 4, 1920, 8.

[21] Gilman Marston Ostrander, *The Prohibition Movement In California, 1848-1933*. (Berkeley: University of California Press, 1957), 159.

[22] "Just What Wright Law Means To California," *Los Angeles Times*, December 10, 1922, II1.

[23] Ostrander, 182.

[24] "Chief of Police Requests New Ordinance To Assist Municipal Enforcement of Prohibition," *Bakersfield Californian*, September 8, 1920, 7 and "City Prohibition Act For Bakersfield Passes Council," *Bakersfield Californian*, September 14, 1920, 9.

[25] "East Side 'Blind Pigs' Are Raided," *Bakersfield Californian*, November 18, 1920, 6.

[26] See "City Prohibition Act For Bakersfield Passes Council," *Bakersfield Californian*, September 14, 1920, 7 and "Italians Fined $250 Each Under Ordinance," *Bakersfield Californian*, October 21, 1920, 6.

[27] " 'Dry' Ordinance Is Passed By County," *Bakersfield Californian*, November 17, 1920, 1.

[28] "Local Liquor Ordinance Is Sustained By State Court," *Bakersfield Californian*, November 9, 1926, 1 and "Bakersfield Liquor Law Repealed," *Bakersfield Californian*, November 29, 1932, 1.

[29] Adjusted for inflation, $317,127 in 1926 has the purchasing power of $1,067,396.47 in 2012.

[30] "Prohibition to Cost U.S. Huge Amount Annually," *Bakersfield Californian*, May 4, 1920, 1.

[31] $6.3 million was spent in 1921, $9.2 million in 1925, and $13.4 million in 1930. See Jeffrey A. Miron and Jeffrey Zwiebel, "Alcohol Consumption During Prohibition," *The American Economic Review* 81, no. 2 (May 1991): 242.

[32] Sinclair, 275.

[33] "Table 8: Population Of The United States, By Divisions," United States Census (1920), 20 and "Table 12: Area And Density," United States Census (1920), 25.

[34] Ostrander, 149.

[35] Ibid., 162.

[36] Joseph K. Willing, "The Profession of Bootlegging," *Annals of the American Academy of Political and Social Science* 125 (May 1926): 40-46.

[37] "Thirsty Hordes From States Cross Line To Revel In Cantu Land," *Bakersfield Californian*, March 29, 1920, 1.

[38] "Giant Drug And Liquor Smuggling Ring Bared," *Bakersfield Californian*, January 13, 1922, 1.

[39] Family lore has my grandfather, Ernie Roux, transporting large orders of sugar to customers in the Greenhorn Mountains. How the Roux Brothers Grocery circumvented detailed accounting of sugar transactions is unclear at this point.

[40] "Big Moonshine Plant Is Found," *Bakersfield Californian*, August 24, 1921, 4.

[41] "Haystacks And Setting Hens Cover Brandy Still," *Bakersfield Californian*, March 15, 1921, 1.

[42] "Rum Raid Stirs Gang War Fear," *Los Angeles Times*, July 14, 1932, 11.

[43] For a small sampling of the many stills discovered within Bakersfield and the surrounding farmlands see "Dry Agents Find Up-To-Date Still," *Bakersfield Californian*, October 8, 1920, 8, "Two More Stills Located in This City by Police," *Bakersfield Californian*, October 11, 1920, 8, "'Ownerless' Still at Jail; Operator Still Out of Jail," *Bakersfield Californian*, January 3, 1921, 8 and "Still Is Seized at Kern Street Home," *Bakersfield Californian*, February 13, 1922, 4.

[44] "Moonshining And Pressure Mining Acts Also Passed," *Bakersfield Californian*, March 29, 1927, 1-2. The new law changed possession of a still from a misdemeanor to a high felony punishable with a sentence in the penitentiary, not jail.

[45] "Owner of Still Admits Felony, Gets Probation," *Bakersfield Californian*, October 5, 1927, 9.

[46] "Owner of Still Is Sentenced To Penitentiary By Judge Lambert," *Bakersfield Californian*, February 23, 1928, 9.

[47] "Convict Three Kern Men, Liquor Charges," *Bakersfield Californian*, April 22, 1932, 13 and "Three Kern Men Are Exonerated On Still Charges By U.S. Jurist," *Bakersfield Californian*, April 26, 1932, 9.

[48] Ibid., 205.

[49] Ibid., 190.

[50] "No Near-Beer to Be Allowed at Veterans' Banquet," *Bakersfield Californian*, August 12, 1921, 4.

[51] "Grape Juice Sales Hurt by Near-Beer," *Bakersfield Californian*, May 27, 1921, 1.

[52] "Dry Raiders Seize Beer," *Los Angeles Times*, September 5, 1928, 8.

[53] "Liquor Raids Jail Many," *Los Angeles Times*, August 1, 1931, sec. A5.

[54] "Sale Of Hops And Malt Is Banned," *Bakersfield Californian*, November 12, 1920, Part 2, 1.

[55] "Think! Wine Grapes Were $10; Now $40," *Bakersfield Californian*, March 1, 1920, Part 2, 1.

[56] "Wine Grape Men of San Joaquin In Quandary As To What To Do," *Bakersfield Californian*, May 17, 1920, Part 2, 1.

[57] "'Kick' Is Reason For Big Planting," *Bakersfield Californian*, April 5, 1921, 7.

[58] "Home-Brewers Cause Shortage Of Grapes," *Bakersfield Californian*, November 17, 1921, 10.

[59] "How Explain It," Editorial, *Bakersfield Californian*, March 10, 1920, 1.

[60] Ostrander, 181.

[61] "Large Amount Of Wine Is Seized," *Bakersfield Californian*, October 23, 1920, 6.

[62] John R. Mears, "The California Wine and Grape Industry and Prohibition," *California Historical Society Quarterly* 46, no. 1 (March 1967): 29.

[63] Ibid., 28.

[64] "Method To Get Liquor For Use As Medicine Is Told By Bureau," *Bakersfield Californian*, January 30, 1920, 4.

[65] "Liquor Manufacture Held Legal," *Bakersfield Californian*, March 9, 1921, 1 and "Pint of Whisky Every Ten Days Is Law's Limit," *Bakersfield Californian*, January 29, 1920, 1.

[66] Sinclair, 191.

[67] Ostrander, 178-179.

[68] "200 Gallons of Wine Is Limit for Family Vats," *Bakersfield Californian*, October 13, 1920, 2.

[69] Ostrander, 178-179.

[70] "New Grape Drink Due," *Los Angeles Times*, March 11, 1931, 12.

[71] Ostrander, 180 and Sinclair, 206.

[72] "Wine Plan Changed," *Los Angeles Times*, November 6, 1931, 1.

[73] Ostrander, 180.

[74] Many protestors of prohibition claimed that it was class legislation. The wealthy and upper middle class was able to purchase supplies of liquor before Prohibition. The poor, dependent on saloons, did not have the financial ability to stock-up for the "dry spell," and thus, were deprived of legal liquor because of their socioeconomic status.

[75] "Trousers and Wine Taken by Thief," *Bakersfield Californian*, September 8, 1920, 1.

[76] "Cellar Door Is Jimmied; Treasure in Liquid Stolen," *Bakersfield Californian*, November 3, 1920, 5.

[77] "Hard-Headed but Thirsty Burglars Rob Local Home," *Bakersfield Californian*, March 25, 1920, 8.

[78] "Ask Warehouses for Storage of Liquor," *Bakersfield Californian*, February 19, 1920, 7.

[79] "Seek Liquor Car Shipper," *Los Angeles Times*, December 20, 1925, 19.

[80] Sinclair, 197.

[81] "Big Kern Booze Mystery," *Bakersfield Californian*, July 25, 1921, 1.

[82] Sinclair, 184.

[83] Ibid.

[84] "Sid Shannon Arrested On Booze Count At Venice," *Bakersfield Californian*, January 31, 1922, 1.

[85] "Probation Granted In Bribe Case," *Los Angeles Times*, February 28, 1924, sec. A8.

[86] "Prohibition Sleuth Slain by L. Lowe," *Bakersfield Californian*, December 19, 1924, 1 and "Louis Lowe Committed To Folsom For Crime," *Bakersfield Californian*, May 6, 1925, 1, 9. This case is covered extensively from May of 1925 to December of 1925.

[87] "Public Hostile To Liquor Laws," *Bakersfield Californian*, April 1, 1921, 7.

[88] "Prohibition Failure, Says Boy-Scout Man," *Bakersfield Californian*, February 20, 1920, 1.

[89] "New State Dry Chief Prepares For Action," *Bakersfield Californian*, June 29, 1921, 6.

[90] "The Remedy," Editorial, *Bakersfield Californian*, May 10, 1920, Part. 2, 4.

[91] "Modification of Volstead Act Sought," *Bakersfield Californian*, May 21, 1920, 1.

[92] "May Ask Congress to Amend Dry Act to Allow Wine, Beer," *Bakersfield Californian*, January 5, 1921, 1.

[93] "California Assembly On Record For Wine, Beer," *Bakersfield Californian*, March 19, 1921, 1.

[94] "Light Wine And Beer Squad Here," *Bakersfield Californian*, August 19, 1921, 4 and "Hope To Bring Back Light Wines And Beer," *Bakersfield Californian*, August 26, 1921, 4.

95 "Bill to Legalize Beer, Wine, Would Aid War Veterans," *Bakersfield Californian*, November 2, 1921, 2.

96 Sinclair, 211. Researcher John F. Padgett argues that plea bargaining was the result of three possible factors. First is caseload. Due to the shortage of court personnel and the potential length of jury trials, plea bargains were brokered to quicken the pace of justice. Second is substantive justice, which is an attempt to implement standardization in sentencing in place of flexible sentencing standards. Last is plea bargaining based on evidentiary quality; the fact that the evidence in some cases was less than solid than in others, so securing a guilty plea to a lesser charge was better than no conviction at all. Padgett also identifies two forms of bargaining—implicit (the defendant pleads guilty based on the expectation that a more lenient sentence will be handed out) and explicit (a plea bargain is secured through overt promises that charges or the sentence will be reduced). See John F. Padgett, "Plea Bargaining and Prohibition in the Federal Courts, 1908-1934," *Law & Society Review* 24, no. 2 (1990): 413-415.

97 Sinclair, 190.

98 Ostrander, 172.

99 More trials may have been requested, but these are the only ones reported in the newspaper.

100 For a sample of cases decided in favor of the defendant see "Jury Disagrees in 'Moonshine' Trial," *Bakersfield Californian*, April 23, 1921, 8, "Mrs. Sadacchi Is Acquitted Today," *Bakersfield Californian*, May 28, 1921, 8, "Polston Freed On Moonshine Charge," *Bakersfield Californian*, October 15, 1921, 9 and "Set New La Selva Trial Tomorrow," *Bakersfield Californian*, October 19, 1921, 4.

101 "Confiscate Coupe In 'Booze' Raid," *Bakersfield Californian*, October 18, 1921, 2. Despite this proclamation, jury trials continued in the Bakersfield Police Court.

102 "Three More Raids Made By Police," *Bakersfield Californian*, December 13, 1920, 2.

103 "Writ Granted In Test Of Dry Act," *Bakersfield Californian*, December 18, 1920, 6.

104 "City of L.A. To Aid In Kern Case," *Bakersfield Californian*, January 4, 1921, 8.

105 Section Two of the Eighteenth Amendment holds that states, such as California, had the concurrent power to enforce prohibition. Grijalva argued that since California had no prohibition enforcement measure, enforcement fell to cities and counties throughout the state. See "Claim Federal Court Has No Jurisdiction In Liquor Case," *Bakersfield Californian*, January 6, 1921, 1.

106 "Dry Law Test Fight at End To Drop Crookshank Appeal," *Bakersfield Californian*, August 4, 1921, 7.

107 "Clogged Sewer Is Clue to Location of Illegal Still," *Bakersfield Californian*, January 11, 1921, 6.

108 "Six Autos, Much Booze Seized At McKittrick," *Bakersfield Californian*, February 16, 1924, 1, 9.

109 "Potato Peeling Booze Cause Of Trouble At Camp," *Bakersfield Californian*, July 9, 1925, 9.

[110] "Federal Agents Take Cheer Out Of Yuletide In Taft Rum World," *Bakersfield Californian*, December 22, 1928, 9 and "Historical Census of Housing Data," U.S. Department of Congress, United States Census Bureau. Accessed June 3, 2013, http://www.census.gov/hhes/www/housing/census/historic/owner.html

[111] "Claim Man Was 'Walking Bar,' Is Caught By Police," *Bakersfield Californian*, January 4, 1921, 8 and "Alleged 'Walking Bar' Jailed Here," *Bakersfield Californian*, June 3, 1921, 9.

[112] "Arrests Are Made Under 'Dry Act'," *Bakersfield Californian*, December 25, 1920, 2.

[113] "Raiders Unable to Locate Liquor; Dig With Good Results," *Bakersfield Californian*, January 25, 1921, 8 and "Stiff Sentence For Dry-Law Violator," *Bakersfield Californian*, April 29, 1921, 8.

[114] "Find New Method in Liquor Case," *Bakersfield Californian*, July 15, 1921, 4.

[115] "50 Arrests Made Here In Night," *Bakersfield Californian*, December 9, 1921, 8.

[116] "Claim Find Liquor in Meat Market," *Bakersfield Californian*, June 14, 1921, 9.

[117] "New York Cuts Hid Illicit Booze," *Bakersfield Californian*, January 27, 1922, 9.

[118] "Now Faces Quartet Of Dry Law Charges," *Bakersfield Californian*, January 10, 1922, 7.

[119] "Officers in Plain Clothes Arrest Pair," *Bakersfield Californian*, November 24, 1921, 2, "American Bar Is Raided by Police," *Bakersfield Californian*, December 24, 1921, 7 and "Arrests Are Made by Bakersfield Police," *Bakersfield Californian*, December 28, 1921, 4.

[120] "More Arrests For Dry Act Violation," *Bakersfield Californian*, February 8, 1921, 8, "Arrested for Third Time in Two Months," *Bakersfield Californian*, August 31, 1921, 6 and "Charge Perjury Against H. Lord," *Bakersfield Californian*, December 5, 1921, 6.

[121] "'Canned Heat Is Latest Beverage With 'Kick' Here," *Bakersfield California*, December 19, 1921, 6.

[122] Sinclair, 174.

[123] "Wood Alcohol Is Potion Of Death," *Bakersfield Californian*, January 16, 1922, 4. The Recreation Park referenced in the story is more than likely present day Hart Park.

[124] Sinclair, 366.

Chapter 4

[1] Mary Grace Paquette, *Lest We Forget: The History of the French in Kern County* (Fresno: Pioneer Publishing Company, 1978), Mary Grace Paquette, *Basques to Bakersfield* (Bakersfield: Kern County Historical Society, 1982), and Donna Tessandori Weeks, *The Italians in Kern County* (Bloomington: Xlibris Corporation, 2011).

[2] Data on place of birth / ethnicity was found for 692 people, but the number for race is 707. The disparity between the data is accounted for by the fact that some individuals are specifically identified by race in newspapers.

[3] University of Virginia, "Historical Census Browser," accessed June 3, 2013, http://mapserver.lib.virginia.edu/.

[4] Jeannie M. Whayne, "Caging the Blind Tiger: Race, Class, and Family in the Battle for Prohibition in Small Town Arkansas," *The Arkansas Historical Quarterly* 71, no. 1 (Spring 2012): 57, 60.

[5] Census data was not found for all 1726 individuals, but gender is accounted for each person. Each and every one of the 191 females were specifically identified as being "female" in newspapers. With this in mind, I assume that each person identified by their first initial and last name is male.

[6] Tanya Marie Sanchez, "The Feminine Side of Bootlegging," *Louisiana History: The Journal of the Louisiana Historical Association* 41, no. 4 (Autumn 2000): 404.

[7] Ibid., 406.

[8] Ibid., 414.

[9] Mary Murphy, "Bootlegging Mothers and Drinking Daughters: Gender and Prohibition in Butte, Montana," *American Quarterly* 46, no. 2 (June 1994): 175. She also asserts that Prohibition changed established gender drinking habits—more women began to drink in public places, changing the perception of what was considered acceptable and unacceptable public behavior for women.

[10] Sanchez, 418, 428. Also, see Murphy, 185.

[11] "Wife Forgot to Obey Husband; Fined $250," *Bakersfield Californian*, October 14, 1927, 11.

[12] "Women Violators of Liquor Laws Fined," *Bakersfield Californian*, July 13, 1922, 2.

[13] Joseph R. Gusfield, *Symbolic Crusade: Status Politics and the American Temperance Movement* (Urbana: University of Illinois Press, 1963), 123.

[14] Ibid., 124.

[15] Ivan Light, "The Ethnic Vice Industry, 1880-1944," *American Sociological Review* 42, no. 3 (1977): 465-466. Light explores this issue through a comparison of prostitution among Chinese immigrants and black Americans, but the conclusions can be expanded to other areas of vice.

[16] Ibid., 475.

[17] The data collected has been dependent on what was, for the most part, reported in newspapers. "Reported" is the key word. A large number of people were arrested for violating Prohibition. Many of the violators are only identified by their first initial and last name, a research problem that is difficult to circumvent.

[18] As with data examined for marital status in Kern County, census and voter registration data is not always from the year of an arrest. For example, a person arrested in 1927 for the possession and sale of alcohol has data on their trade found in the 1920 or 1930 census, or perhaps in voter registration records from 1922. The trade of that individual might be totally different in 1927 from that recorded in available documents. Therefore, this examination of trade is based on available data—data that may or may not be definitively accurate. However, it is based upon the best information available and paints a picture of violators under the theory that an educated assumption is better than no data at all.

[19] "Table 1: Real Average Weekly or Daily Earnings for Selected Occupations, 1920 to 1930," Accessed April 8, 2013, http://eh.net/encyclopedia/article/smiley.1920s.final

[20] "Five Arrested On Dry Law Charges," *Bakersfield Californian*, September 9, 1924, 9. Information on Labovitch's trade has not been found, but it is assumed that the lack of data indicates a lack of permanence in one location, a characteristic often found among unskilled workers.

[21] "Poor Bootlegger Pays $995 Fine And Gets Freedom," *Bakersfield Californian*, December 15, 1924, 9.

[22] "Prisoner Taxed on Liquor Used for Evidence in Case," *Bakersfield Californian*, June 30, 1921, 7. Hickman is identified in the 1920 Census as a "Rig Builder" on an Oil Lease.

[23] "Oil Worker Of Long Beach Is Held Prisoner Following Race," *Bakersfield Californian*, July 15, 1929, 9.

[24] As with other categories of analysis, data on home analysis has not been found for all of the individuals arrested for violating Prohibition. Additionally, data that has been found may not be relevant to the time of the person's arrest.

[25] "Historical Census of Housing Data," U.S. Department of Congress, United States Census Bureau. Accessed June 3, 2013, http://www.census.gov/hhes/www/housing/census/historic/owner.html

[26] According to election data for 1920, 49.01 percent of voters in Kern County were Republicans, 42.20 percent were Democrats, and 8.79 percent voted for "other" political party candidates. See "Report From 145 Precincts At Hand," *Bakersfield Californian*, November 4, 1920, 1.

Chapter 5

[1] In all, there were 2111 arrests in Kern County between 1918 and 1933. Discounting the arrests made under Wartime Prohibition, there were 2106 arrests.

[2] "Enforcement of Dry Law At Present Is Failure," *Bakersfield Californian*, October 18, 1927, 1.

[3] "Dance Halls, Liquor Trade Hit By Grand Jury Report," *Bakersfield Californian*, May 29, 1928, 1, 7.

[4] "Rum Informers Will Be 'Tipped' by Government," *Bakersfield Californian*, July 13, 1928, 11 and "Award Schedule For Snooping In Rum Cases Given By "Dry" Agents," July 14, 1928, 7. According to the stories, payments have to be approved of by officials in Washington, D.C. The pay schedule was as follows: Seizure of autos-- $25 to $100 and Other Information--$5 to $200.

[5] "Taft Council Dooms All Hidden Kick in Liquor," *Bakersfield Californian*, March 7, 1928, 9.

[6] "Bakersfield "Vice Squad" Abolished by Chief Webster," *Bakersfield Californian*, February 17, 1932, 9.

[7] Title II, Sect. 21 of the Volstead Act states that any "place where intoxicating liquor is manufactured, sold, kept, or bartered in violation of this title, and all intoxicating liquor and property kept and used in maintaining the same, is hereby declared to be a common nuisance...." This statement was interpreted to allow a federal injunction to be issued on the location, resulting in the "padlock" provision. For a discussion on the "Common Nuisance" clause of the Volstead Act see "The Test of a Common Nuisance under the Volstead Act," *University of Pennsylvania Law Review and American Law Register* 72, no. 3 (March 1924): 289-293.

[8] "Federal Padlock Is Put on Local Place," *Bakersfield Californian*, December 6, 1928, 11.

[9] "Prohi Officials Padlock Alleged Rum Dispensary," *Bakersfield Californian*, March 15, 1930, 9.

[10] "Kern Too "Hot" for Racketeers Is Word Spread Over Gangland," *Bakersfield Californian*, August 3, 1929, 9.

[11] "Agent Must Search Only If Possessed Of Warrant," *Bakersfield Californian*, August 9, 1928, 1.

[12] "Those Who Sell Barrel, Label, Bottle, Liable," *Bakersfield Californian*, May 5, 1930, 2.

[13] "Sleuths Instructed as to New Ruling," *Bakersfield Californian*, May 23, 1930, 2. Interestingly enough, a major producer of yeast, Fleischman, pled no contest to charges of conspiracy to violate Prohibition and paid $3000 in fines. See "Fleischman Yeast Firm Fined $3000," *Bakersfield Californian*, September 18, 1931, 2.

[14] "Dry Agents' Cars Must Bear Metal Shields 17 by 20," *Bakersfield Californian*, August 20, 1930, 1. Imposters used their false authority to hijack liquor supplies and steal money, or collect bribes from violators of Prohibition.

[15] "Material Sought For Rum Agents," *Bakersfield Californian*, July 28, 1928, 9 and "Uncle Sam Is in Market for Liquor Sleuths," *Bakersfield Californian*, October 23, 1928, 9.

[16] "Federal Agents Are Transferred," *Bakersfield Californian*, January 20, 1930, 9.

[17] "Rigid Dry Enforcement Defeated," *Bakersfield Californian*, December 17, 1928, 1 and "$24,000,000 Extra Voted For Dry Law Enforcement," *Bakersfield Californian*, January 23, 1929, 1.

[18] "Ogden Requests Emergency Bill Creating Fund To Aid Crusades," *Bakersfield Californian*, May 14, 1929, 11. It was reported on May 29 that Ogden died at his desk in his private office. See "City Manager Succumbs At His Desk In Heat Spell," *Bakersfield Californian*, May 29, 1929, 1.

[19] "Dry Squad Raid In Taft Echoes As Man Claims $5000 Damages," *Bakersfield Californian*, January 3, 1928, 9 and "Judge Will Rule In Suit Against Federal Agents," *Bakersfield Californian*, January 4, 1928, 9. Results of the lawsuit were not listed and have not been found.

[20] "Case Involving Police Officers Of Bakersfield Is Under Probe," *Bakersfield Californian*, April 24, 1930, 11, "Shannon Is Accused Of Attempt To "Frame" Dry," *Bakersfield Californian*, April 25, 1930, 1, 2, "Shannon Denies Accusations Of Alleged Scheme Against Mathias," *Bakersfield Californian*, April 26, 1930, 11, "Validity of Charges Attacked by Officers," *Bakersfield Californian*, June 7, 1930, 9, "Trial Starts Monday for Shannon, Others," *Bakersfield Californian*, October 2, 1930, 11, "Former Federal Officer Witness Against Shannon," *Bakersfield Californian*, October 7, 1930, 9, 15, "Defense In Shannon Trial Dealt Blow," *Bakersfield Californian*, October 8, 1930, 9, 21, "Government Will End Case Today Against Shannon," *Bakersfield Californian*, October 9, 1930, 9, 21, "Shannon Defense Witness Tells of Liquor Gift," *Bakersfield Californian*, October 10, 1930, 13, "Mayor, Judge and Department Head in Shannon Case," *Bakersfield Californian*, October 10, 1930, 13, "Shannon's Fate Rests In Hands Of Jury," *Bakersfield Californian*, October 11, 1930, 9 and "Shannon Acquitted On Conspiracy Count," *Bakersfield Californian*, October 13, 1930, 9, 15.

[21] "Patterson Sought on Accusation of Disabled Veteran," *Bakersfield Californian*, February 25, 1931, 9, "U.S. Attorney to Defend Patterson; Civil Suit Filed," *Bakersfield Californian*, February 26, 1931, 13 and "Patterson Wins Federal Trial on Charge of Slugging Disabled Man," *Bakersfield Californian*, February 28, 1931, 9.

[22] "Carlock And Webster In Battle Following Discussion On Liquor," *Bakersfield Californian*, February 9, 1933, 11 and "Bakersfield Mayor Has Fist Fight With Chief," *The Los Angeles Times*, February 10, 1933, 7. Carlock stated that the claims against

Officer Otto Heckman needed to be investigated. The only casualty of the fight was Patrolman Bill Richardson who was accidentally punched in the jaw while trying to break up the uneventful fight. Investigation of Heckman was turned over to members of the Bakersfield Police Commission. See "Council Names Commission To Consider Issue," *Bakersfield Californian*, February 15, 1933, 9.

[23] Jeffrey A. Miron and Jeffrey Zwiebel, "Alcohol Consumption During Prohibition," *The American Economic Review* 81, no. 2 (May 1991): 242.

[24] Ibid.

[25] Ibid., 245.

[26] J.C. Burnham, "New Perspectives On The Prohibition 'Experiment' Of The 1920s," *Journal of Social History* 2, no. 1 (Autumn 1968): 52.

[27] Ibid., 58-59.

[28] Ibid., 64.

[29] Ibid., 61, 67.

[30] Herbert Brucker, "How Long, O Prohibition," *The North American Review* 234, no. 4 (October 1932): 347.

[31] Ibid., 349.

[32] Ibid., 350.

[33] Ibid., 351.

[34] David E. Kyvig, "Women Against Prohibition," *American Quarterly* 28, no. 4 (1976): 465. Over 10,000 amendment resolutions have been submitted to Congress. Only thirty-three were approved by two-thirds majority of both houses in Congress, and only twenty-seven were ratified. See Michael Munger and Thomas Schaller, "The Prohibition-Repeal Amendments: A Natural Experiment in Interest Group Influence," *Public Choice* 90, no. ¼ (March 1997): 140.

[35] "Dry Law Unjust, Claims Emmons," *Bakersfield Californian*, June 30, 1927, 9.

[36] "Pollock Avers Dry Act Leading U.S. To Slavery, Narcotics, Ultimate Disaster," *Bakersfield Californian*, September 17, 1927, 1 and "Federal Judge Raps Prohibition Policy," *Bakersfield Californian*, September 24, 1927, 2.

[37] "Judge Rules Law Cannot Be Applied In California Case," *Bakersfield Californian*, March 25, 1929, 1. While the Jones Act remained on the books in its original incarnation it was not enforced. The Senate eventually reduced the fines and jail time ($500 and up to six months in jail) for non-habitual offenders. See "Jones Law Penalty Reduced By Senate," *Bakersfield Californian*, July 2, 1930, 1.

[38] "New President Emphasizes Necessity for Law Enforcement," *Bakersfield Californian*, March 4, 1929, 6.

[39] John C. Gebhart, "Movement Against Prohibition," *Annals of the American Academy of Political and Social Science* 163 (September 1932): 175.

[40] Ibid.

[41] "Petitions Started For Dry Referendum," *Bakersfield Californian*, March 15, 1930, 9 and "Many Local Names on Dry Referendum," *Bakersfield Californian*, March 19, 1930, 11. The Association hoped to collect at least 35 million signatures to force the referendum.

[42] Gebhart, 172.

[43] Walter F. Wilcox, "An Attempt to Measure Public Opinion About Repealing the Eighteenth Amendment," *Journal of the American Statistical Association* 26, no. 175 (1931): 249, 256.

[44] Ibid., 244.

[45] Ibid., 252.

[46] "Bakersfield Is Voting Wet in National Poll by Publication," *Bakersfield Californian*, April 5, 1930, 11.

[47] "Bakersfield Still Wet in Digest Poll," *Bakersfield Californian*, May 20, 1930, 11.

[48] Gebhart: 173. More than twenty million ballots were mailed out by the *Literary Digest*, and despite postage for return paid for by the *Digest* less than 25 percent of the ballots were returned. Those who wish to maintain Prohibition have no real incentive to participate in the straw ballot. Many of the participants indicating their desire for repeal would most likely support modification to allow "less than intoxicating" beverages. See H.H. Mitchell, "Prohibition and the Straw Ballot," *The Scientific Monthly* 35, no. 5 (November 1932): 443, 448.

[49] "Bakersfield Votes 5 To 1 Against Dry Law," *Bakersfield Californian*, March 31, 1932, 13.

[50] "Kansas, N. Carolina Only "Dry" States in Literary Digest Poll," *Bakersfield Californian*, April 15, 1932, 2, 8.

[51] Kyvig, 466-467. They did have an auxiliary group for women called the Molly Pitcher Club. By 1928 the Molly Pitcher Club ceased to exist.

[52] Ibid., 467.

[53] Ibid., 468.

[54] Ibid., 469.

[55] "Organized Labor Enters Fight To Nullify Part Of Prohibition Act," *Bakersfield Californian*, July 8, 1931,11.

[56] "American Bar Association Ballots Wet," *Bakersfield Californian*, September 17, 1931, 1 and "Urges Repeal Of 18th Amendment," *Bakersfield Californian*, January 18, 1932, 1.

[57] "Federal Agents To Ignore Home Brewers Unless Sale Is Proven," *Bakersfield Californian*, August 20, 1930, 9 and "Home Brewers Safe, U.S. Official States," *Bakersfield Californian*, October 30, 1930, 2.

[58] "Senate Votes, 32-5, To Keep Wright Act," *Bakersfield Californian*, May 5, 1931, 1.

[59] "Congress To Vote On Prohibition," *Bakersfield Californian*, December 2, 1931, 1.

[60] "Only One Prohibition Vote To Be Granted," *Bakersfield Californian*, December 30, 1931, 3.

[61] "Wet Republicans Fight Dry Law," *Bakersfield Californian*, December 16, 1931, 1-2.

[62] "Legalization of Beer Advocated," *Bakersfield Californian*, January 20, 1932, 1.

[63] "Wets Lose In House, 227 To 187," *Bakersfield Californian*, March 14, 1932, 1.

[64] "Wets Claim Majority In Lower House In November," *Bakersfield Californian*, March 15, 1932, 1, 3.

[65] "Petitions To Annul State Dry Act Filed With Jordan," *Bakersfield Californian*, April 9, 1932, 1.

[66] "Wright-Act Repeal on Ballots," *Bakersfield Californian*, April 16, 1932, 1. If voters approved of the proposition, the state legislature would have the power to regulate liquor, allow liquor to be sold in eating places, ban the establishment of saloons, bars, or similar businesses, and allow alcohol to be sold at retail stores, but not consumed at the premises.

[67] "Roosevelt's Liquor Plan Reiterated," *Bakersfield Californian*, April 18, 1932, 2 and "Roosevelt Sees Dry-Act Change," *Bakersfield Californian*, June 8, 1932, 1.

[68] "House Defeats 2.75 Beer Bill," *Bakersfield Californian*, May 23, 1932, 1 and "2.75 Beer Is Again Rejected," *Bakersfield Californian*, May 25, 1932, 1.

[69] This is another example of pressure and punctuation politics. For more on this see Mark Lawrence Schrad, "Constitutional Blemishes: American Alcohol Prohibition and Repeal as Policy Punctuation," *The Policy Studies Journal* 35, no. 3 (2007): 437-463.

[70] "G.O.P. Straddles Prohibition," *Bakersfield Californian*, June 15, 1932, 1 and "G.O.P. Prohibition Plank," *Bakersfield Californian*, June 16, 1932, 1. The actual process the Republicans favored was eventually explained, but it was no different than a lesson on how amendments can be added to the Constitution according to Article Five. See "Process Of Making Dry-Law Change Under G.O.P. Platform Is Explained," *Bakersfield Californian*, June 17, 1932, 2.

[71] "California To Caucus On Rum," *Bakersfield Californian*, June 15, 1932, 1.

[72] "President In Favor Of Changes In Law To Give Control Of Liquors To States," *Bakersfield Californian*, August 12, 1932, 12.

[73] "Woman Seeks Right To Sell Beer, Wine," *Bakersfield Californian*, July 5, 1932, 9 and "Light Wines, Beer Permit Sought Here," *Bakersfield Californian*, July 12, 1932, 9.

[74] "Resolution For Repeal Introduced," *Bakersfield Californian*, May 24, 1932, 1-2.

[75] "33 Californians Vote For Repeal," *Bakersfield Californian*, June 30, 1932, 3.

[76] "Jackson Mahon Files Papers; Urges Repeal of Prohibition Laws," *Bakersfield Californian*, June 4, 1932, 7, "Mahon Attacks U.S. Dry Laws," *Bakersfield Californian*, June 8, 1932, 9 and "Tariff Measure Scored By Kern Contestant For Congress Seat," *Bakersfield Californian*, June 14, 1932, 9. The Tenth Congressional District included parts of Kern, Tulare, San Luis Obispo, Santa Barbara, and Ventura counties.

[77] "Congress Candidate Favors Beer, Wines," *Bakersfield Californian*, July 11, 1932, 9 and "Crites Gives Stand On Liquor Question," *Bakersfield Californian*, July 20, 1932, 9.

[78] "Wardell Scores Costs Involved In Enforcement Of Liquor Laws," *Bakersfield Californian*, August 23, 1932, 9.

[79] "Wardell, Mahon Win Support Of Women Opposed To Liquor Laws," *Bakersfield Californian*, August 26, 1932, 9.

[80] "Complete Kern Vote," *Bakersfield Californian*, September 1, 1932, 1.

[81] Even though McAdoo was a "dry," he did support modification of the Volstead Act to allow the sale of light wines and beer. See "Senate Passes Beer Bill 43-36," *Bakersfield Californian*, March 20, 1933, 1.

[82] "Democrats Win 472 Votes In Electoral College; Hoover, 59," *Bakersfield Californian*, November 9, 1932, 1 and "Californians Desert G.O.P.," *Bakersfield Californian*, November 9, 1932, 1-2.

[83] "Wright Act Hit By Kern Voters," *Bakersfield Californian*, November 9, 1932, 1.

[84] "State Vote On Propositions," *Bakersfield Californian*, November 10, 1932, 2.

[85] "Prisoners Under Wright Act Are To Be Released," *Bakersfield Californian*, November 17, 1932, 9.

[86] "Gov. Rolph Also May Give Pardon to Many Jones-Law Violators," *Bakersfield Californian*, November 19, 1932, 10.

[87] "Rolph Frees 128 Liquor Violators," *Bakersfield Californian*, December 19, 1932, 1 and "Rolph Pardons 248 Prisoners," *Bakersfield Californian*, January 6, 1933, 6.

[88] "Council Considers Repeal of Bakersfield Liquor Ordinance," *Bakersfield Californian*, November 9, 1932, 9, 13.

[89] "Council Fails To Repeal City Liquor Law," *Bakersfield Californian*, November 22, 1932, 9, 13.

[90] "Bakersfield Liquor Law Repealed," *Bakersfield Californian*, November 29, 1932, 1.

[91] "City Liquor Law Repeal Is Effective Today," *Bakersfield Californian*, December 28, 1932, 7.

[92] "Prompt Vote Demanded By Two Parties," *Bakersfield Californian*, November 26, 1932, 1-2.

[93] "Vote Is 272 To 144 Which Is 6 Short Of Two-Thirds Needed," *Bakersfield Californian*, December 5, 1932, 1.

[94] "Beer And Wine Bills Are Approved," *Bakersfield Californian*, December 15, 1932, 1.

[95] "Grape Growers Of County Join Fight For Wine," *Bakersfield Californian*, December 28, 1932, 7. Grape producers wanted legalization of wine to help increase prices for grapes. In the early years of Prohibition prices for grapes reached record prices. Because of this, increasing numbers of grape producers entered the market driving prices down by 1932.

[96] "Committee Rejects Wine Bill," *Bakersfield Californian*, December 16, 1932, 1-2.

[97] For a sample of the slow progress modification of the Volstead Act took see "Beer-By-Christmas Act Blocked," *Bakersfield Californian*, December 23, 1932, 1, "Practicable Test Of 3.2 PCT. Beer Urged," *Bakersfield Californian*, December 31, 1932, 2 and "Collier's Beer Bill Is Scored," *Bakersfield Californian*, January 7, 1933, 1-2.

[98] "State Assembly Votes 54-21 for Dry-Act Repeal," *Bakersfield Californian*, January 12, 1933, 1.

[99] "Two Seek Right to Sell Wines, Beer in County," *Bakersfield Californian*, January 9, 1933, 9.

[100] "Dry Amendment Repeal Approved," *Bakersfield Californian*, January 9, 1933, 1-2.

[101] "Dry States Are Assured Protection," *Bakersfield Californian*, February 16, 1933, 1.

[102] "Congress Votes Dry-Act Repeal," *Bakersfield Californian*, February 20, 1933, 1.

[103] "U.S. Dry Agents Told Not to Molest "Speakeasies,"" *Bakersfield Californian*, March 8, 1933, 1.

[104] "Volstead-Act Change Asked Of Congress," *Bakersfield Californian*, March 13, 1933, 1, 10.

[105] "House Passes Beer Bill, 316-97," *Bakersfield Californian*, March 14, 1933, 1, "Reduces Alcohol Content Of Beer," *Bakersfield Californian*, March 16, 1933, 1, "Beer Bill To Be Effective April 4," *Bakersfield Californian*, March 17, 1933, 1-2, "Senate Passes Beer Bill 43-36," *Bakersfield Californian*, March 20, 1933, 1 and "Cullen Bill Is Made Law By President," *Bakersfield Californian*, March 22, 1933, 1-2.

[106] "Many Cities Of Valley Closed To Beer Sales," *Bakersfield Californian*, March 20, 1933, 7.

[107] "City, County Given Power to Regulate," *Bakersfield Californian*, April 24, 1933, 1. A previous beer regulation bill was passed by the Assembly. See "State Acts To Regulate Beer," *Bakersfield Californian*, March 21, 1933, 1. An "on sale" license allowed an individual to sell alcohol to be consumed at the site of their business, whereas an "off sale" license only allowed a person to sell alcohol to be consumed in another location.

[108] "Gov. Rolph Approves Beer Regulation Act," *Bakersfield Californian*, April 28, 1933, 1.

[109] "Action On Beer Sales Expected," *Bakersfield Californian*, March 27, 1933, 7.

[110] "Applications To Sell Beer, Wine Prove Numerous," *Bakersfield Californian*, March 27, 1933, 7.

[111] "Display Beer Mugs at Redlick's Store," *Bakersfield Californian*, April 7, 1933, 13.

[112] "Beer Trucks Race To City," *Bakersfield Californian*, April 7, 1933, 13.

[113] "Beer Truck Hits Auto; Passenger Killed Instantly," *Bakersfield Californian*, April 18, 1933, 7.

[114] "Come Rain, Rum Or Repeal, Taft "Dry"," *Bakersfield Californian*, December 21, 1932, 9.

[115] "Taft Plans Special Election On Beer Issue," *Bakersfield Californian*, March 29, 1933, 9.

[116] "Official Urges Repeal of Taft Anti-Beer Rule," *Bakersfield Californian*, April 5, 1933, 9.

[117] "Barbeque-Picnic To Welcome "3.2 Beer"," *Bakersfield Californian*, April 3, 1933, 7.

[118] "Beer Judging Will Be West Side Event," *Bakersfield Californian*, April 21, 1933, 9.

[119] "Local Option Measure Under Fire In Battle To Legalize 3.2 Beer," *Bakersfield Californian*, April 27, 1933, 11, "Beer Ballot Is Reported Heavy, Taft," *Bakersfield Californian*, April 28, 1933, 11, "Option Law Of West Side City Is Voted Down," *Bakersfield Californian*, April 29, 1933, 7 and "3.2 Beer Is Made Legal, City Of Taft," *Bakersfield Californian*, May 2, 1933, 7. Taft passed a law regulating beer sales, requiring businesses selling beer to serve a light lunch (sandwich), and that distributors must acquire a regular business license costing $20 a year, a license to sell beer on-site for $35 a year with an application fee of $2, or a license to sell off-site for $10 a year plus a $2 application fee. The law, scheduled to go into effect July 1, 1933, was cancelled by the city trustees of Taft due to the County's failure to act on an overall licensing plan and the looming repeal of the Eighteenth Amendment. See "New Taft Beer Statute Passed," *Bakersfield Californian*, June 21, 1933, 7 and "Beer Ordinance At Taft Is Rescinded," *Bakersfield Californian*, June 29, 1933, 9.

[120] "Beer Law Asked By Delano Group," *Bakersfield Californian*, April 6, 1933, 6.

[121] "Regulation For Selling Beer Is Topic For Meet," *Bakersfield Californian*, May 5, 1933, 11.

[122] "State Submits Regulations On Beer Dispensing," *Bakersfield Californian*, May 8, 1933, 7.

[123] A grape grower and former president of the Kern County Farm Bureau, H.W. Mellen, the Agricultural Commissioner L.A. Burtch, M.A. Lindsay (a farm advisor), and Secretary of the Chamber of Commerce, L.B. Nourse pledged to aid the cause for natural light wine in Kern County. See "Grape Growers To Battle For Light Wine Measure," *Bakersfield Californian*, March 22, 1933, 7.

[124] "California Vintners Not To Make Wine," *Bakersfield Californian*, March 23, 1933, 2.

[125] "Citizens Would Aid Grape Men," *Bakersfield Californian*, March 25, 1933, 7.

[126] "Wine Bill Urged In Group Report," *Bakersfield Californian*, March 31, 1933, 11.

[127] "$85,000 Winery Will Be Built At Delano," *Bakersfield Californian*, August 2, 1933, 7. Perelli-Minetti was elected one of nineteen directors of the Wine Producers Association. The committee's goal was to guide California's wine industry and maintain the high quality of wine produced. See "Winemakers In State Organize," *Bakersfield Californian*, August 31, 1933, 11 and "Kern Vintner Is State Director," *Bakersfield Californian*, September 7, 1933, 11.

[128] This assertion is made based on the number of times I noticed a story concerning the WCTU in Kern County and noted the date. Surely, the probability that there were other mentions of the WCTU that I missed is great.

[129] "Late W.C.T.U. News Notes," *Bakersfield Californian*, January 17, 1931, 5.

[130] "Board of Strategy Formed by 'Drys' of Bakersfield," *Bakersfield Californian*, August 23, 1932, 9. It was expected that Rev. Frank O. Belden (Pastor of the First Baptist Church) would have the Chairmanship, Rev. J.D. Page would be the Executive Secretary, and Miss Mariana Bohna would be the Secretary Treasurer.

[131] "Kern County Strategy Board Discusses 18th Amendment," *Bakersfield Californian*, November 2, 1932, 3.

[132] "Annual W.C.T.U. Picnic Tuesday," *Bakersfield Californian*, May 20, 1933, 7.

[133] "Famous Prohibition Authority Coming," *Bakersfield Californian*, October 9, 1933, 9.

[134] "Late W.C.T.U. News Notes," *Bakersfield Californian*, November 19, 1932, 5.

[135] "Late W.C.T.U. News Notes," *Bakersfield Californian*, September 25, 1933, 3, "Late W.C.T.U. News Notes," *Bakersfield Californian*, October 23, 1933, 3 and "Late W.C.T.U. News Notes," *Bakersfield Californian*, October 30, 1933, 5.

[136] "Study Of Liquor From Scientific Angle Is Slated," *Bakersfield California*, September 25, 1933, 9.

[137] "Many Problems Follow Repeal," *Bakersfield Californian*, November 8, 1933, 2. Some "dry" advocates stressed the idea that high taxes on alcohol might be used as a viable tool to promote or maintain temperance, a potential positive outcome of repeal.

[138] "Drys Move to Block State Vote on Repeal," *Bakersfield Californian*, May 27, 1933, 2.

[139] "Drys Fail To Block Early Repeal Vote," *Bakersfield Californian*, May 29, 1933, 3 and "Drys May Appeal To U.S. Supreme Court," *Bakersfield Californian*, May 30, 1933, 1.

[140] "Californian To Ballot On 11 Proposals," *Bakersfield Californian*, June 26, 1933, 1, 13.

[141] "Bakersfield, Kern Vote 3 To 1 Repeal Of Prohibition Law," *Bakersfield Californian*, June 28, 1933, 1, 9.

[142] "Dry-Act Convention May Be Postponed," *Bakersfield Californian*, July 12, 1933, 1 and "Dry's Stand May Hinder Convention," *Bakersfield Californian*, July 13, 1933, 1-2.

[143] "California Formally Votes Dry Repeal," *Bakersfield Californian*, July 24, 1933, 1.

[144] "U.S. Prohibition Office in Bakersfield Closes Down," *Bakersfield Californian*, August 25, 1933, 11.

[145] "Distributors Of Beer Form Unit," *Bakersfield Californian*, August 30, 1933, 9.

[146] "$150,000 Brewery Will Be Erected Here," *Bakersfield Californian*, September 18, 1933, 9, "'Bakersfield Beer' In March Predicted," *Bakersfield Californian*, September 29, 1933, 13, "Consider Sites For Beer Plant," *Bakersfield Californian*, October 2, 1933, 7 and "Brewery Site Is Chosen; Plan To Begin Work Soon," *Bakersfield Californian*, October 30, 1933, 9.

[147] "14,000,000 Vote Wet And 5,000,000 Dry," *Bakersfield Californian*, November 9, 1933, 1.

[148] "Ohio, Pennsylvania, Utah Ballot Wet," *Bakersfield Californian*, November 8, 1933, 1-2 and "Utah Is 36th State To Ratify," *Bakersfield Californian*, December 5, 1933, 1.

[149] "Restrictions On Drinking Few, Slight," *Bakersfield Californian*, December 2, 1933, 1, 11.

[150] "Prohibition A Thing Of The Past," *Bakersfield Californian*, December 5, 1933, 14.

[151] "Asks People Avoid Curse Of Excesses," *Bakersfield Californian*, December 6, 1933, 1.

[152] "Liquor Licenses May Be Applied for on Monday," *Bakersfield Californian*, November 23, 1933, 13 and "Liquor License Forms Delayed," *Bakersfield Californian*, November 28, 1933, 9.

[153] "Fast Cars Will Transport Kern Stock Of Liquor," *Bakersfield Californian*, December 5, 1933, 9.

[154] "Hanning, Williams Open Liquor Store," *Bakersfield Californian*, December 5, 1933, 9. Liquor ads began to appear in the *Bakersfield Californian* beginning on December 5, 1933.

[155] "Repeal Taken With Calmness," *Bakersfield Californian*, December 9, 1933, 12.

[156] "Daily Comment By Will Rogers," *Bakersfield Californian*, December 6, 1933, 1.

Bibliography

"$7500 Total Fines Under City Dry Act In 5 Weeks," *Bakersfield Californian*, December 21, 1920, 1.

"$24,000,000 Extra Voted For Dry Law Enforcement," *Bakersfield Californian*, January 23, 1929, 1.

"$85,000 Winery Will Be Built At Delano," *Bakersfield Californian*, August 2, 1933, 7.

"$150,000 Brewery Will Be Erected Here," *Bakersfield Californian*, September 18, 1933, 9.

"1 Dead, 3 Injured, Result Federal Raid," *Bakersfield Californian*, March 9, 1920, Part 2, 2.

"2.75 Beer Is Again Rejected," *Bakersfield Californian*, May 25, 1932, 1.

"2.75 Beer Is Held Illegal," *Bakersfield Californian*, January 5, 1920, 1.

"3.2 Beer Is Made Legal, City Of Taft," *Bakersfield Californian*, May 2, 1933, 7.

"33 Californians Vote For Repeal," *Bakersfield Californian*, June 30, 1932, 3.

"50 Arrests Made Here In Night," *Bakersfield Californian*, December 9, 1921, 8.

"200 Gallons of Wine Is Limit for Family Vats," *Bakersfield Californian*, October 13, 1920, 2.

"5,000 Dealers Fail To Report Liquor Stock," *Bakersfield Californian*, March 20, 1918, 1.

"1,500,000 Gallons Of Wine Exported From Fresno," *Bakersfield Californian*, January 15, 1920, 1.

"14,000,000 Vote Wet And 5,000,000 Dry," *Bakersfield Californian*, November 9, 1933, 1.

"A Big Question In 1918," Editorial, *Bakersfield Californian*, February 7, 1918, 10.

"A Patriotic Duty," Editorial, *Bakersfield Californian*, January 26, 1918, 12.

"Action On Beer Sales Expected," *Bakersfield Californian*, March 27, 1933, 7.

"Action On Liquor Licenses set For Wednesday," *Bakersfield Californian*, January 7, 1918, 6.

Advertisement, "Come And Hear The Other Side," *Bakersfield Californian*, October 21, 1911, 3.

Advertisement, "Crime Is Mostly Due To Booze," *Bakersfield Morning Echo*, October 22, 1911, 16.

Advertisement, "I Am Still Strong For The Boy," *Bakersfield Morning Echo*, October 29, 1911, 16.

Advertisement, "Maier Select," *Bakersfield Californian*, May 21, 1921, 5.

Advertisement, "This Is The Way To Vote Wet," *Bakersfield Morning Echo*, October 31, 1911, 6.

Advertisement, "Wet or Dry," *Bakersfield Californian*, October 28, 1911, 6.

"Agent Must Search Only If Possessed Of Warrant," *Bakersfield Californian*, August 9, 1928, 1.

"Agents Unable to Stop 'Moonshining'," *Bakersfield Californian*, April 29, 1920, 1.

"Alcohol In Beer To Be Reduced To 3 Per Cent," *Bakersfield Californian*, November 27, 1917, 7.

"Alien Enemies To Be Registered Feb. 4 To 9," *Bakersfield Californian*, January 24, 1918, 4.

"All But Families Must Report In Food Survey," *Bakersfield Californian*, January 1, 1918, 7.

"Alleged Blind Pig Raided Here," *Bakersfield Californian*, May 4, 1920, 8.

"Alleged 'Walking Bar' Jailed Here," *Bakersfield Californian*, June 3, 1921, 9.

"American Bar Is Raided by Police," *Bakersfield Californian*, December 24, 1921, 7.

"American Bar Association Ballots Wet," *Bakersfield Californian*, September 17, 1931, 1.

"Annual W.C.T.U. Picnic Tuesday," *Bakersfield Californian*, May 20, 1933, 7.

"Anti-Saloon League Declares for General Local Option Elections," *Bakersfield Californian*, May 6, 1911, 1, 6.

"Anti-Saloon League Reassures Timid Ones," *Bakersfield Californian*, September 2, 1911, 6.

"Anti-Saloonists Organized By Precincts," *Bakersfield Californian*, May 18, 1911, 1.

"Anti's To Wage War On Saloons," *Bakersfield Californian*, February 9, 1910, 1.

"Applications To Sell Beer, Wine Prove Numerous," *Bakersfield Californian*, March 27, 1933, 7.

"Arrested for Third Time in Two Months," *Bakersfield Californian*, August 31, 1921, 6.

"Arrests Are Made by Bakersfield Police," *Bakersfield Californian*, December 28, 1921, 4.

"Arrests Are Made Under 'Dry Act'," *Bakersfield Californian*, December 25, 1920, 2.

"Ask Injunction To Stop Prohibition Enforcement," *Bakersfield Californian*, January 8, 1920, 1.

"Ask Warehouses for Storage of Liquor," *Bakersfield Californian*, February 19, 1920, 7.

"Asks People Avoid Curse Of Excesses," *Bakersfield Californian*, December 6, 1933, 1.

"Award Schedule For Snooping In Rum Cases Given By "Dry" Agents," *Bakersfield Californian* July 14, 1928, 7.

"Bakers Must Observe Rules For Using Flour," *Bakersfield Californian*, February 22, 1918, 1.

""Bakersfield Beer" In March Predicted," *Bakersfield Californian*, September 29, 1933, 13.

Bakersfield City Directory, 1911 (San Francisco: The Polk-Husted Directory Co., 1911).

Bakersfield City Directory, 1919 (San Francisco: The Polk-Husted Directory Co., 1919).

Bakersfield City Directory, 1920 (San Francisco: The Polk-Husted Directory Co., 1920).

"Bakersfield Is Voting Wet in National Poll by Publication," *Bakersfield Californian*, April 5, 1930, 11.

"Bakersfield Kern Vote 3 To 1 Repeal Of Prohibition Law," *Bakersfield Californian*, June 28, 1933, 1, 9.

"Bakersfield Lands W.C.T.U. State Convention," *Bakersfield Californian*, March 23, 1918, 4.

"Bakersfield Liquor Law Repealed," *Bakersfield Californian*, November 29, 1932, 1.

"Bakersfield Mayor Has Fist Fight With Chief," *The Los Angeles Times*, February 10, 1933, 7.

"Bakersfield Still Wet in Digest Poll," *Bakersfield Californian*, May 20, 1930, 11.

"Bakersfield "Vice Squad" Abolished by Chief Webster," *Bakersfield Californian*, February 17, 1932, 9.

"Bakersfield Virtue Spasm," *Los Angeles Times*, July 15, 1911, sec. J15.

"Bakersfield Votes 5 To 1 Against Dry Law," *Bakersfield Californian*, March 31, 1932, 13.

"Bakersfield Votes Wet By Majority of 1,134," *Bakersfield Californian*, November 1, 1911, 1.

"Bakersfield's Regeneration," *Los Angeles Times*, March 29, 1906, sec. J7.

"Bar German Study From Schools Of Kern County," *Bakersfield Californian*, April 11, 1918, 1.

"Barbeque-Picnic To Welcome "3.2 Beer"," *Bakersfield Californian*, April 3, 1933, 7.

"Bars Are Ordered To Close When Troops Arrive," *Bakersfield Californian*, October 4, 1917, 6.

"Bartenders Aid Shelter Fund," *Bakersfield Californian*, January 9, 1918, 1.

"Bartenders Entertain at Informal Dance," *Bakersfield Californian*, January 29, 1918, 6.

"Beer And Wine Bills Are Approved," *Bakersfield Californian*, December 15, 1932, 1.

"Beer Ballot Is Reported Heavy, Taft," *Bakersfield Californian*, April 28, 1933, 11.

"Beer Bill To Be Effective April 4," *Bakersfield Californian*, March 17, 1933, 1-2.

"Beer-By-Christmas Act Blocked," *Bakersfield Californian*, December 23, 1932, 1.

"Beer Judging Will Be West Side Event," *Bakersfield Californian*, April 21, 1933, 9.

"Beer Law Asked By Delano Group," *Bakersfield Californian*, April 6, 1933, 6.

"Beer Ordinance At Taft Is Rescinded," *Bakersfield Californian*, June 29, 1933, 9.

"Beer Trucks Race To City," *Bakersfield Californian*, April 7, 1933, 13.

"Beer Truck Hits Auto; Passenger Killed Instantly," *Bakersfield Californian*, April 18, 1933, 7.

Behr, Edward. *Prohibition: Thirteen Years That Changed America*. New York: Arcade Publishing, 2011.

"Big Force To Be Used To Guard Liquor," *Bakersfield Californian*, January 15, 1920, 2.

"Big Kern Booze Mystery," *Bakersfield Californian*, July 25, 1821, 1.

"Big Moonshine Plant Is Found," *Bakersfield Californian*, August 24, 1921, 4.

"Big Shipments of Liquor On Way," *Bakersfield Californian*, January 7, 1920, 1.

"Bill to Legalize Beer, Wine, Would Aid War Veterans," *Bakersfield Californian*, November 2, 1921, 2.

"Board of Strategy Formed by "Drys" of Bakersfield," *Bakersfield Californian*, August 23, 1932, 9.

Boole, Ella A. *Give Prohibition Its Chance*. Evanston: National Women's Temperance Union Publishing House, 1929.

"Both Sides Claim Victory At Close Of Long Campaign,"

Bakersfield Californian, October 28, 1911, 1.

Boyd, William Harland. *Lower Kern River Country 1850-1950: Wilderness To Empire*. Bakersfield, CA: Kern County Historical Society, Inc., 1997.

"Brewery Site Is Chosen; Plan To Begin Work Soon," *Bakersfield Californian*, October 30, 1933, 9.

Brown, L. Ames. "Prohibition," *The North American Review* 202, no. 720 (November 1915): 702-729.

Brucker, Herbert. "How Long, O Prohibition," *The North American Review* 234, no. 4 (October 1932): 347-357.

Brunk, Gregory G. "Freshmen vs. Incumbents: Congressional Voting Patterns on Prohibition Legislation during the Progressive Era," *Journal of American Studies* 24, no. 2 (August 1990): 235-242.

Burnham, J.C. "New Perspectives on the Prohibition "Experiment" of the 1920s," *Journal of Social History* 2, no. 1 (Autumn 1968): 51-68.

"Business Men Protest Against Prohibition," *Bakersfield Californian*, October 21, 1911, 1.

"CA Wine Men To Intervene in R.I.," *Bakersfield Californian*, January 9, 1920, 5.

"California Assembly On Record For Wine, Beer," *Bakersfield Californian*, March 19, 1921, 1.

"California Formally Votes Dry Repeal," *Bakersfield Californian*, July 24, 1933, 1.

"California To Caucus On Rum," *Bakersfield Californian*, June 15, 1932, 1.

"California Vintners Not To Make Wine," *Bakersfield Californian*, March 23, 1933, 2.

"Californian To Ballot On 11 Proposals," *Bakersfield Californian*, June 26, 1933, 1, 13.

"Californians Desert G.O.P.," *Bakersfield Californian*, November 9, 1932, 1-2.

"Call Read For Local Option Convention," *Bakersfield Californian*,

May 8, 1911, 1.

"Calls Upon Congress To Arrange For Referendum," *Bakersfield Californian*, September 24, 1931, 1-2.

"Can Horse Drink Champagne Under New Amendment," *Bakersfield Californian*, April 1, 1920, 1.

"'Canned Heat' Is Latest Beverage With 'Kick' Here," *Bakersfield California*, December 19, 1921, 6.

"Carlock And Webster In Battle Following Discussion On Liquor," *Bakersfield Californian*, February 9, 1933, 11.

Carter, Paul A. "Prohibition and Democracy: The Noble Experiment Reassessed," *The Wisconsin Magazine of History* 56, no. 3 (Spring 1973): 189-201.

Cartoon, "The Great American Home," *Bakersfield Californian*, February 16, 1921, 4.

"Case Involving Police Officers Of Bakersfield Is Under Probe," *Bakersfield Californian*, April 24, 1930, 11.

"Cellar Door Is Jimmied; Treasure in Liquid Stolen," *Bakersfield Californian*, November 3, 1920, 5.

"Chairman Jastro Takes Stand Against Local Option Petition," *Bakersfield Californian*, July 14, 1908, 1.

"Charge Perjury Against H. Lord," *Bakersfield Californian*, December 5, 1921, 6.

"Chief of Police Requests New Ordinance To Assist Municipal Enforcement of Prohibition," *Bakersfield Californian*, September 8, 1920, Part 2, 1.

"Citizens Would Aid Grape Men," *Bakersfield Californian*, March 25, 1933, 7.

"City, County Given Power to Regulate," *Bakersfield Californian*, April 24, 1933, 1.

"City Liquor Law Repeal Is Effective Today," *Bakersfield Californian*, December 28, 1932, 7.

"City Manager Succumbs At His Desk In Heat Spell," *Bakersfield Californian*, May 29, 1929, 1.

"City of L.A. To Aid In Kern Case," *Bakersfield Californian*, January

4, 1921, 8.

"City Prohibition Act For Bakersfield Passes Council," *Bakersfield Californian*, September 14, 1920, 7.

"Claim Federal Court Has No Jurisdiction In Liquor Case," *Bakersfield Californian*, January 6, 1921, 1.

"Claim Find Liquor in Meat Market," *Bakersfield Californian*, June 14, 1921, 9.

"Claim Man Was 'Walking Bar;' Is Caught By Police," *Bakersfield Californian*, January 4, 1921, 8.

"Clogged Sewer Is Clue to Location of Illegal Still," *Bakersfield Californian*, January 11, 1921, 6.

"Close Bars, Serve Beer Sans Meals Brewers' Plan," *Bakersfield Californian*, February 9, 1918, 9.

"Collier's Beer Bill Is Scored," *Bakersfield Californian*, January 7, 1933, 1-2.

"Colorado Going After Wine and Beer," *Bakersfield Californian*, April 29, 1920, 2.

"Colored Voters Express Opposition To Prohibition," *Bakersfield Californian*, October 26, 1911, 4.

"Come Rain, Rum Or Repeal, Taft "Dry"," *Bakersfield Californian*, December 21, 1932, 9.

"Committee Rejects Wine Bill," *Bakersfield Californian*, December 16, 1932, 1-2.

"Complete Kern Vote," *Bakersfield Californian*, September 1, 1932, 1.

"Confiscate Coupe In 'Booze' Raid," *Bakersfield Californian*, October 18, 1921, 2.

"Congress Candidate Favors Beer, Wines," *Bakersfield Californian*, July 11, 1932, 9.

"Congress To Vote On Prohibition," *Bakersfield Californian* December 2, 1931, 1.

"Congress Votes Dry-Act Repeal," *Bakersfield Californian*, February 20, 1933, 1.

"Consider Sites For Beer Plant," *Bakersfield Californian*, October 2,

1933, 7.

"Convict Three Kern Men, Liquor Charges," *Bakersfield Californian*, April 22, 1932, 13.

"Council Cites Two Saloon Men To Appear Monday," *Bakersfield Californian*, April 2, 1918, 6.

"Council Considers Repeal of Bakersfield Liquor Ordinance," *Bakersfield Californian*, November 9, 1932, 9, 13.

"Council Declines To Raise Saloon License Charge," *Bakersfield Californian*, February 26, 1918, 6.

"Council Fails To Repeal City Liquor Law," *Bakersfield Californian*, November 22, 1932, 9, 13.

"Council Names Commission To Consider Issue," *Bakersfield Californian*, February 15, 1933, 9.

"County Officials In Open Revolt Against Revenue Men Trying To Enforce Dry Law," *Bakersfield Californian*, February 23, 1920, 1.

"Crites Gives Stand On Liquor Question," *Bakersfield Californian*, July 20, 1932, 9.

"Cullen Bill Is Made Law By President," *Bakersfield Californian*, March 22, 1933, 1-2.

"Daily Comment By Will Rogers," *Bakersfield Californian*, December 6, 1933, 1.

"Dance Halls, Liquor Trade Hit By Grand Jury Report," *Bakersfield Californian*, May 29, 1928, 1, 7.

"Dealers Asked To Observe Food Rules," *Bakersfield Californian*, January 4, 1918, 8.

"Defense In Shannon Trial Dealt Blow," *Bakersfield Californian*, October 8, 1930, 9, 21.

"Democrats Win 472 Votes In Electoral College; Hoover, 59," *Bakersfield Californian*, November 9, 1932, 1.

"Display Beer Mugs at Redlick's Store," *Bakersfield Californian*, April 7, 1933, 13.

"Distilled Spirits May Be Imported Is Ruling," *Bakersfield Californian*, October 22, 1917, 5.

"Distillers Also File Brief on Dry Act," *Bakersfield Californian*, March 6, 1920, 1.

"Distributors Of Beer Form Unit," *Bakersfield Californian*, August 30, 1933, 9.

"Drink Book Gets Official Kibosh," *Bakersfield Californian*, April 16, 1920, 5.

"'Drive Nails In Saloon Coffin,'" *Bakersfield Californian*, October 19, 1911, 3.

"Dry-Act Convention May Be Postponed," *Bakersfield Californian*, July 12, 1933, 1.

"Dry Agents Find Up-To-Date Still," *Bakersfield Californian*, October 8, 1920, 8.

"Dry Agents' Cars Must Bear Metal Shields 17 by 20," *Bakersfield Californian*, August 20, 1930, 1.

"Dry Amendment Repeal Approved," *Bakersfield Californian*, January 9, 1933, 1-2.

"Dry Law Test Fight at End To Drop Crookshank Appeal," *Bakersfield Californian*, August 4, 1921, 7.

"Dry Law Unjust, Claims Emmons," *Bakersfield Californian*, June 30, 1927, 9.

"Dry Petition Filed With Clerk," *Bakersfield Californian*, August 23, 1911, 1.

"Dry Raiders Seize Beer," *Los Angeles Times*, September 5, 1928, 8.

"Dry Squad Raid In Taft Echoes As Man Claims $5000 Damages," *Bakersfield Californian*, January 3, 1928, 9.

"Dry States Are Assured Protection," *Bakersfield Californian*, February 16, 1933, 1.

"Dry To Have Street Meetings," *Bakersfield Californian*, October 26, 1911, 2.

"'Dry' Ordinance Is Passed By County," *Bakersfield Californian*, November 17, 1920, 1.

"Dry's Stand May Hinder Convention," *Bakersfield Californian*, July 13, 1933, 1-2.

"Drys Fail To Block Early Repeal Vote," *Bakersfield Californian*,

May 29, 1933, 3.

"Drys Hold Good Meeting," *Bakersfield Californian*, September 18, 1911, 1.

"Drys Lose in City by 1158 Majority," *Bakersfield Morning Echo*, November 1, 1911, 1.

"Drys May Appeal To U.S. Supreme Court," *Bakersfield Californian*, May 30, 1933, 1.

"Drys Move to Block State Vote on Repeal," *Bakersfield Californian*, May 27, 1933, 2.

"East Side 'Blind Pigs' Are Raided," *Bakersfield Californian*, November 18, 1920, 6.

"Editorial: Our Neighbors," *Bakersfield Californian*, March 28, 1906, 2.

"Election Auto Runs Down Woman," *Bakersfield Californian*, October 31, 1911, 1.

"El Tejon Liquors Company," *Bakersfield Californian*, December 6, 1933, 8.

"Enforcement of Dry Law At Present Is Failure," *Bakersfield Californian*, October 18, 1927, 1.

"Ex-Bakersfield Man Seized As German Spy In Tucson," *Bakersfield Californian*, January 14, 1918, 1.

"Extent Of The Majority A Surprise," *Bakersfield Californian*, November 1, 1911, 1.

"Famous Prohibition Authority Coming," *Bakersfield Californian*, October 9, 1933, 9.

"Farmers Want Kern Saloons Closed," *Bakersfield Californian*, April 27, 1918, 1.

"Fast Cars Will Transport Kern Stock Of Liquor," *Bakersfield Californian*, December 5, 1933, 9.

"Federal Agents Are Transferred," *Bakersfield Californian*, January 20, 1930, 9.

"Federal Agents Take Cheer Out Of Yuletide In Taft Rum World," *Bakersfield Californian*, December 22, 1928, 9.

"Federal Agents To Ignore Home Brewers Unless Sale Is Proven,"

Bakersfield Californian, August 20, 1930, 9.

"Federal Judge Raps Prohibition Policy," *Bakersfield Californian*, September 24, 1927, 2.

"Federal Padlock Is Put on Local Place," *Bakersfield Californian*, December 6, 1928, 11.

"Find New Method in Liquor Case," *Bakersfield Californian*, July 15, 1921, 4.

"Five Arrested On Dry Law Charges," *Bakersfield Californian*, September 9, 1924, 9.

"Fleischman Yeast Firm Fined $3000," *Bakersfield Californian*, September 18, 1931, 2.

"Food Pledge Card Total To Date Is 5,300," *Bakersfield Californian*, November 3, 1917, 1.

"Formed A Law And Order League," *Bakersfield Californian*, March 28, 1906, 3.

"Former Federal Officer Witness Against Shannon," *Bakersfield Californian*, October 7, 1930, 9, 15.

Garbutt, Mary Alderman. *Victories of Four Decades: A History of the Women's Christian Temperance Union of Southern California, 1883-1924*. Women's Christian Temperance Union, 1924.

Gebhart, John C. "Movement Against Prohibition," *Annals of the American Academy of Political and Social Science* 163 (September 1932): 172-180.

"German Arrested For Failure To Register," *Bakersfield Californian*, February 21, 1918, 6.

"German Intrigue Is Suspected In Placards," *Bakersfield Californian*, January 3, 1918, 7.

"Giant Drug And Liquor Smuggling Ring Bared," *Bakersfield Californian*, January 13, 1922, 1.

"G.O.P. Prohibition Plank," *Bakersfield Californian*, June 16, 1932, 1.

"G.O.P. Straddles Prohibition," *Bakersfield Californian*, June 15, 1932, 1.

"Gov. Edwards of N.Y. Is Fighting Prohibition Act Along Two Lines," *Bakersfield Californian*, February 14, 1920, 5.

"Gov. Rolph Also May Give Pardon to Many Jones-Law Violators," *Bakersfield Californian*, November 19, 1932, 10.

"Gov. Rolph Approves Beer Regulation Act," *Bakersfield Californian*, April 28, 1933, 1.

"Government Will End Case Today Against Shannon," *Bakersfield Californian*, October 9, 1930, 9, 21.

"Grand Jury Files Its Report and Adjourns," *Bakersfield Californian*, April 24, 1918, 7.

"Grand Jury Would Close Bars July 1st," *Bakersfield Californian*, February 10, 1918, 1.

"Grape Growers Of County Join Fight For Wine," *Bakersfield Californian*, December 28, 1932, 7.

"Grape Growers To Battle For Light Wine Measure," *Bakersfield Californian*, March 22, 1933, 7.

"Grape Growers to Seek New Markets; Stop 'Dry' Battle," *Bakersfield Californian*, February 24, 1920, 2.

"Grape Juice Sales Hurt by Near-Beer," *Bakersfield Californian*, May 27, 1921, 1.

"Great Increase In Production Aim Of Farm Bureau," *Bakersfield Californian*, January 1, 1918, 1.

"Greater Bakersfield's Vote May Exceed 3000," *Bakersfield Californian*, October 31, 1911, 1.

"Guns Trained On Saloons," *Los Angeles Times*, February 12, 1910, sec. JJ10.

Gusfield, Joseph R. "Social Structure and Moral Reform: A Study of the Woman's Christian Temperance Union," *The American Journal of Sociology* 61, no. 3 (1955): 221-232.

---. *Symbolic Crusade: Status Politics and the American Temperance Movement*. Urbana: University of Illinois Press, 1963.

"Hanning, Williams Open Liquor Store," *Bakersfield Californian*, December 5, 1933, 9.

"Hard-Headed but Thirsty Burglars Rob Local Home," *Bakersfield Californian*, March 25, 1920, 8.

"Haystacks And Setting Hens Cover Brandy Still," *Bakersfield*

Californian, March 15, 1921, 1.

"Historical Census of Housing Data," U.S. Department of
Congress, United States Census Bureau. Accessed June 3,
2013,
http://www.census.gov/hhes/www/housing/census/historic/
owner.html

"History of the Anti-Saloon League." Accessed January 26, 2013,
http://www.wpl.lib.oh.us/AntiSaloon/history/

"History of the Bakersfield Police Department." 2001. Accessed
October 18, 2006.
http://www.bakersfieldcity.us/police/Chiefs/index.htm.
The link is no longer active and the Bakersfield Police
Department no longer has this information listed on their
website.

"History: Woodmen of the World's Storied History." Accessed
January 26, 2013,
http://www.woodmen.org/about/history.cfm

"Holds Fate Of War-Time Beer," *Los Angeles Times*, August 5,
1919, I11.

"Home-Brewers Cause Shortage Of Grapes," *Bakersfield Californian*,
November 17, 1921, 10.

"Home Brewers Safe, U.S. Official States," *Bakersfield Californian*,
October 30, 1930, 2.

"Hope To Bring Back Light Wines And Beer," *Bakersfield Californian*,
August 26, 1921, 4.

"Hope to Prevent Vineyardists' Loss," *Bakersfield Californian*,
January 24, 1920, 4.

"House Defeats 2.75 Beer Bill," *Bakersfield Californian*, May 23,
1932, 1.

"House Passes Beer Bill, 316-97," *Bakersfield Californian*, March 14,
1933, 1.

"House Passes 'Dry' Measure 282 To 128," *Bakersfield Californian*,
December 17, 1917, 1.

"How Explain It," Editorial, *Bakersfield Californian*, March 10, 1920,

1.

"Hundred Women Register Today With Clerk," *Bakersfield Californian*, October 16, 1911, 1.

"Index of Registration: Kern County, 1912," *Great Register of Vote, 1900-1944* (Sacramento: California State Library, 1986).

"Italians Fined $250 Each Under Ordinance," *Bakersfield Californian*, October 21, 1920, 6.

"Jackson Mahon Files Papers; Urges Repeal of Prohibition Laws," *Bakersfield Californian*, June 4, 1932, 7.

"Jones Law Penalty Reduced By Senate," *Bakersfield Californian*, July 2, 1930, 1.

"Judge Rules Law Cannot Be Applied In California Case," *Bakersfield Californian*, March 25, 1929, 1.

"Judge Will Rule In Suit Against Federal Agents," *Bakersfield Californian*, January 4, 1928, 9.

"Jury Disagrees in 'Moonshine' Trial," *Bakersfield Californian*, April 23, 1921, 8.

"Just What Wright Law Means To California," *Los Angeles Times*, December 10, 1922, II1.

"Kansas, N. Carolina Only "Dry" States in Literary Digest Poll," *Bakersfield Californian*, April 15, 1932, 2, 8.

Kennedy, David M. *Over Here: The First World War and American Society*. Oxford: Oxford University Press, 1980.

"Kern County Organizes To Fight Pro-Germans," *Los Angeles Times*, September 1, 1918, 14.

"Kern County Strategy Board Discusses 18th Amendment," *Bakersfield Californian*, November 2, 1932, 3.

"Kern Too "Hot" for Racketeers Is Word Spread Over Gangland," *Bakersfield Californian*, August 3, 1929, 9.

"Kern Vintner Is State Director," *Bakersfield Californian*, September 7, 1933, 11.

Kerr, K. Austin. "Organizing for Reform: The Anti-Saloon League and Innovation in Politics," *American Quarterly* 32, no. 1 (1980): 37-53.

"'Kick' Is Reason For Big Planting," *Bakersfield Californian*, April 5, 1921, 7.

Kyvig, David E. "Women Against Prohibition," *American Quarterly* 28, no. 4 (1976): 465-482.

"Large Amount Of Wine Is Seized," *Bakersfield Californian*, October 23, 1920, 6.

"Last Chance to Move Liquor Supply," *Bakersfield Californian*, January 15, 1920, 1.

"Late W.C.T.U. News Notes," *Bakersfield Californian*, January 17, 1931, 5.

"Late W.C.T.U. News Notes," *Bakersfield Californian*, November 19, 1932, 5.

"Late W.C.T.U. News Notes," *Bakersfield Californian*, September 25, 1933, 3.

"Late W.C.T.U. News Notes," *Bakersfield Californian*, October 23, 1933, 3.

"Late W.C.T.U. News Notes," *Bakersfield Californian*, October 30, 1933, 5.

"Legalization of Beer Advocated," *Bakersfield Californian*, January 20, 1932, 1.

"Legalize 2.75 Per Cent Beer in N.Y.," *Bakersfield Californian*, April 24, 1920, 1.

"Legislature Cannot Repeal Ratification," *Bakersfield Californian*, January 13, 1920, 2.

Lewis, Michael. "Access to Saloons, Wet Voter Turnout and Statewide Prohibition Referenda, 1907-1919," *Social Science History* 32, no. 3 (Fall 2008): 373-404.

Light, Ivan, "The Ethnic Vice Industry, 1880-1944," *American Sociological Review* 42, no. 3 (1977): 464-479.

"Light Wine And Beer Squad Here," *Bakersfield Californian*, August 19, 1921, 4.

"Light Wines, Beer Permit Sought Here," *Bakersfield Californian*, July 12, 1932, 9.

"Liquor And Cigars Being Listed For Taxes Here," *Bakersfield*

Californian, October 5, 1917, 1.

"Liquor Elections Planned On West Side," *Bakersfield Californian*, February 2, 1918, 7.

"Liquor Interests to Renew Battle Against Dry Act," *Bakersfield Californian*, January 6, 1920, 1.

"Liquor License Forms Delayed," *Bakersfield Californian*, November 28, 1933, 9.

"Liquor Licenses May Be Applied for on Monday," *Bakersfield Californian*, November 23, 1933, 13.

"Local Option Measure Under Fire In Battle To Legalize 3.2 Beer," *Bakersfield Californian*, April 27, 1933, 11.

"Liquor License Forms Delayed," *Bakersfield Californian*, November 28, 1933, 9.

"Liquor Licenses May Be Applied for on Monday," *Bakersfield Californian*, November 23, 1933, 13.

"Liquor Manufacture Held Legal," *Bakersfield Californian*, March 9, 1921, 1.

"Liquor Raids Jail Many," *Los Angeles Times*, August 1, 1931, A5.

"Liquor Worth Million Sent Into Mexico," *Bakersfield Californian*, January 14, 1920, 4.

"Local Liquor Ordinance Is Sustained By State Court," *Bakersfield Californian*, November 9, 1926, 1

"Local Lodge, Wet Ass'n, Gives $100 To Shelter," *Bakersfield Californian*, January 10, 1918, 1.

"Local Option Bill Goes To Governor," *Bakersfield Californian*, March 16, 1911, 1.

"Local Option Measure Under Fire In Battle To Legalize 3.2 Beer," *Bakersfield Californian*, April 27, 1933, 11.

"Local Women Take Hand In Dry Fight," *Bakersfield Californian*, September 11, 1911, 1.

"Look In The Woodpile," Editorial, *Bakersfield Californian*, January 7, 1918, 6.

"Louis Lowe Committed To Folsom For Crime," *Bakersfield Californian*, May 6, 1925, 1, 9.

"M. Plantier Fined $150 in Los Angeles," *Bakersfield Californian*, January 15, 1920, 8.

Macnaghten, Russell. "Local Option and After," *The North American Review* 190, no. 648 (November 1909): 628-641.

"Mahon Attacks U.S. Dry Laws," *Bakersfield Californian*, June 8, 1932, 9.

"Man Arrested Here Under Espionage Law Clause," *Bakersfield Californian*, December 5, 1917, 1.

"Man Held As Agent Of Germany At Visalia," *Bakersfield Californian*, January 12, 1918, 2.

"Many Cities Of Valley Closed To Beer Sales," *Bakersfield Californian*, March 20, 1933, 7.

"Many Local Names on Dry Referendum," *Bakersfield Californian*, March 19, 1930, 11.

"Many Problems Follow Repeal," *Bakersfield Californian*, November 8, 1933, 2.

Martin, Michael and Leonard Gelber, *Dictionary of American History*. Philosophical Library, Inc., 1978.

"Material Sought For Rum Agents," *Bakersfield Californian*, July 28, 1928, 9.

"May Ask Congress to Amend Dry Act to Allow Wine, Beer," *Bakersfield Californian*, January 5, 1921, 1.

"Mayor, Judge and Department Head in Shannon Case," *Bakersfield Californian*, October 10, 1930, 13.

Meers, John R. "The California Wine and Grape Industry and Prohibition," *California Historical Society Quarterly* 46, no. 1 (March 1967): 19-32.

"Meetings By The Wets and Drys," *Bakersfield Californian*, October 21, 1911, 1.

"Merchants Did Not Sign 'Dry' Petition," *Bakersfield Californian*, September 2, 1911, 6.

"Method To Get Liquor For Use As Medicine Is Told By Bureau," *Bakersfield Californian*, January 30, 1920, 4.

"Minister Opposed To Prohibition," *Bakersfield Californian*,

October 25, 1911, 2.

"Minors Must Keep Out of Saloons," *Bakersfield Californian*, August 11, 1911, 2.

Miron, Jeffrey A. and Jeffrey Zwiebel, "Alcohol Consumption During Prohibition," *The American Economic Review* 81, no. 2 (May 1991): 242-247.

Mitchell, H.H. "Prohibition and the Straw Ballot," *The Scientific Monthly* 35, no. 5 (November 1932): 443-448.

"Modification of Volstead Act Sought," *Bakersfield Californian*, May 21, 1920, 1.

"Mojave Saloonman Has Hearing On Serious Charge," *Bakersfield Californian*, January 8, 1918, 6.

"Moonshining And Pressure Mining Acts Also Passed," *Bakersfield Californian*, March 29, 1927, 1-2.

"More Arrests For Dry Act Violation," *Bakersfield Californian*, February 8, 1921, 8.

"More Votes For Wet And Dry," *Bakersfield Californian*, November 2, 1911, 1.

"Mothers-Parent-Teachers Elect," *Los Angeles Times*, May 26, 1917, 14.

"Mrs. Sadacchi Is Acquitted Today," *Bakersfield Californian*, May 28, 1921, 8.

Munger, Michael and Thomas Schaller, "The Prohibition-Repeal Amendments: A Natural Experiment in Interest Group Influence," *Public Choice* 90, no. ¼ (March 1997): 139-163.

Murphy, Mary. "Bootlegging Mothers and Drinking Daughters: Gender and Prohibition in Butte, Montana," *American Quarterly* 46, no. 2 (June 1994): 174-194.

"Must Report Cellar Stock 10 Days From January 17," *Bakersfield Californian*, January 1, 1920, 1.

"New German Spy System Broken Up," *Bakersfield Californian*, January 10, 1918, 1.

"New Grape Drink Due," *Los Angeles Times*, March 11, 1931, 12.

"New Licenses May Be Revoked At Any Time," *Bakersfield*

Californian, January 9, 1918, 6.

"New Meatless And Wheatless Days Decreed," *Bakersfield Californian*, January 22, 1918, 1.

"New President Emphasizes Necessity for Law Enforcement," *Bakersfield Californian*, March 4, 1929, 6.

"New Ruling On Sale of Wine Found By Seizure," *Bakersfield Californian*, January 7, 1920, 1.

"New 'Rum Route' Is One Long Lane That Has No Turning; Is Much Patronized Highway," *Bakersfield Californian*, March 13, 1920, 9.

"New State Dry Chief Prepares For Action," *Bakersfield Californian*, June 29, 1921, 6.

"New Taft Beer Statute Passed," *Bakersfield Californian*, June 21, 1933, 7.

"New York Cuts Hid Illicit Booze," *Bakersfield Californian*, January 27, 1922, 9.

"Newspaper Archive," accessed February 7, 2013, http://access.newspaperarchive.com.ezproxy.lapl.org/.

Nicholson, S.E. "The Local-Option Movement," *Annals of the American Academy of Political and Social Science* 32, Regulation of the Liquor Traffic (November 1908): 471-475.

"No Liquor From One To Six Is Ordinance," *Bakersfield Californian*, October 3, 1911, 4.

"No Near-Beer to Be Allowed at Veterans' Banquet," *Bakersfield Californian*, August 12, 1921, 4.

"Now Faces Quartet Of Dry Law Charges," *Bakersfield Californian*, January 10, 1922, 7.

"Petition For 'Dry' Election Filed Today," *Bakersfield Californian*, August 29, 1911, 1.

"Officers Discover 'Moonshiners' On East Side," *Bakersfield Californian*, January 8, 1920, 8.

"Officers in Plain Clothes Arrest Pair," *Bakersfield Californian*, November 24, 1921, 2.

"Official Urges Repeal of Taft Anti-Beer Rule,"

Bakersfield Californian, April 5, 1933, 9.

"Ogden Requests Emergency Bill Creating Fund To
    Aid Crusades," *Bakersfield Californian*, May 14, 1929, 11.

"Ohio, Pennsylvania, Utah Ballot Wet," *Bakersfield Californian*,
    November 8, 1933, 1-2.

"Oil Worker Of Long Beach Is Held Prisoner Following Race,"
    Bakersfield Californian, July 15, 1929, 9.

Okrent, Daniel. *Last Call. The Rise and Fall of Prohibition*. New York:
    Scribner, 2010.

"Only One Prohibition Vote To Be Granted," *Bakersfield Californian*,
    December 30, 1931, 3.

"Option Law Of West Side City Is Voted Down," *Bakersfield
    Californian*, April 29, 1933, 7.

"Organize Forces to Clasp Screws to Bone-Dry Lid," *Bakersfield
    Californian*, January 3, 1920, 1.

"Organized Labor Enters Fight To Nullify Part Of Prohibition
    Act," *Bakersfield Californian*, July 8, 1931, 11.

Ostrander Gilman Marston. *The Prohibition Movement in California,
    1848-1933*. Berkeley: University of California Press, 1957.

"Out of Dry Territory in One Short Jump," *Bakersfield Californian*,
    December 21, 1920, 5.

"Owner of Still Admits Felony, Gets Probation," *Bakersfield
    Californian*, October 5, 1927, 9.

"Owner of Still Is Sentenced To Penitentiary By Judge Lambert
    Bakersfield Californian, February 23, 1928, 9.

"'Ownerless' Still at Jail; Operator Still Out of Jail," *Bakersfield
    Californian*, January 3, 1921, 8.

Padgett, John F. "Plea Bargaining and Prohibition in the Federal
    Courts, 1908-1934," *Law & Society Review* 24, no. 2,
    Longitudinal Studies of Trial Courts (1990): 413-450.

Paquette, Mary Grace. *Basques to Bakersfield*. Bakersfield: Kern
    County Historical Society, 1982.

---. *Lest We Forget: The History of the French in Kern County*. Fresno:
    Pioneer Publishing Company, 1978.

""Patterson Sought on Accusation of Disabled Veteran," *Bakersfield Californian*, February 25, 1931, 9.

"Patterson Wins Federal Trial on Charge of Slugging Disabled Man," *Bakersfield Californian*, February 28, 1931, 9.

"Peace Conference in Liquor Rebellion," *Bakersfield Californian*, February 27, 1920, 2.

"Petitions Started For Dry Referendum," *Bakersfield Californian*, March 15, 1930, 9.

"Petitions Started On Rominger Bill," *Bakersfield Californian*, October 8, 1917, 7.

"Petitions To Annul State Dry Act Filed With Jordan," *Bakersfield Californian*, April 9, 1932, 1.

"Pilsner Beer Advertisement," *Bakersfield Californian*, June 17, 1933, 2.

"Pint of Whisky Every Ten Days Is Law's Limit," *Bakersfield Californian*, January 29, 1920, 1.

"Police Raid N.Y. Café; Seize Booze," *Bakersfield Californian*, April 7, 1920, Part 2, 2.

"Pollock Avers Dry Act Leading U.S. To Slavery, Narcotics, Ultimate Disaster," *Bakersfield Californian*, September 17, 1927, 1.

"Polston Freed On Moonshine Charge," *Bakersfield Californian*, 15 October 15, 1921, 9.

"Poor Bootlegger Pays $995 Fine And Gets Freedom," *Bakersfield Californian*, December 15, 1924, 9.

"Potato Peeling Booze Cause Of Trouble At Camp," *Bakersfield Californian*, July 9, 1925, 9.

"Practicable Test Of 3.2 PCT. Beer Urged," *Bakersfield Californian*, December 31, 1932, 2.

"President In Favor Of Changes In Law To Give Control Of Liquors To States," *Bakersfield Californian*, August 12, 1932, 12.

"Prisoner Taxed on Liquor Used for Evidence in Case," *Bakersfield Californian*, June 30, 1921, 7.

"Prisoners Under Wright Act Are To Be
Released," *Bakersfield Californian*, November 17, 1932, 9.

"Probation Granted In Bribe Case," *Los Angeles Times*, February 28,
1924, A8.

"Process Of Making Dry-Law Change Under G.O.P. Platform Is
Explained," *Bakersfield Californian*, June 17, 1932, 2.

"Pro-German Forced To Kiss U.S. Flag," *Bakersfield Californian*,
December 4, 1917, 6.

"Prohi Officials Padlock Alleged Rum Dispensary," *Bakersfield
Californian*, March 15, 1930, 9.

"Prohibition Act Violates States Rights Claim Of R.I.," *Bakersfield
Californian*, March 1, 1920, 2.

"Prohibition A Thing Of The Past," *Bakersfield Californian*,
December 5, 1933, 14.

"Prompt Vote Demanded By Two Parties," *Bakersfield Californian*,
November 26, 1932, 1-2.

"Prohibition Controversy In Michigan Still Heated," *Bakersfield
Californian*, February 25, 1920, 2.

"Prohibition Failure, Says Boy-Scout Man," *Bakersfield Californian*,
February 20, 1920, 1.

"Prohibition Party Asks Nation Wide Temperance For Duration
Of War," *Bakersfield Californian*, March 5, 1918, 2.

"Prohibition Party Is Defeated At Convention," *Bakersfield
Californian*, February 6, 1918, 9.

"Prohibition Sleuth Slain by L. Lowe," *Bakersfield Californian*,
December 19, 1924, 1.

"Prohibition to Cost U.S. Huge Amount Annually," *Bakersfield
Californian*, May 4, 1920, 1.

"Public Hostile To Liquor Laws," *Bakersfield Californian*, April 1,
1921, 7.

"Put Limit On Highway Fund," *Los Angeles Times*, March 22, 1919,
13.

"Raiders Unable to Locate Liquor; Dig With Good Results,"
Bakersfield Californian, January 25, 1921, 8.

"Railroad Has No Means To Drive Out Saloons," *Bakersfield Californian*, January 3, 1913, 8.

"Rally Of Drys On Sunday," *Bakersfield Californian*, October 9, 1911, 4.

"Record of Political Events," *Political Science Quarterly*, 34, no. 3, Supplemental (1919), 73-100.

"Reduces Alcohol Content Of Beer," *Bakersfield Californian*, March 16, 1933, 1.

"Registration In City Is 6348," *Bakersfield Californian*, October 24, 1911, 4.

"Registration Of German Aliens Next Monday," *Bakersfield Californian*, February 2, 1918, 6.

"Regulation For Selling Beer Is Topic For Meet," *Bakersfield Californian*, May 5, 1933, 11.

"Regulation VS. Prohibition," *Los Angeles Times*, October 20, 1911, sec. I13.

"Repeal Taken With Calmness," *Bakersfield Californian*, December 9, 1933, 12.

"Report From 145 Precincts At Hand," *Bakersfield Californian*, November 4, 1920, 1.

"Resolution For Repeal Introduced," *Bakersfield Californian*, May 24, 1932, 1-2.

"Restricted Sales To Be Enforced," *Bakersfield Californian*, January 21, 1918, 7.

"Restrictions On Drinking Few, Slight," *Bakersfield Californian*, December 2, 1933, 1, 11.

"Rev. Shaw Discusses Work Of Law An Order League," *Bakersfield Californian*, April 5, 1906, 3.

"Rigid Dry Enforcement Defeated," *Bakersfield Californian*, December 17, 1928, 1.

Rogers, Lindsay. "American Government and Politics," *The American Political Science Review* 14, no. 1 (1920), 74-92.

Rogers, Will. *Rogers-Isms: The Cowboy Philosopher on Prohibition.* Stillwater: Oklahoma State University Press, 1975.

"Rolph Frees 128 Liquor Violators," *Bakersfield Californian*, December 19, 1932, 1.

"Rolph Pardons 248 Prisoners," *Bakersfield Californian*, January 6, 1933, 6.

"Rominger Petitions For Signers Here," *Bakersfield Californian*, October 11, 1917, 3.

"Roosevelt Sees Dry-Act Change," *Bakersfield Californian*, June 8, 1932, 1.

"Roosevelt's Liquor Plan Reiterated," *Bakersfield Californian*, April 18, 1932, 2.

Rose, Kenneth D. "Wettest in the West: San Francisco & Prohibition in 1924," *California History* 65, no. 4 (December 1986): 284-295.

"Rum Informers Will Be "Tipped" by Government," *Bakersfield Californian*, July 13, 1928, 11.

"Rum Raid Stirs Gang War Fear," *Los Angeles Times*, July 14, 1932, 11.

"Sale Of Hops And Malt Is Banned," *Bakersfield Californian*, November 12, 1920, Part 2, 1.

"Saloon Closing As War Measure," *Bakersfield Californian*, February 13, 1918, 1.

"Saloonmen Before Council Get Coat Of Whitewash," *Bakersfield Californian*, April 9, 1918, 6.

"Saloons Are Charged by Defense Council," *Bakersfield Californian*, April 1, 1918, 6.

Sanchez, Tanya. "The Feminine Side of Bootlegging," *Louisiana History: The Journal of the Louisiana Historical Association* 41, no. 4 (Autumn 200): 403-433.

"Says Revolution Likely To Follow US Prohibition," *Bakersfield Californian*, January 9, 1920, 2.

Schrad, Mark Lawrence. "Constitutional Blemishes: American Alcohol Prohibition and Repeal as Policy Punctuation," *The Policy Studies Journal* 35, no. 3 (2007): 437-463.

"Seek Liquor Car Shipper," *Los Angeles Times*, December 20, 1925,

19.

"Senate Also Approves U.S. Dry Measure," *Bakersfield Californian*, December 18, 1917, 1.

"Senate Passes Beer Bill 43-36," *Bakersfield Californian*, March 20, 1933, 1.

"Senate Votes, 32-5, To Keep Wright Act *Bakersfield Californian*, May 5, 1931, 1.

"Set New La Selva Trial Tomorrow," *Bakersfield Californian*, October 19, 1921, 4.

"Set Date To Hear Beer Test Case," *Los Angeles Times*, July 26, 1919, I15.

"Shannon Acquitted On Conspiracy Count," *Bakersfield Californian*, October 13, 1930, 9, 15.

"Shannon Defense Witness Tells of Liquor Gift," *Bakersfield Californian*, October 10, 1930, 13.

"Shannon Denies Accusations Of Alleged Scheme Against Mathias," *Bakersfield Californian*, April 26, 1930, 11.

"Shannon Is Accused Of Attempt To "Frame" Dry," *Bakersfield Californian*, April 25, 1930, 1-2.

"Shannon's Fate Rests In Hands Of Jury," *Bakersfield Californian*, October 11, 1930, 9.

"Sid Shannon Arrested On Booze Count At Venice," *Bakersfield Californian*, January 31, 1922, 1.

"Sierra Beer Advertisement," *Bakersfield Californian*, June 19, 1933, 5.

Sinclair, Andrew. *Era of Excess: A Social History of the Prohibition Movement*. New York: Harper Colophon Books, 1964.

"Six Autos, Much Booze Seized At McKittrick," *Bakersfield Californian*, February 16, 1924, 1, 9.

"Sixty Saloons To Close At 1 Tonight," *Bakersfield Californian*, July 13, 1911, 1.

"Sleuths Instructed as to New Ruling," *Bakersfield Californian*, May 23, 1930, 2.

"Soldiers May Have Liquor In Homes," *Bakersfield Californian*,

February 20, 1918, 1.

"Special Officers Search City for Illicit Liquor," *Bakersfield California*, March 19, 1920, 1.

"State Acts To Regulate Beer," *Bakersfield Californian*, March 21, 1933, 1.

"State Assembly Votes 54-21 for Dry-Act Repeal," *Bakersfield California*, January 12, 1933, 1.

"State Submits Regulations On Beer Dispensing," *Bakersfield California*, May 8, 1933, 7.

"State Vote On Propositions," *Bakersfield Californian*, November 10, 1932, 2.

"Stiff Sentence For Dry-Law Violator," *Bakersfield Californian*, April 29, 1921, 8.

"Still Is Seized at Kern Street Home," *Bakersfield Californian*, February 13, 1922, 4.

"Study Of Liquor From Scientific Angle Is Slated," *Bakersfield California*, September 25, 1933, 9.

"Table 1: Real Average Weekly or Daily Earnings for Selected Occupations, 1920 to 1930," Accessed April 8, 2013, http://eh.net/encyclopedia/article/smiley.1920s.final

"Table III: Composition And Characteristics Of The Population, For Cities of 10,000 To 25,000: 1910," United States Census (1910), 182.

"Table 8: Population Of The United States, By Divisions," United States Census (1920), 20.

"Table 12: Area And Density," United States Census (1920), 25.

"Table No. 323: Distilled Spirits, Wines, and Malt Liquors: Quantities Consumed and Average Annual Consumption Per Capita in the United States, 1850 To 1920," United States Census (1920), 561.

"Taft Council Dooms All Hidden Kick in Liquor," *Bakersfield Californian*, March 7, 1928, 9.

"Taft Goes Dry; Maricopa, McKittrick Stay Wet," *Bakersfield*

Californian, April 9, 1918, 7.

"Taft Plans Special Election On Beer Issue," *Bakersfield Californian*, March 29, 1933, 9.

"Tariff Measure Scored By Kern Contestant For Congress Seat," *Bakersfield Californian*, June 14, 1932, 9.

"Temperance Speaker Has Praise for the Trustees' Cleaning Up Activities," *Bakersfield Californian*, July 24, 1911, 1.

"The Anti-Saloon Men Hold First Meeting," *Bakersfield Californian*, March 22, 1906, 3.

"'The Bootlegger' Without A Kick," *Bakersfield Californian*, April 22, 1920, 7.

"The Grape Men," Editorial, *Bakersfield Californian*, February 13, 1918, 2.

"The Remedy," Editorial, *Bakersfield Californian*, May 10, 1920, Part 2, 4.

"The Shadow Across the Land," *Bakersfield Californian*, April 6, 1921, 9.

"The Test of a Common Nuisance under the Volstead Act," *University of Pennsylvania Law Review and American Law Register* 72, no. 3 (March 1924): 289-293.

"Think! Wine Grapes Were $10; Now $40," *Bakersfield Californian*, March 1, 1920, Part 2, 1.

"Thirsty Hordes From States Cross Line To Revel In Cantu Land," *Bakersfield Californian*, March 29, 1920, 1.

"Those Who Sell Barrel, Label, Bottle, Liable," *Bakersfield Californian*, May 5, 1930, 2.

"Three Hundred Women Register," *Bakersfield Californian*, October 18, 1911, 1.

"Three Kern Men Are Exonerated On Still Charges By U.S. Jurist," *Bakersfield Californian*, April 26, 1932, 9.

"Three More Raids Made By Police," *Bakersfield Californian*, December 13, 1920, 2.

"To Make Syrup From Wine Grapes," *Bakersfield Californian*, February 28, 1920, 2.

"To Test 'Dry' Law On Beer," *Los Angeles Times*, July 10, 1919, I11.

Tomkins, Floyd W. "Prohibition," *Annals of the American Academy of Political and Social Science* 109, Prohibition and Its Enforcement (September 1923): 15-25.

Towle, Katherine A. "The Presidential Veto Since 1889," *The American Political Science Review* 31, no. 1 (1937), 51-56.

"Trial Starts Monday for Shannon, Others," *Bakersfield Californian*, October 2, 1930, 11.

"Trousers and Wine Taken by Thief," *Bakersfield Californian*, September 8, 1920, 1.

"Two Districts Are Dry And Three Wet," *Bakersfield Californian*, November 1, 1911, 1.

"Two More Stills Located in This City by Police," *Bakersfield Californian*, October 11, 1920, 8.

"Two Seek Right to Sell Wines, Beer in County," *Bakersfield Californian*, January 9, 1933, 9.

"Uncle Sam Is in Market for Liquor Sleuths," *Bakersfield Californian*, October 23, 1928, 9.

University of Virginia, "Historical Census Browser," accessed January 27, 2013, http://mapserver.lib.virginia.edu/.

"Urges Repeal Of 18th Amendment," *Bakersfield Californian*, January 18, 1932, 1.

"US Whiskey Moving Out Over Border," *Bakersfield Californian*, January 13, 1920, 1.

"U.S. Attorney to Defend Patterson; Civil Suit Filed," *Bakersfield Californian*, February 26, 1931, 13.

"U.S. Dry Agents Told Not to Molest "Speakeasies,"" *Bakersfield Californian*, March 8, 1933, 1.

"U.S. Prohibition Office in Bakersfield Closes Down," *Bakersfield Californian*, August 25, 1933, 11.

"Use of Bootleg Warned Against," *Bakersfield Californian*, January 7, 1920, 4.

"Utah Is 36th State To Ratify," *Bakersfield Californian*, December 5, 1933, 1.

"Validity of Charges Attacked by Officers," *Bakersfield Californian*, June 7, 1930, 9.

"Volstead-Act Change Asked Of Congress," *Bakersfield Californian*, March 13, 1933, 1, 10.

"Vote Is 272 To 144 Which Is 6 Short Of Two-Thirds Needed," *Bakersfield Californian*, December 5, 1932, 1.

"Wants Names Here To Put Rominger Bill On Ballot," *Bakersfield Californian*, November 19, 1917, 2.

"Wardell, Mahon Win Support Of Women Opposed To Liquor Laws," *Bakersfield Californian*, August 26, 1932, 9.

"Wardell Scores Costs Involved In Enforcement Of Liquor Laws," *Bakersfield Californian*, August 23, 1932, 9.

"Warns Gin Dispensers," *Los Angeles Times*, June 15, 1911, sec. J13.

Wasserman, Ira M. "Prohibition and Ethnocultural Conflict: The Missouri Prohibition Referendum of 1918," *Social Science Quarterly* 70, no. 4 (December 1989): 886-901.

"W.C.T.U. Now Aims To Buy Trench Kitchen," *Bakersfield Californian*, February 14, 1918, 2.

"W.C.T.U. Prepares For War Relief Drive Here," *Bakersfield Californian*, January 22, 1918, 2.

"W.C.T.U. Would Raise $2000 In The County For War Activity Fund," *Bakersfield Californian*, March 14, 1918, 5.

Weeks, Donna Tessandori. *The Italians in Kern County*. Bloomington: Xlibris Corporation, 2011.

"'Wet and Dry' Is New Kolb and Dill Vehicle Here Next Wed. and Thurs.; 'Up In Mabel's Room' Coming Monday Night," *Bakersfield Californian*, January 24, 1920, 3.

"Wet and Dry Issue on West Side Today," *Bakersfield Californian*, April 8, 1918, 7.

"Wet Federation In Annual Meeting Decides To Oppose Rominger Bill," *Bakersfield Californian*, March 7, 1918, 7.

"Wet Or Dry Campaign In Kern County Near End With Both Sides Confident," *Bakersfield Morning Echo*, October 29,

1911, 1.

"Wet Republicans Fight Dry Law," *Bakersfield Californian*, December 16, 1931, 1-2.

"Wets Claim Majority In Lower House In November," *Bakersfield Californian*, March 15, 1932, 1, 3.

"Wets Lose In House, 227 To 187," *Bakersfield Californian*, March 14, 1932, 1.

Whayne, Jeannie M. "Caging the Blind Tiger: Race, Class, and Family in the Battle for Prohibition in Small Town Arkansas," *The Arkansas Historical Quarterly* 71, no. 1 (Spring 2012): 44-60.

"Whiskey Valued at $10,000 Is Burglars' Prize," *Bakersfield Californian*, January 8, 1920, 1.

"Who's Who On 'Dry' Petition," *Bakersfield Californian*, September 1, 1911, 1, 4.

"Wife Forgot to Obey Husband; Fined $250," *Bakersfield Californian*, October 14, 1927, 11.

Wilcox, Walter F. "An Attempt to Measure Public Opinion About Repealing the Eighteenth Amendment," *Journal of the American Statistical Association* 26, no. 175 (1931): 243-261.

"Will Enforce Regulations," *Los Angeles Times*, July 3, 1911, sec. J17.

Willard, Frances. "Address Before The Second Biennial Convention Of The World's Woman's Christian Temperance Union," Accessed January 26, 2013, http://gos.sbc.edu/w/willard.html.

Willing, Joseph K. "The Profession of Bootlegging," *Annals of the American Academy of Political and Social Science* 125, Modern Crime: Its Prevention and Punishment (May 1926): 40-48.

"Wine Bill Urged In Group Report," *Bakersfield Californian*, March 31, 1933, 11.

"Wine Grape Men of San Joaquin In Quandary As To What To Do," *Bakersfield Californian*, May 17, 1920, Part 2, 1.

"Wine Plan Changed," *Los Angeles Times*, November 6, 1931, 1.

"Winemakers In State Organize," *Bakersfield Californian*, August 31, 1933, 11.

"Woman Arrested as Spy at Hanford," *Bakersfield Californian*, January 11, 1918, 1.

"Woman Seeks Right To Sell Beer, Wine," *Bakersfield Californian*, July 5, 1932, 9.

"Women Organize To Fight West," *Bakersfield Californian*, September 14, 1911, 1.

"Women Start With Petitions," *Bakersfield Californian*, January 28, 1911, 4.

"Women Violators of Liquor Laws Fined," *Bakersfield Californian*, July 13, 1922, 2.

"Wood Alcohol," Letter To The Editor, *Bakersfield Californian*, January 3, 1920, 12.

"Wood Alcohol Is Potion Of Death," *Bakersfield Californian*, January 16, 1922, 4.

"Would Limit Saloon Hours," *Bakersfield Californian*, January 23, 1911, 1.

"Wright Act Hit By Kern Voters," *Bakersfield Californian*, November 9, 1932, 1.

"Wright-Act Repeal on Ballots," *Bakersfield Californian*, April 16, 1932, 1.

"Writ Granted In Test Of Dry Act," *Bakersfield Californian*, December 18, 1920, 6.

"Wylie Spoke---To Tour Through County," *Bakersfield Californian*, October 16, 1911, 1.

"Wylie to Speak Twice Sunday," *Bakersfield Californian*, October 14, 1911, 6.

"Zero Hour For John Barleycorn To Be Struck At Midnight, Jan 16," *Bakersfield Californian*, January 15, 1920, 12.

INDEX

268

CPSIA information can be obtained at www.ICGtesting.com
Printed in the USA
LVOW01s2307150514

386029LV00016B/226/P